The Colditz Story

P.R. REID
MBE MC

First published in Great Britain in 1952 by Hodder & Stoughton
An Hachette UK company

This edition published in 2014

1

Copyright © P.R. Reid 1952
Copyright © Diana McLeod & Henry Reid 2014

The right of P.R. Reid to be identified as the Author of the Work has
been asserted by him in accordance with the Copyright, Designs and
Patents Act 1988.

A CIP catalogue record for this title is available from the British Library

Paperback ISBN 978 1 444 79568 4
eBook ISBN 978 1 444 79569 1

Typeset in Bembo by Hewer Text UK Lt, Edinburgh

Printed and bound by Clays Ltd, St Ives plc

Hodder & Stoughton policy is to use papers that are natural, renewable
and recyclable products and made from wood grown in sustainable
forests. The logging and manufacturing processes are expected to
conform to the environmental regulations of the country of origin.

Hodder & Stoughton Ltd
338 Euston Road
London NW1 3BH

www.hodder.co.uk

Apologia

Escape books are sometimes said to make escaping more difficult for the future, but the escape stories of the First World War made the majority of POWs in the Second World War escape-conscious. In the First World War escapers were an uncommon breed of men. A spirit was created by the early books which throve and bore fruit.

Minor escape techniques may have been made public by these early books, but they are never criticized for that by the escapers of the Second World War. Besides, much was left unsaid, and that applies even more to the stories of today – thanks to the authors who have deliberately omitted many details of enthralling interest. The different conditions of life in Germany were what our generation was really up against: the Gestapo, the Allied bombing and the Hitler Youth. Big Bertha cannot be compared to Allied air bombardment, nor can Allied air bombardment be compared to guided, stratospheric, atomic warhead rocket missiles. It will be the new conditions which will be the obstacles in the future, not escape books. The inspiration of escape books lives in men's memories and serves to keep alive the spirit of adventure.

Acknowledgments

This book, written ten years after the events it portrays would not have materialized without the help of many friends. They are, one and all, former Colditz POWs.

It has been necessary to omit from this edition the drawings by John Watton (who shared my captivity) with which the cloth-bound editions published by Hodder & Stoughton Ltd. are illustrated.

Other officers, former Colditz inmates, who have helped me are: Flight Lieutenant H. D. Wardle, Lieutenant-Commander W. L. Stephens, Major P. Storie Pugh, Lieutenant-Colonel A. Neave, Captain K. Lockwood, Captain R. Howe, Colonel G. German, Major H. A. V. Elliott, Major R. R. F. T. Barry and Captain A. M. Allan. Major Elliott's many contributions and unstinted help have been of especial value, and I am grateful to Captain Allan for his correction of the German in the text.

I have been fortunate, too, in finding the whereabouts, on the Continent, of several ex-Colditz POWs of the Allied armies: Dutch, French, and Polish. Lieutenant-General C. Giebel, Major P. Mairesse Lebrun and Lieutanant F. Jablonowski (in the U.K.), in particular, have kindly given me their assistance.

Lastly, to my wife I owe much, for her comments and for her untiring help in the preparation of the material of the book.

P.R.R.

A plan of Colditz Castle is on pages 68–69

Contents

Contents

Prologue

WHEN I was a boy at school, I read with avidity three of the greatest escape books of the First World War. They were: *The Road to En-Dor* by E. H. Jones, *The Escape Club* by A. J. Evans, and *Within Four Walls* by H. A. Cartwright and M. C. C. Harrison. All of them, as exciting reading, are as fresh today as when they were first published. These three epics lived long in my memory, so that when the fortunes of war found me a prisoner in an enemy land the spirit enshrined in them urged me to follow the example of their authors.

A. J. Evans said that escaping is the greatest sport in the world. In my early twenties I thought that to ride in the Grand National Steeplechase at Aintree would be the epitome of sporting excitement – more so even than big-game hunting. I longed to do both. Since the war and my experiences as an escaper, my one-time ambitions have died a natural death. I feel I have quaffed deeply of the intoxicating cup of excitement and can retire to contemplate those 'unforgettable moments' of the past. I can think of no sport that is the peer of escape, where freedom, life, and loved ones are the prize of victory, and death the possible though by no means inevitable price of failure.

The Second World War had just come to a close when A. J. Evans wrote some further memoirs in a book he called *Escape and Liberation, 1940–1945*. In it he wrote:

> The whole story of Colditz will, no doubt, one day be told, and it will make an enthralling story; but it must be written by one of the men who was there.

This book is the story of Colditz. I was one of the men imprisoned there.

We called Colditz 'the bad boys' camp'; the Germans called it the *Straflager*. An officer had to pass an entrance exam before being admitted through its sacred – the French would say its *sacré* – portals. The qualifying or passing-out test was the performance of at least one escape from any one of the many 'Prep.-school' camps that were dotted all over Germany. Naturally, the qualifying escape exam was not set by the Germans, nor were 'full marks' a guarantee of entry – in fact, the contrary, for the hundred per cent candidate was never available to take up his vacancy. He was out of bounds and, happily for him, 'expelled' for good!

Unfortunately, the nearer the applicant's marking came to a hundred without actually attaining it, the more certain he was of finding a wooden trestle bed and straw palliase awaiting him in Colditz.

The reader of this book, I feel, would also like to qualify before entering Colditz. He should run the gauntlet as hundreds of us did and pass the exam. So, in order to get him into training, he will, I hope, forgive me if he does not reach Colditz until Chapter IV. If he has read many escape books and is an old-timer, he may skip the early chapters. But at least in my qualifying exam I escaped as a woman – almost the only feminine interest in the book, I am sorry to say – so it might be worth while . . .

When the reader eventually arrives at Colditz, I shall not waste his time with details that every escaper knows. All the other inhabitants are professionals, and professionals do not demean themselves with the lesser problems. In fact, there will not be time to go into all the details, for that was Colditz.

It was supposed to be impregnable and certainly looked like it for a long time. It was the German fortress from which there was no escape. It had been escape-proof in the 1914–18 War and was to be so again in this war, according to the Germans.

The garrison manning the camp outnumbered the prisoners at all times. The Castle was floodlit at night from every angle, in spite of the blackout. Notwithstanding the clear drops of a hundred feet or so on the outside from barred windows, there were sentries all round the camp within a palisade of barbed wire. Beyond the palisade were precipices of varying depth. A detailed description of the plan and elevations of the Castle is impossible, but the above outline gives an indication of what we were up against.

But the Germans overlooked the fact that successful escapes depend mostly on the accumulation of escape technique, and they gathered together in one place, in Colditz, all the escape technicians of the Allied forces from all over the world. Together with this, they concentrated in Colditz the highest morale it is possible to imagine.

To cite an example, let me mention 'Never-a-dull-moment' Paddon – Squadron Leader B. Paddon, RAF, in other words. He earned his title well, for he was never out of trouble. Time after time his escape preparations were discovered, or he was caught red-handed by the German 'snoops' wielding a contraband file or saw. He earned months of solitary confinement for himself and others, as well as the stopping of 'privileges' for the whole prisoner contingent. Colditz was proud of Paddon long before he escaped successfully. It was ironical that the opportunity for his last escape should have been provided by a court-martial charge earned by him in earlier days when he was busy qualifying for Colditz.

'Never a dull moment' might well have been the motto on the Castle's armorial bearings. If there were not three hundred and sixty-five escape attempts in a year at Colditz, there were not far short of that number in the four and a half years of its war history.

If the reader feels in a mood to launch into the feverish underground activity of a camp full of diehards, let him read on. But he should remember, as I said before, that a little preliminary training may be of advantage. It was at Laufen that not a few of the Colditz escapers began their studies, myself among them.

PART ONE
Apprentice

I

Escape Reconnaissance

IT WAS JUNE 5th, 1940. We arrived at Laufen, about eighteen miles north-east of Salzburg, on the tenth day of my captivity. It was our final destination and we disembarked. My first impression was of a charming village on the banks of a murmuring river, the Salzach. The inhabitants lined the road and watched in silence as we marched by. The Salzach separates Bavaria from Austria at this point. We saw beside the river an enormous block-like building which looked a little like a medieval Schloss and a great deal like a huge asylum. It was the ancient palace of the Archbishop of Salzburg, sentimentally revered as the place where Mozart composed and played many of his works. To us, it was remarkable, on first inspection, only for the amazing number of windows it possessed; in one wall-face alone I counted over sixty. This was to be our permanent home.

We were the first arrivals. Everything was prepared for us in the way of barbed wire and guards falling over each other. We were paraded while the Commandant made an appearance, surrounded by his hierarchy, and delivered a speech. For the first time, we were searched individually and thoroughly. Our heads were shaven under riotous protest, and we were each given a small aluminium disc with a number on it. Our photos were taken and we were let loose into a small compound as fully recognized prisoners-of-war. Captain Patrick Reid, RASC, had become *Kriegsgefangenennummer* 257. The prison was Oflag VII C.

* * *

June 12th brought two hundred more arrivals, making our total four hundred. We were told that when the camp was full it would hold fifteen hundred officers. Many of the newcomers were allotted to our room, No. 66, and among them was Captain Rupert Barry of the 52nd Light Infantry. From the moment of our first meeting we talked escape.

He was sitting on a bench in front of a long kitchen-type table, playing patience with a pack of cards which he had made out of pieces of paper, when I came into the room.

I sat opposite him in silence for a long time, my chin in my hands. My mind wandered hundreds of miles away to a home in England.

The man in front of me continued his game, deliberately, carefully smoothing out and adjusting his pieces of paper. Occasionally he twirled his large guardee moustache with a slow controlled movement of his long fingers. My thoughts switched to him.

'Control. Yes, the man in front of me has certainly taught himself control. Maybe he has need of it. Still waters run deep,' I mused.

He looked up from his game. His dark eyes smouldered, but withal there was kindliness somewhere within and his smile was pleasant.

'I'm determined to get out of this place within three months,' I said, wondering in the next instant why I had confided in him.

'You're an optimist. Why the hurry?'

'I've got a date for Christmas which I don't want to miss. If I leave early in September, I could hope to get a sailing from Gibraltar or Lisbon in time.'

'I wouldn't mind joining you,' Rupert Barry said. 'My wife will never forgive me if I don't escape from here. She'll accuse me of not caring for her any more.'

'She sounds as if she's rather a strong personality.'

'That's one of the things I like about her,' he said, and added: 'You're obviously not married.'

'No, I'm a bachelor and what little eligibility I ever possessed is fading rapidly with every day that passes here.'

'How about a systematic reconnaissance of the premises?'

'Good, let's start.'

* * *

Rupert was twenty-nine, about five feet eleven inches tall, and well-proportioned. Considering the circumstances, he was dressed smartly and was an imposing personality with his handsome, rather sallow-complexioned face set off by the big dark guardee moustache and a large chin. Straight-nosed, brown-eyed, with dark-brown hair (after it had grown again!); a man who could play havoc with the female sex, but, in fact lived only for his wife 'Dodo' and his two children. He was a professional soldier and had been educated at King's School, Canterbury.

For several days we scoured the camp together on our reconnaissance tour. We examined all the possibilities of passing the barbed-wire entanglements in the compounds, discussed the pros and cons of rushing the gates, and argued over wall-climbs blatantly suicidal. When the floodlights were switched on at night, we judged the depths and positions of shadows, timed sentries on their beats, and stayed up for hours on end peering cautiously through windows to see if the guards became lazy or changed their habits in the early hours, giving us a possible opening. In the end we found ourselves concentrating on one particular corner of a tall building in the inner quadrangle, and our ideas filtered down to two opposing schemes.

The first, Rupert's idea, was simply a tunnel; the second, mine, involved a long roof-climb and a rope-descent. These were the embryos from which the first escape attempt from Laufen developed. Rupert's plan involved tedious work for months on end. Mine was a 'blitz'. We agreed it was worth making an experiment on my scheme before deciding what plan to adopt. We needed two helpers to act as observers while I did a trial run over the roofs. Sailor Nealy, a Lieutenant of the Fleet Air Arm, and Kenneth Lockwood, a Captain of the Queen's Royal Regiment, joined us. Both of them, without being over-curious, had expressed interest in our 'snooping' and had told us of their intention of making a break. We all four lived in room 66.

We held a meeting and I opened the proceedings. I told Nealy and Kenneth of the alternatives and of our intention to start with the roof. I went on:

'For the trial run we need a night with no moon – the darker the night the better.'

'Yes, but you don't want rain,' said Nealy. 'You'll career off the roof like a toboggan, and you'll have to wear gym shoes anyway.'

'A wind wouldn't matter. In fact it should help,' said Kenneth.

'You see the idea. We need all these conditions if possible. Rupert

5

is the strongest of us, so I suggest he lets me down on the sheet-rope to the flat inter-connecting roof.'

'We'll need at least two sheets; better have three for the twelve-foot drop,' put in Kenneth.

'I'll drop and then carry on to the main roof. Kenneth, you'll have to watch my whole journey and check for visibility, shadows, and noise. Sailor, you'd better keep your eye on each sentry in turn as I come into his line of vision and area of responsibility, and watch for reactions.'

'The idea,' said Rupert, 'is that Pat will go to the far end of the long roof and see if it is practicable to make a sheet-descent outside the prison. There's a sentry in the roadway round the corner, but we don't know how much he can see. Pat can check on that too. A lot depends on the depth of shadow in which the descent will be made.'

'The moon will be nearly gone on June 30th. That's a Sunday,' I went on, 'and the guards should have drunk some beer and may be more sleepy than usual. I suggest we agree on that date provided the weather is reasonable.'

The date was agreed and we discussed all the details of the climb. We were complete beginners – pioneers – and we had only enthusiasm and determination behind us. I suddenly had an idea:

'Wouldn't it make the climb a cakewalk if we could fuse all the lights? I believe I could do it.'

'How?'

'You know the wires run round the walls of the buildings on insulators, and they're only about eighteen inches apart. It's just a matter of shorting them.'

'And how do you think you can do that?'

I thought for a moment. 'I know. One of the windows in room 44 is only about four feet above the wires and is in pretty good shadow. If we can collect about forty razor-blades I'll attach these with drawing-pins to a piece of wood, forming a conductor and sharp knife at the same time. I can screw the piece of wood on to a broom-handle and there we are.'

'A good idea,' said Rupert, 'and if June 30th is our zero date, then the sooner the fusing is done the better.'

'I meant to fuse them on the 30th.'

6

'I don't think that's wise. It might create an uproar, and they might get the lights working again just when you were hanging somewhere in mid-air. It would be better to make the fusing a try-out too. Then we can see how long it takes them to repair the fuse.'

'All right,' I agreed, 'then I'll do the job, and while I'm fusing, you three had better take up positions around the buildings to note if any sections of the lighting do not go out with the rest.'

In due course the fusing was carried out. The razor-edged 'short-circuit' worked perfectly. I cut through the heavy insulation in a matter of a minute with a gentle sawing motion. There was a brilliant flash and all the floodlights I could see went out. There was some shouting and running about near the guard-house. In three minutes the lights went on again. This interval of time would not be enough for our purposes.

One of the main problems in escaping, which in course of time and through bitter experience we recognized, was that of deciding at a moment's notice whether all the conditions for an escape were right, or if not, which of them could be ignored. An opportunity once missed might not occur again for months or years, which made one keen to take it; yet if it were taken under adverse conditions, or if more important conditions were misjudged as being of less importance, then the escape was ruined. Another chance was gone and another gap in the enemy's defences closed for good.

There was a second problem. Whether a sentry would shoot or not on detection was entirely a matter for conjecture; probably he would. His orders were to shoot; this had been explicitly pointed out to us by the Camp Commandant at his memorable parade on our arrival. He had delivered a long harangue, and on the subject of escaping had said, 'It is useless to try to escape. Look around you at the impregnable barriers, the formidable array of machine-guns and rifles. To escape is impossible. Anyone attempting it will be shot.' He spoke English well and he spat out the word 'shot' with a malicious staccato that was no doubt intended to put escaping out of our minds for ever. 'These are my strict orders to the guards, who will carry out the command to the letter.' Awed silence was followed by roars of laughter as he added with Teutonic seriousness, 'If you escape a second time, you will be sent to a special camp.'

June 30th was a fine day. Evening approached and the stars came out – not a breath of wind, not a cloud! At 10.30 pm Rupert and I crept from our room and along the corridors, which were irregularly patrolled, to the room where the job was to begin. We looked carefully through the window, and listened. It was disconcertingly light outside, but the shadows were correspondingly dark and there was a new sound which we had not noticed before. The river, the pleasant gurgling stream rushing talkatively down from the mountains, made up for the silence reigning elsewhere. Yes, it was worth trying.

Rupert fetched Nealy and Lockwood, who took up positions at key windows. I estimated the trip would take about an hour and said I would not return earlier than that. Zero hour was 11.30 pm.

The drop was in full view of a sentry about fifty yards away, who could play a searchlight at will on any desired spot. I dropped quietly and quickly to the flat roof as the sentry's footbeats indicated his back was turned. I had stockings on my feet, old stockings cut out as mittens on my hands, and a borrowed balaclava helmet concealing the greater part of my face. All was well. Once on the flat roof I was hidden from view and I continued to the higher sloping roof which ran at right angles to the flat one. I had just succeeded, making a certain amount of noise, in climbing the five feet of the gutter in full view of a second sentry but helped by a shadow, when a commotion began among the guards, a running hither and thither with torches flashing and orders shouted. I lay like a dead thing, spread-eagled on the roof. The commotion increased, but it did not approach the quarter where I was. At midnight a continuous sound of murmuring voices broke out in the most distant of the four courtyards and, after listening for some time, I decided that the noise must be due to the arrival of another batch of prisoners. I continued with a lighter heart, for though the noise was far off, it would help me. As I moved, slates cracked like pistol-shots, so it seemed to me, and broken pieces slid to the eaves with a long-drawn-out rattle. I had to cross over the ridge of the roof, because on the near side I was visible as soon as I left the gable end. On the far side I was out of sight and in deep shadow. I tried to spread my weight as evenly as possible and found the best way to move was to lie on my back with arms and legs stretched out and move slowly crabwise. The roof was forty yards long and the drop to the ground was sixty feet. One piece of luck that came my way on this long stretch of the journey was a roof walkway for chimney sweeps running about half the length, but even this made the most terrifying creaks and groans. It frightened the wits out of me, especially when a loose plank fell right off and slid, rattling loudly, down to the edge. I watched, transfixed with horror, waiting for the moment when it would topple over, and then it stopped, wedged in the gutter. I had to control my movements to such an extent that I was in continual danger of cramp. At the far end of the roof I could peer over the gable end and do my reconnaissance.

The end wall of the building descended to a narrow alley outside the prison. There was a sentry who marched to and fro along the street running parallel with the building. By studying his routine and timing his beat, we had previously established that a blind interval of some three minutes might be expected in the alley at each turn of the sentry's walk. We hoped to make use of this, provided there was sufficient deep shadow or other concealment in the alley. That was the purpose of the reconnaissance – a survey of the alley and of its precincts at the time of night when the escape was projected. There were other points to be established too; whether the climb was feasible, the speed at which we could move without making a noise loud enough to attract attention, and whether at the exposed points of the climb the darkness was sufficient.

Three and a half hours later I returned, having spent about half an hour at the prospective point of descent. I nearly failed at the twelve-foot climb back through the window. I was tired and a month's starvation diet had told on me. Rupert hauled me in. I made a most unholy row, but the sentry must have been only half-awake. It was 3 am. The next day we held a second meeting, and I gave my opinion.

'The proposed point of descent isn't good. The nearest anchor for a rope will mean carting along with us about twenty-five sheets or blankets. We would also have ruck-sacks and boots. The alley is a cul-de-sac, but I'm afraid the shadows are not helpful. The rope would be clearly visible in any position.'

'I heard you distinctly on several occasions,' reported Kenneth, to which Nealy added:

'Once I thought you had fallen off the roof. I couldn't see you because you were on the far side, but there was a long rumble and a crash against the gutter.'

'I think we may as well call it off,' said Rupert. 'If one man without luggage makes all that din, what are four going to do? Frankly, Pat, I think you were saved by the noise of the new arrivals. And, to clinch it, if the rope has got to dangle in the limelight, we shall never get away with it. I couldn't descend sixty feet on a home-made rope and give you time to heave it up again all within three minutes.'

We all agreed and decided to prospect further along the lines of Rupert's tunnel idea.

As for the new arrivals of the night, they turned out to be four hundred officers of the 51st Division who had been captured at St Valéry on the north coast of France on about June 12th. This meant crowding in the rooms, and our No. 66 finished up with fifty-seven occupants. The room was about fifteen yards by twelve yards by twelve feet high. In this space there were nineteen wooden three-tier bunks, half a dozen tables, a heating stove, and ten small wardrobe cupboards. Fifty-seven officers ate, slept and lived in this room, for at that time day-rooms were unheard of.

While I had been concentrating on my idea of escaping over the roofs, Rupert had been doing some quiet 'snooping' on his own. The word 'snooping' soon became recognized camp terminology. It meant touring the camp in a suspicious manner and was applied to both Germans and British. The Germans employed professional snoopers who became familiar figures in the camp. It was extraordinary how few people snooped effectively. Snoopers could usually be distinguished in a crowd a mile away, looking like habitual burglars searching for another safe to break.

Rupert was a good snooper chiefly because it was impossible for anyone to look at him without taking him for a man too honest and proud to demean himself. He noted a small locked room in the corner of the building backing against the alley (cul-de-sac) that I had examined from the roof-tops, and discovered that the room was a semi-basement. One day, while Kenneth kept watch for the German snoopers, Rupert, Nealy, and I undid the lock of the door and went in. We found some steps leading down to the floor, which was about five feet below the outside ground-level. Rupert proposed piercing the wall at floor-level, digging a tunnel across the street, and through or under the foundations of an old stone building at the other side. Nealy preferred crossing under the alley and coming up inside a small lean-to shed against a private house. The walls of the shed were made of vertical wooden slats with gaps in between. We could see piles of wooden logs inside. We adopted Nealy's suggestion because we thought we would have no heavy foundations to circumvent at the far end of our tunnel. As things turned out we were right, although even in this direction we did not know what form our exit would take.

We started to break through the wall on July 14th. I thought it was a propitious day – the anniversary of the storming of the Bastille!

We decided to work two shifts of two hours each per day, and in the afternoon, this being the quietest time from the point of view of internal camp disturbance, and at the same time the noisiest for external street sounds which would help to cover up the sound of our working. We kept the tunnel a complete secret except for one officer, Major Poole, who had been a prisoner-of-war in the 1914–18 War, and whose advice we sought. The routine was simple enough; one man worked at the wall-face, another man sat on a box inside the room with his eye glued to the keyhole of the door looking along the passage, a third man read a book, or otherwise behaved innocently, seated on the stone steps at the only entrance to the building a few yards away from the passage, a fourth man lounged, or exercised, in the farthest courtyard. After a couple of hours the two men outside and the two men inside would change places. Warning of the approach of any German was passed by noncommittal signals, such as the blowing of a nose, along the line, depending upon the direction from which he appeared. The man on the wall-face would immediately stop work on receipt of the signal.

The door of the room was opened by removing the screws holding the latch of the padlock. The latch was screwed up during each shift. The room contained lumber, including a large variety of rifle-range targets. There were painted French soldiers and English Tommies – lying, kneeling, and charging, as well as the usual bull's-eye type. If a German decided to come into the room, the only hope for the men inside was to hide amongst the lumber or in a small triangular space underneath the stone steps. The entrance to the tunnel was in the farthest corner of the room and was hidden in the darkness under an old table. For tools, we began with three stout six-inch nails. After some days we received an addition of a small hammer.

The hammer was the cause of one of the first major camp 'incidents', and gave us a 'friend in need' in a Royal Tank Regiment lieutenant called O'Hara, who as time went on became 'Scarlet O'Hara', one of the most notorious POWs in Germany. His face was so ruddy that the slightest excitement made it live up to the name.

On this particular day, a lorry came into one of the courtyards to deliver goods to the canteen, and although it was guarded by a sentry, O'Hara, with a confederate, 'Crash' Keeworth, secured the hammer and a very fine road-map of Germany from the tool-kit under the driver's seat. Keeworth pretended to steal something from the back of the lorry, distracting the sentry enough to ensure that Scarlet could perform his task with the utmost ease. The loss was, of course, soon discovered. The guard was called out and a special *Appell*, or parade, sounded. Incidentally, this *Appell* gave us some anxious moments, for we had to extract our two men from the room in double-quick time: a contingency for which we always had to be prepared, as we never knew what mischief the other prisoners might be up to.

The Commandant appeared at the parade foaming at the mouth. All his subordinates duly followed suit and shouted themselves into paroxysms of rage which were encouraged by derisive laughter from the British ranks. After interminable haranguing, both in English and German, we were given to understand that all privileges would be withdrawn until the hammer and map were returned. The parade then broke up with catcalls, hoots, and jeers. Scarlet had pulled off his job superbly, and we found a muffled hammer a much better tool than a roughly shaped stone!

★ ★ ★

After three weeks our tunnel had progressed three feet. We had pierced the stone and brick wall and found loose earth on the other side. Great was our rejoicing. Progress would be much faster now, but it was also obvious that shoring and timbering would be necessary to keep the roof of the tunnel from caving in. We found some lengths of three-inch by two-inch timber in the target-room where we worked, and these, together with 'bed-boards', of which there was an unlimited supply, carried us the whole length of the tunnel.

Our wooden bunks supported the human body by means of about ten boards spanning the width of the bed. They were about three-quarters of an inch thick and two feet six inches long, and they became invaluable in innumerable ways as time went on. They were the escaper's most important raw material. Bed-boards could be used for roof timbers in a tunnel, carved into dummy pistols or German bayonets, and made into false doors and cupboards. Jumping ahead a little in time (in fact, about a year), a tunnel was built at Laufen under the direction of Captain Jim Rogers, R.E., in which no fewer than twelve hundred bed-boards were used.

We learned by experience how best to carry these boards about, and eventually we were confident enough to meet and pass a German officer with a couple of them nursed tenderly under a negligently worn overcoat.

The tunnel now progressed more rapidly. So much so that it became impossible to get rid of the soil quickly enough by the method we employed at first, which was that of taking the rubble out in our pockets, especially elongated for the purpose to reach our knees, and emptying it surreptitiously as we lay on the grass in the compound. Rupert and I were one day carrying out this thankless task.

'At this rate, Pat,' protested Rupert, 'the tunnel will take us six months.'

'The only alternative is to pile up the soil in the target-room, and I don't like that,' I retorted.

'We can hide it in the corner under the steps.'

'Not all of it. The space isn't big enough.'

'We can cover what remains with old targets and rubbish.'

'If the Jerries take more than a glance at the room, they can't fail to notice it.'

'And if we plod on for six months, the Jerries will find the tunnel anyway,' rejoined Rupert.

'Why?'

'It's only a matter of time before we're caught. We take risks every day, and the longer we work the shorter the odds become against us.

One day a Jerry will just be in the wrong place at the wrong time. The longer we work the more chance there is of that happening.'

'All right,' I concluded, 'then I agree. We'll make a "blitz" of it.'

In the week following our decision, we progressed three yards.

On the right of the tunnel we ran along the side of an old brick wall. Curiosity as to the purpose of this wall led to a lucky discovery and also to an unlucky incident. We made further measurements and found that we were not outside the main wall of the building as we had thought, but were running beside what was a completely sealed-up room under the lavatories on the first floor. By using a small mirror held out of the lavatory window we could see a manhole cover in the alleyway adjacent to the sealed chamber. We assumed that the chamber was an old sewage-pit, of which the manhole cover was the exit. If we could enter the sewage-pit and go out by the manhole cover, we would have a perfect exit to the tunnel which could be used over and over again. We decided to risk breaking through the wall on our right. It was lucky we made the measurements, for if we had proceeded with the tunnel, thinking we were outside the main wall, we would always have been three yards short in our calculation of the length of the tunnel.

But we nearly wrecked the whole scheme by breaking through the wall on our right! I was working away at the wall, which came away easily. As I removed a final brick, a flood of foul sewage rushed out at me, extinguishing the light. (Light was provided by German cooking-fat in a cigarette-tin with a pyjama-cord wick.) I lay prone in total darkness with a gushing torrent sweeping round me. I shouted to Rupert who was keeping guard:

'There's a flood coming in. I've got to stop it. The stench is asphyxiating. For God's sake, pull me out of the tunnel if I pass out.'

I heard Rupert say:

'I can smell it from here. I'll call you every half-minute and if you don't answer I'll come for you.'

I set about the hole as best I could with bricks and clay mud, in feverish anxiety. The tunnel was built downhill and the flood was mounting! Fortunately the pressure could not have been great on the other side, and after five minutes of frantic work I managed to reduce the torrent to a small trickle. I wormed my way back out of the tunnel. Rupert nearly fell off his box when he saw the appalling object which rose from the hole. Not much sewage had come into the room because of the downward slope of the tunnel made to provide ventilation at the working end. We knocked off for the day to let the flood settle. I cleaned myself up in the bathroom next door, and dry clothing was produced.

Next day I went in again with a light and made a proper dam of puddled clay, of which there was no lack, supported by boards driven into the floor of the tunnel. Needless to say, we abandoned the pit scheme and carried on in a forward direction. There always remained a small leak which necessitated our putting duck-boards along the whole length of the tunnel. As luck had it, the tunnel-level carried us just beneath the base of the main external wall. It would have been a heartbreaking job to tackle three feet of masonry in the confined space of the tunnel. Without further incident, towards the end of August we arrived under the lean-to woodshed at the other side of the alleyway.

Nealy had been given orders, in the middle of August, that he would move at short notice to a naval camp, as he belonged to the Fleet Air Arm. At the same time, with the lengthening of the tunnel we needed more workers. We sought Major Poole's advice. Finally, we asked 2nd Lieutenant 'Peter' Allan, Captain 'Dick' Howe, and Captain Barry O'Sullivan to join us, which they did with alacrity.

Our choice fell on Peter first because he could speak German fluently, and in fact was used as an interpreter with the Germans on many occasions. When the escape took place, it would be helpful to have a German speaker. The rest of us knew nothing of the language. Major Poole warned us to be careful to check up on his credentials: Where had he learnt German? The reply was – at school in Germany. Why was he at school in Germany? His father had business relations with Germany. These and other pointers as to his past were probed, mostly indirectly and unostentatiously through officers who said they knew him before the war.

All this goes to show how, from the start, in prisoner-of-war camps we were suspicious of the possibility of the planting of an 'agent provocateur' in our midst. Officers had read how these were placed in camps in the First World War to spy, and we certainly thought Nazi Germany would be capable of it in this war. Later these agents became known as 'stool pigeons'.

Peter passed the tests – we often laughed about it in later days – and he was as keen as mustard. A 2nd lieutenant of the Cameron Highlanders, standing only five feet six inches, he nevertheless swung his kilt as well as the tallest, and his tough legs showed he could walk long distances. He was fit in spite of the starvation. Educated at Tonbridge, he played both rugby and soccer well, and was an excellent bridge and chess player. He always managed to drive opponents into a frenzy by his unvarying stratagem of taking a pawn or two early in the game, and swopping like piece for like. He and Rupert were a match at bridge.

Dick Howe and Barry O'Sullivan were likewise tested. Neither proved difficult to check up on. Barry was the son of a British General and Dick had been known in England by a large number of the prisoners now at Laufen. Both belonged to the Royal Tank Regiment. Barry was of an effervescent nature and had been for some time in India. He was recommended by Poole for our acceptance on account of his keenness and determination to escape at all costs. The recommendation proved well founded.

Dick Howe was our own choice. He lived in room 66 with us and showed initiative combined with good sense, which made him the possible leader of a second group to escape via our tunnel. Already we had ideas of concealing our tunnel exit so that it could be used repeatedly.

Dick was a Londoner educated at Bedford Modern School and possessing a flair for mechanical engineering, and for wireless theory and practice. He had just been awarded the MC for his gallantry at Calais, where he had been landed with his group at a moment's notice to fight an action postponing the capture of that port by the Germans for several precious days.

He was good-looking and strongly built, if anything burly, and was about five feet ten inches tall. He laughed with a neigh like a horse, had a great sense of humour, and went about everything in a quiet manner with a slight grin as if he was looking for the funniest way of doing it.

Nealy left towards the end of August. I agreed to write to his parents if the escape was successful to let them know how he was faring.*

A few days later we had a bad scare. Barry O'Sullivan was digging at the face, I was hauling back the earth in improvised boxes – a tiring job crawling back and forth on one's tummy – and Peter Allan was doing 'keyhole' watch. From outside he received the signal – 'danger, cease work'. No sooner had he warned us than a German non-commissioned officer came down the corridor and, without hesitating, approached our door, unlocked the padlock, and pushed. The door did not open. We had devised a safety-catch on the inside – a rough-and-ready affair. It was our last defence for just such an event as this. The German swore, pulled the door with all his strength, tearing the latch off, then pushed again and peered through the narrow chink, to discover a rough piece of iron barring his way. This delaying action gave Peter Allan just sufficient time to jump down the steps and crawl behind the targets and into the tunnel. We all wore soft-soled shoes, otherwise Peter would have been heard.

A moment later the Jerry burst open the door. What he thought I do not know, but he must have been deceived by our safety-catch. This was made of rusty-looking material and fell downwards into position very easily so that the explanation might offer itself to a person finding an empty room barred on the inside, that it had fallen into position of its own accord on the last occasion when the door was shut. This we knew was about two or three months before. It was a long chance, but our only one, and it worked. Peter reported action at our end and later we heard the rest from our confederates. The Jerry came in, pushed the targets farther against our tunnel corner and went out again. After an interval Peter was sent out to inspect, but soon scuttled back saying, 'Jerries are returning!' This time several came in, carrying an assortment of targets which they piled up wherever there was room. They then nailed on the latch with some four-inch nails, turning them over on the inside, locked the padlock, and departed. Five minutes later a surreptitious knock on the door told us our own guard was outside. Peter and I went to the door and I whispered:

---

* Nealy escaped from Stalag Luft III in the 'Great Escape' of March 1944, when fifty out of seventy-six officers were shot by the Gestapo. Nealy was a survivor.

'We can't get out. They've driven in four-inch nails and turned them over on the inside. You'll never be able to remove the latch.'

'A prison within a prison,' mused Kenneth from outside. 'Can't you bend the nails?'

'Not a hope! The wood will split if we try. The nails are as thick as my little finger.'

'Well, what a pity! You'll just have to stay there until you've starved enough to crawl out under the door.'

'Shut up that nonsense, Kenneth! I've got an idea. Can you fetch me a file?'

'Why, certainly, old man! The ironmonger's shop is just around the corner,' and I heard him chuckling maddeningly on the other side of the door.

'It's not at all funny. You're on the right side of the door, but we're on the wrong side. I'm sure Scarlet O'Hara can produce a file. For heaven's sake, hurry!'

The file was produced in a very short time and passed under the door. I filed the nails through at the point where they were bent over. Kenneth on the outside levered the latch from the woodwork, drawing out the bitten-off nails. We left the room, replacing the nails quickly, and departed. The next day, in the interest of silence, we again shortened the nails and, rebending the filed-off ends, stuck them into their original positions, leaving no trace of the tampering.

The tunnel progressed. We were all interviewed and recommended to have a medical examination to see that we were fit enough for the arduous trek to the frontier. The examination included running up and down four flights of stairs at full speed, followed by a heart test. The result of the medical exam was reported, and unfortunately Barry O'Sullivan was asked to stand down in favour of someone else. His trouble was recurring malaria, contracted in the East. He was far too honest to conceal it from the doctor. The latter considered it a serious handicap and with reason.

We were very sorry to lose Barry. Although it consoled nobody at the time, it is pleasant to recall that Barry escaped shortly afterwards from another camp, and was about the first British escaper to reach Switzerland safely.

We chose Harry Elliott, a captain in the Irish Guards, to take his place. He passed all his tests, and his inclusion was agreed, so that the first escaping party still consisted of six officers. I hoped that others would be able to follow subsequently.

I had an important reason for limiting the first batch to six persons. Our sortie would be made from the woodshed and thence up the side street, for about thirty yards, to the main road. The side street was in full view of a permanent day-and-night sentry-post on a cat-walk about forty yards away from the woodshed alley. Although we would be walking away from him, the sentry would see each one of us. Six men appearing from a little-used cul-de-sac was quite a mouthful to swallow. So much so that I planned we should leave by ones and twos at intervals and, moreover, that at least two of us should dress up as women for the occasion. We also decided that after the escape we should separate for good into two parties of three each. Rupert and Peter Allan agreed to join me as one party, and the other three formed the second. My party made plans to go to Yugoslavia, while the other three were to head for Switzerland.

I asked that Scarlet O'Hara should be placed at the top of the list for any subsequent escape from the tunnel. He was already a man marked down by the Germans as dangerous, and wherever he was seen by a 'snoop,' there suspicion followed. He was never long out of trouble and was quite irrepressible. Scarlet soon possessed a wide range of useful tools and implements, odd civilian attire, maps and other escape paraphernalia, which he concealed in various hide-outs all over the camp. He was a Canadian, small and wiry, and he loathed the Jerries so much that he was unable to pass one without muttering semi-audible curses and insults. He had a nature that craved excitement and intrigue; he was never so happy as when he was tinkering with some implement with a view to breaking out of the camp. He and 'Crash' Keeworth were the pet aversions of the Germans.

One day Scarlet was going through one of his hides. It was behind the cleaning-hatch of a chimney-flue. He had a square key to fit the hatch and used the large space within as an extra cupboard – mostly for contraband. The hatch was at the corner of a corridor, about nine feet from the ground.

The Camp Commandant had just declared that Army mess-tins were to be handed in as being illegal escape equipment. Any officer retaining a tin would be liable to heavy punishment. So Scarlet was busy hiding several mess-tins. His 'stooge,' that is the officer keeping watch, passed him up the tins one after the other. As he handed the last one, a Goon (the senior Sergeant, or *Feldwebel* as it happened) surprised them. The stooge had only time to say, 'Goons,' giving Scarlet's trousers a tug at the same time, and then walk away unconcerned as the Goon approached and stared up at Scarlet. Scarlet's head was inside the hatch and he did not hear the operative word. He shouted:

'What in hell's name do you think you're doing, trying to knock me off my stool?'

No answer.

'There's not enough room in this b— hole. I reckon some of you guys'll have to find your own holes. I'm not a b— storage contractor, anyway. B— those b— Huns. I'd like to wring their necks and knock their square heads together till their gold teeth fall out. Hey! Hold this tin! I've got to make more space.'

Silence.

'Take the b— tin, I said.'

The mess-tin was taken from his hand by the *Feldwebel*, who started pulling violently at the seat of his pants.

'For crying out loud! You'll have me over. What in hell's name do you want?'

At this juncture Scarlet's ruddy face appeared from the hatch and surveyed his mortal enemy beneath him holding one of his precious mess-tins.

* * *

It was obvious that Scarlet was not the right person to assist in building the tunnel. He was too conspicuous. So he was allotted the task of closing it up after our six had departed, with a view to his learning the job and going with the second batch.

Harry Elliott was introduced to tunnel work in a curious way. On his first shift he was given the post of keyhole stooge. Incidentally, this usually entailed suffering from a strained bloodshot eye for several days after the shift. No sooner had Harry taken up his position on this, his first day, than one of the camp's 'athletic types' approached the door. We had various 'athletic types'. Some ran round the compound for hours on end, others walked as if the devil was after them, others again did physical jerks and acrobatics, appearing to stand on their hands for more hours per day than their feet.

The particular 'athletic type' that approached the door was a boxer. Harry told us the story afterwards:

'The man was obviously punch-drunk from his earliest child-hood. His nose told his life-story. I thought he was heading for the bathroom next door. He certainly needed a shower – he was perspiring so much, as a matter of fact, that he looked as if he'd just come from one. He was shadow-boxing his way down the corridor with massive gloves on his fists. He started snorting vigorously as he passed out of my keyhole line of vision. The next thing I knew was a terrific crash against the door which sent me reeling backwards. I quickly put my eye to the keyhole again to see what was the matter. I was sent reeling again as the door shuddered under another blow. Another and another followed in quick succession. He was a formi-dable opponent even with a door between us. I shouted at him through the keyhole, but between his loud snorts and the drum-like blows, a ship's siren couldn't have been heard. I just gave up and disappeared into the tunnel. I thought it the best place to be when the Jerries arrived.

'After ten minutes, when the door showed signs of decomposing, the athletic type retired – I suppose finally to cool himself off in the bathroom. The silence that followed made me feel I was in a tomb rather than a tunnel.'

Harry had an infectious laugh, almost a giggle, which was irresist-ible. When he told a story, listeners invariably started to laugh at the beginning and did not stop for a day or two. He was an Harrovian, older than most of us, and had several children. He loathed being a prisoner more than anyone else I knew in the camp, but he never showed it except when he took 'time-off' to express his feelings for the German race, the *Herrenvolk*, with a picturesque invective diffi-cult to equal. He was small and wiry, with darting blue eyes set in a sunburnt face. His voice was reminiscent of the 'Colonel Sahib' home from India after years of polo and pigsticking. He said he could always tell whether a man was an 'officer and a gentleman' by asking him to repeat one sentence, namely, 'I saw thousands and thousands of Boy Scouts routing around in their brown trousers.' He tested many officers, roaring with laughter at the result. No offence was ever taken or implied. It was Harry having his fun!

The tunnel grew towards completion and we were under the lean-to shed which I have mentioned before and which we now called the woodshed. We had to determine our exact position. The woodshed contained a pile of logs each about one yard long, and we dare not break cover under the passage of the shed immediately beyond the logs. I found a thin-steel rifle ramrod about three feet long in the target-room. While Rupert observed with a mirror the ground outside the shed from the lavatory window above, I made a small vertical hand-hole in the roof of the tunnel and slowly pushed the rod upwards. As soon as Rupert saw it he was to kick the lavatory wall once and make a mental note of its position. The alarm signal was two knocks in case of danger. The sound carried down the wall and was to be reported to me by a listener in the tunnel immediately beneath the wall foundations. I started at a point I estimated to be just outside the woodshed and pushed the rod upwards, digging away with the same hand until I began to think our tunnel was deeper underground than we had estimated. Suddenly the double knock was heard. I withdrew the rod like lightning and awaited a report. Some minutes later it came – whispered up the tunnel (noise carries like thunder in a tunnel). My rod had been waving about two feet above the roadway, but was so close to the shed that even Rupert had not noticed it for some time.

Now we continued with confidence, and after a few days I broke the surface under the wood-pile and first smelt wholesome fresh air. I was delighted, for whereas I had envisaged perilously removing logs to leave a natural archway, I found the logs were on a platform of wood raised some six inches above the earth. Furthermore, by inspection I found that a wainscot board had been placed along the shed passage against the platform, closing it off down to the ground.

The next thing to figure out was how to make a concealed exit. We were determined this tunnel should work for several escapes. Besides, the position of the exit and of the woodshed made it danger-ous to attempt sending off a large number of officers at one time.

Eventually I decided to dig away the ground just inside the wainscot and to support the earth of the passage-way with narrow wooden horizontal slats backed against two stakes driven vertically into the floor of the tunnel. Actually Dick did most of the work on his shift, and had to work very carefully and silently, hammering the stakes into the ground. The vertical wall of comparatively loose earth was thus held up by a little wooden dam. We christened it 'Shovewood'. The scheme of opening was simple. When all was ready, the slats would be removed and an opening quickly made at an angle of forty-five degrees upwards and out into the passage-way, pulling the earth into the tunnel.

The escaping party having scrambled out, one person remaining behind would close up the tunnel again by replacing the slats one by one and filling the earth back behind them. Everything that would speed up this process was seized upon. Thus to save putting back earth that needed tamping, a couple of small strong wooden boxes were made ready which, placed behind the slats, would fill up much space and save valuable seconds. The final slat immediately beneath the wainscot was only two inches wide. In this way the last layer of earth outside could be spread, then tamped with a flat board and made to merge with the passage-way, the slat would be put in, and the earth backed up behind. It could not be a perfect job, but it was the best we could do, and we estimated that the owner of the wood-shed would imagine that a chicken had been there and scratched about, or maybe that a rat had been at work.

The tunnel was ready on August 31st. It had taken just under seven weeks to build, and was eight yards long.

We were pleased with our work, especially when we thought of the slow progress made in the early days when we had stood a pint of beer to the one amongst us who had extracted the largest stone from the wall in each series of working shifts. I remember the first winner was Rupert, with a stone the size of an egg, then I won a pint with a half-brick. We closed the competition with two pints for Rupert when he cleared the wall by removing a piece of masonry twice the size of a man's head, which we could hardly lift.

The next decision ahead of us was the date and time of the escape. It was essential to be able to forecast the movements of the household which occupied the building beside the woodshed. From behind the wainscot in the tunnel, a watch was kept through a tiny peephole, which revealed a doorway into the house, a window and a washing-machine, but alas! not enough of a slatted door opening on to the roadway to allow us to ascertain what kind of a lock, if any, was on this door, which was to be our gateway to freedom. I made a mental note that, when we escaped, I would take a screwdriver with me. It might be useful!

The watch was maintained at first over the whole day, quickly shortening to concentrate on the more quiet periods. A graph was made of movements against the hours. A German woman spent much of her time in the shed.

We needed a definite 'all-quiet' period of at least half an hour, esti-mated thus: five minutes to open up, twelve minutes (two minutes per person) to sortie, and thirteen minutes to close up the tunnel again.

Two periods showed promise, but not the certainty, of half an hour's quiet. A sentry came on before dusk at the woodshed corner, and left after dawn. In fact, he spent most of the night leaning against the shed, and one fine morning had the audacity to relieve himself immediately over my head. The two periods were: one, immediately prior to the sentry's arrival, and the other immediately after his departure. He usually left at 6 am, and was followed by a patrol. These patrols had always to be reckoned with; some were at regular intervals, but most of them were irregular. They were always a nuisance, and much more so now in the final stage of arranging the getaway.

On the morning of September 4th, our watchers informed us that the woodshed sentry had departed at 5 am. This was good news and placed the early-morning escape in the most favourable light. The woman, according to the graph, could be relied upon not to enter the woodshed before 6.30 am, and usually she arrived a little later. Thus, at the best we would have an hour and a half, and at the worst half an hour. We decided to waste no further time, and to escape next morning. Our zero hour was 5 am on Thursday, September 5th.

2

The First Bid for Freedom

WE ATE WELL on September 4th and prepared our kit, putting the final touches to our clothing. Maps – good survey maps which had been found, and others carefully traced on thin lavatory paper – were distributed. Our staple diet of raw oatmeal mixed with sugar provided at the expense of the German kitchen, was packed. My portion of staple diet went into two small sacks of strongly sewn canvas which were to be hung round my neck so as to fall over my chest and form a buxom bust, for I was to escape as a woman. I still possessed a large brown canvas pouch, which I had found in a caserne at Charleville. This I could carry by hand when dressed as a woman, and later on my back as a man. There was no room for my boots, so I made a brown paper parcel of them.

My female attire consisted of a large red spotted handkerchief for my head, a white sports-shirt as blouse, and a skirt made of an old grey window-curtain, which I had also picked up during the trek into Germany. My legs were shaved and 'sunburnt' with iodine, and I wore black plimsolls.

Once clear of the camp, I would change into a man again, wearing a green-grey Tyrolean hat, cleverly made and dyed from khaki by a British sergeant (a former tailor), a heavy pullover to go over my shirt, a small mackintosh groundsheet for wet weather (also picked up during the journey to Germany), a pair of dark-blue shorts cut from a Belgian airman's breeches (obtained by barter), white Bavarian woollen stockings of the pattern common to the country, purchased at a shocking price in the German canteen, and my brown army boots dyed black.

The others had similar clothing, with minor individual differences. The tailor had devised enough Tyrolean hats to go round and had fashioned an Austrian cloak for Harry Elliott. Lockwood was also to make his exit disguised as a woman, and his costume was more or less like mine. Rupert had an old grey blanket which he converted into a cloak. We were a motley crowd and hardly fit to pass close inspection by daylight, for we had not the experience required to produce really finished garments from scratch. But the idea was that we were young Austrian hikers, and we would only be seen at dusk or dawn.

That night our room-mates made dummies in our beds, good enough to pass the cursory glance of the German night patrol through the room. We all slept in different rooms in the same building as the tunnel, doubling up with other officers, and these arrangements were made as secretly as possible to avoid any hubbub or infectious atmosphere of excitement. The Senior Officers of the rooms in question, who had to declare nightly to the German Officer on the rounds the number of officers present, were not even aware of the additions to or subtractions from their flock.

We were to rise at 4 am. None of us slept much, though we took precautions against oversleeping by having a couple of 'knockers up' in reserve. I remember banging my head on the pillow four times – an old childhood habit which for some unaccountable reason usually worked. It was hardly necessary on this occasion. I passed a most unpleasant night with the cold sweat of nervous anticipation upon me, and with that peculiar nausea of the stomach which accompanies tense nerves and taut muscles. My mind turned over the pros and cons a hundred times; the chances of success, immediate and later, and the risks. If they shot, would they shoot to kill? If they caught us sooner or later, what were our chances – to be liquidated or to disappear into a Concentration Camp? At that period of the war, nobody knew the answers. It was the first escape from this prison, probably the first escape of British officers from any organized prison in Germany. We were the guinea-pigs.

We undertook the experiment with our eyes open, choosing between two alternatives: to attempt escape and risk the ultimate price, or face up to the sentence of indefinite imprisonment. There were many who resigned themselves from the beginning to the second of these alternatives. They were brave, but their natures differed from those of the men who escaped and failed, and escaped again; who having once made the choice between escape and resignation, could not give up, even if the war lasted the remainder of their lives. I am sure that the majority of the men who sought to escape did it for self-preservation. Instinctively, unconsciously, they felt that resignation meant not physical but mental death – maybe lunacy. My own case was not exceptional. One awful fit of depression sufficed to determine my future course as a prisoner. One dose of morbidity in which the vista of emptiness stretched beyond the horizon of my mind was quite enough.

★　★　★

At 4 am, in grisly darkness, I fastened my bosom in place, put on my blouse and skirt. We crept downstairs to our collecting-point in the washroom beside the tunnel-room. A tap was turned on quietly to fill a water-bottle. It went on dripping. The sound of the drops was loud and exasperating. A sentry stood only thirty yards away by the court-yard gate. I felt he must hear it . . . It was nerves. Captain Gilliat, one of the assistants, wore a gas-cape. Why he chose this garment for the occasion I never knew. It crackled loudly with every movement and nearly drove us mad. A watcher was by now at the end of the tunnel, waiting to pass the signal when the sentry near the tunnel exit went off duty. Other stooges were posted at vantage-points to give the alarm in case a patrol suddenly appeared in the buildings. We waited.

At 5.15 am the sentry outside the tunnel still remained at his post. It was probable now he would not leave till 6 am. There was nothing to do but wait quietly while our hearts pounded through our ribs with suppressed excitement.

There was a thundering crash and a reverberating clang as if fifty dinner-gongs had been struck hard with hammers all at once. There was a second crash and a third, diminishing in intensity, and, finally, some strident squeaks. This must be the end – but no one was allowed to move. We had our stooges and we had time after a warning to disappear. The men in the tunnel-room were safely locked in and could hide in the tunnel. A panic would have been dangerous.

Dick Howe and Peter Allan, tired of the long wait, had leant against one of the twelve-foot-long, solid cast-iron troughs which were used as communal washbasins, and finally they had sat on the edge of it. The next instant the whole trough collapsed on to the concrete floor. If I had tried for weeks I doubt if I could have thought of a better way of making the loudest noise possible with the least effort. The succeeding crashes and squeaks which kept our hair standing on end were caused by Dick and Peter who, having made a frantic attempt to save the crash, were extricating themselves from the wreckage and bringing the trough to rest quietly on the floor.

We waited for the signal to return. A minute passed, five minutes passed, and then – and we began to breathe again. No Germans appeared. I never found out why they did not come. The noise woke up most of the officers in the building, which was a large one, and the sentry thirty yards away near the courtyard must have jumped out of his skin. Yet for some unaccountable reason he did not act.

Six o'clock chimed out from a distant steeple. We waited more anxiously as every minute passed. At last, at 6.15 am, the signal came through: 'All clear!' In a moment the door was unlocked and we hustled into the tunnel. I crawled quickly to the end, listened for a second, and then set to work like a demon. Down went the slats and I shovelled earth and cinders to my right and below me as fast as I could. It was light outside. As the hole enlarged I could see the various shed details. All the usual household cleaning equipment, piles of cardboard boxes at one end, clothes drying on a line, and then the slatted door and its lock – a large and formidable-looking padlock on a hasp. Once I tried to get through, but the opening was still too small. I enlarged it further and then squirmed upwards and into the shed. I pulled Rupert and then Peter through after me, telling Dick, who was next, to wait below while we found the way out. We searched quickly. The padlock would not open to a piece of wire which I inserted as a key. I climbed the cardboard boxes to reach a large opening in the slats near the roof and slipped, nearly bringing the boxes down on top of me. Peter held them and we readjusted the pile. We tried the door into the house; it was locked. Then in a flash I thought of the screwdriver. (I had asked Scarlet to lend me one – just in case.) I looked more closely at the hasp on which the padlock was bolted. What a fool I was!

The way was clear. With hands fumbling nervously, I unscrewed three large screws securing the hasp to the wood and the door swung open. I looked at my watch.

'Dick!' I whispered hoarsely down into the tunnel. 'You'd better come up quick, it's 6.30.'

As he started to worm himself up through the hole, there came the sound of an approaching horse and cart.

'Hold everything, Dick!' I said, 'don't move,' and to the others: 'Flatten yourselves against the walls!'

A moment later the cart appeared. Dick remained rigid like a truncated man at floor-level! The driver did not look our way and the cart passed on. We pulled Dick out of the hole. I repeated to him what he already knew.

'We're late. Our safe half-hour is already over and the woman may come in at any moment. Someone's got to replace this.' I pointed at the hasp and padlock. 'It will take five minutes. Add to this twenty minutes to clear the six of us.'

'It will take Scarlet fifteen minutes to close and camouflage the hole,' said Dick. 'It's now 6.35. That means 7.15 before everything is clear.'

We looked at each other and I knew he read my thoughts. We had gone over the timetable so often together.

'I'm sorry, Dick! The graph has never shown the woman to be later than 7 o'clock, and she may arrive any minute. You'll have to lock up and follow tomorrow,' and I handed him the screwdriver.

'Make a good job of closing up our "Shovewood",' I added. 'Your escape depends on it.'

We quickly brushed each other down. I was worried about the back of my skirt, which had suffered in the exit as we had come out on our backs. I repeated nervously:

'Is my bottom clean? Is my bottom clean?'

For the sentry, about forty yards away on the trestle walkway, would see my back view and I did not want him to see a dirty skirt.

I tied my spotted handkerchief around my head, opened the door, and walked out into the sunlight. I turned the corner into the side street leading to the main road, and felt a gooseflesh sensation up my back and the sentry's stare burning through my shoulder-blades. I waited for the shot.

For thirty yards up the side street I walked with short steps imitating what I thought to be the gait of a middle-aged peasant woman, and thereby prolonging the agony of every yard. At last I reached the main road. There was no alarm and I turned the corner.

The road was almost deserted. A few people were cleaning their shop-windows, a restaurant manager was pinning up his menu, and a girl was brushing the pavement. A cyclist or two passed. The hush of dawn and of sleep still lay over the town. I received casual glances, but did not attract any stares.

After I had gone about two hundred yards I heard the heavy footsteps of two persons following me, marching in step. I turned into a square and crossed it diagonally towards the bridge over the river. The footsteps grew louder and nearer. I was being followed: a patrol had been sent after me by the suspicious sentry. They did not run for fear of making me run. I was finished – the game was up – but, I thought, I may as well play it to the end and I ambled along with my bundles across the bridge, not daring to turn round. How those footsteps echoed, first in the street, now on the bridge! The patrol came alongside and passed me without accosting me. I raised my head and to my relief saw two young hikers. They were Rupert and Peter, walking briskly away from me. I had never expected them so soon.

About a hundred yards past the bridge I turned right, following the other two. This route brought me alongside a local railway line and towards the outskirts of the town. We could see the line from the camp, and it had been arranged we should follow the path beside it and rendezvous in the woods about a quarter of a mile out of the town.

As I turned the corner, a little girl, playing with a toy, looked up at me and caught my eye. Astonishment was written all over her face. I might take in a casual adult observer, but I could not pass the keen observation of a child. She continued to look wide-eyed at me as I passed and when I was a few yards farther on I heard her running into a house – no doubt to tell her parents to come and look at the extraordinary man dressed up as a woman. Nobody came, so I presumed they just did not believe her. Grown-ups always know better than their children!

It was a misty morning heralding a hot day. I followed the railway into the woods, where it swept to the left in a big curve. I heard a train approaching and made for cover among the trees. It passed and I continued a short distance, expecting to see the other two waiting for me. There was no sign of them and I began to worry. I whistled, but there was no answer. I continued slowly, whistling 'We're going to hang out our washing on the Siegfried Line . . .' They must be close by the woods. Still no answer. Then I heard shots in the distance and dogs barking. I immediately dashed into the woods and decided to hide and change rapidly. I could not go on in my makeshift skirt. Maybe the child's parents had phoned the camp or the police. They might search for someone with a skirt on!

I found myself close to the river and was soon in among high reeds, where I started to change. It was about 7.15 am. Shots continued spasmodically and the barking of dogs increased. I was at my wits' end and sure the 'hunt was up,' and I had lost the other two. Rupert had the only compass – a good army one given him by a fellow-officer, who had managed to conceal it through all searches. I could not travel far without one.

I suddenly heard people approaching along a wood path close to the reeds. I crouched and waited until I saw them. Thank God, it was my two hikers once more!

'I thought I'd lost you for good,' I said, quickly completing my change and hiding my skirt in the reeds. 'I was already bothering about how I was going to reach Yugoslavia without a compass.'

'What's all the shooting about?' said Peter.

'I haven't the foggiest idea. I don't like it. They've probably discovered something and are shooting up the camp. They'll be after us in no time. We'll have to hide up.'

'It sounds to me like rifle-range shooting,' said Rupert.

'Well, why have we never heard it before, then?' I questioned, 'and how do you account for the dogs?'

'Probably the village dogs barking at the gunfire.'

'The fact is, Rupert, we've never heard shooting like this before, and besides, it's still misty in places. I believe they're after us and we'd better hide up quickly.'

'I bet you five pounds it's range-shooting. Anyway, it's no use hiding here. We're much too close. Come on, let's make tracks!'

We made for the top of a high wooded hill which lay in our

general direction southwards. From it we could see all the surrounding country. We crossed the railway, then a road and some open fields before entering the friendly cover of more woods. We simply scuttled across the fields, Rupert, who was the calmest, doing all he could to make us walk normally. In the woods we disturbed some chamois which fled away noisily, giving us the fright of our lives.

We had left tracks in the dew-laden grass of the fields and we were out of breath from the steep uphill going. We rested for a moment and smeared our boots with German mustard, which we had brought for the purpose of putting dogs off the scent, and then continued, climbing steeper and steeper. We heard woodcutters at work and kept clear of them. Eventually, at about 9 am, we reached the top of the hill.

The shooting and the barking of dogs had ceased. We gained confidence. Either the hunters had lost track of us or it had been a false alarm, as Rupert thought.

The camp *Appell*, that is, roll-call, was due and soon we should have an important matter decided. We had arranged that, from a window high up in the camp building, a sheet would be hung, as if to air; white for 'all clear,' blue check if our absence had been discovered.

The Germans held two separate *Appells*, one for the Officers, and immediately afterwards one for the Other Ranks – in another courtyard. This gave us an opening of which we were not slow to avail ourselves. I had arranged with six 'good men and true' that they would stand in for the Officers' *Appell* and then do a rapid change in a lavatory into orderlies' attire and appear on the Other Ranks parade. Only three of them would be necessary today.

It was a glorious morning and I climbed a tree to look down into the valley, now clear of mist and bathed in luxurious sunshine. The view was beautiful, rich in September fruitfulness, with the river in the foreground rushing over its pebbly bed, a ribbon of sparkling light.

I could see our prison in the distance reflecting a warm golden colour from its walls. I had never thought that our Archbishop's Palace could be called beautiful, but from a distance it certainly was so. Then I realized why; I could not distinguish the windows in the walls. We were farther away than we had estimated, and the sunlight was at a bad angle. There was no hope of seeing a sheet of any colour. Later, when the sun had moved round, Peter climbed the tree, but he could scarcely distinguish the windows and, although his sight was keen, could see no sign of a sheet.

We hid the whole day in a copse of young fir-trees on the top of the hill. We were only disturbed once, by a woodman who passed close by but did not see us. We reconnoitred the southern slope of the hill along the route we were to take that night, but it was wooded for a long distance so we soon gave up, letting the darkness bring what it might. We were in very good hiding. I believe only dogs would ever have found us.

We lay in long grass in an open patch among the trees, dozing from time to time, scarcely ever talking. The sun shone in a cloudless sky. It was good to be alive, to breathe the air of freedom, the scent of pines and dry grass, to hear the murmur of flying insects around and the distant chopping of a woodman's axe, to listen to a lark above one's head – a fluttering speck against the infinity of the clear blue sky. We were free at last. A restful calm, a silent relish of this precious day spread over us. There was a hush on the sunbathed, pleasant countryside. We felt attuned to it. Our hearts were full of thanksgiving. Animals do not need to speak, I thought.

At meal-time we sat up and ate our meagre ration. We had worked it out to last us twelve days. We drank a mouthful of water each from a small bottle, exchanged a few remarks on the chances of Dick and the others the next day and then returned to our dreaming.

A beautiful autumnal evening set in, and with it came a chill in the air as the sun sank peacefully over the horizon. I have seldom in my life spent a happier day. The war did not seem to exist.

We clothed ourselves, put chalk in our socks and boots, and, as darkness approached, set off downhill through the woods – southwards to Yugoslavia. It was about one hundred and fifty miles away across the mountains of the Austrian Tyrol. We hoped to make it in ten days.

3

The Price of Failure

W E HAD A large-scale survey map which covered the first sixty
miles of our journey. It showed all the contours, and even
tiny villages and mountain paths. Its acquisition deserves an
explanation.

Our camp was formerly the depot of the 100th Gebirgs-jäger
Regiment – mountain troops. At the top of one of our buildings was
a staircase leading up to an attic. The former was entirely shut off by
a wood partition and a door made of slats which was heavily chained
and padlocked. We could not see far up the staircase, but its situation
was intriguing and invited inspection.

One day Scarlet O'Hara solved the problem of how to by-pass the
door. The stair passed diagonally across a window, the springer being
about eight inches away from the glass. The sill of this window could
be reached from the flight of stairs below by climbing on a man's
shoulder. A thin man could worm himself up through the eight-inch
gap on to the forbidden staircase, and thus the secrets of the attic
were revealed. A few doors with very simple locks were no barrier to
Scarlet, and an old storeroom was found in which there were many
copies of survey maps of the district around Laufen. Other useful
things, such as small hatchets, screws and nails, pens and coloured
inks, were found, and even badges of the mountain regiment. We
took away a small portion of everything, hoping the stock had never
been accurately counted.

Before we escaped, someone a little too fat had tried the window
route and split the glass. The Jerries realized what was happening and
barred off the window completely. There was not much left in the
attic by that time. The Germans created a big fuss and searched the
camp and the prisoners individually. The search lasted a day, but

nothing seriously incriminating was found, and our tunnel, being behind German locks, was not troubled.

Rupert's compass had survived many such searches by employing the following simple ruse. Before being searched, the owner of the compass demanded urgently to go to the lavatory, meeting there by arrangement a friend who had been searched already. Although the owner was accompanied by a sentry while carrying out this simple duty, a moment always arrived when it was possible to slip the article to the friend unobserved. The method required good synchronization and deft handling of an opportunity, or even the making of an opportunity by diverting the attention of the sentry.

There was no moon and it soon became pitch-dark in the woods. We were in thick undergrowth and brambles and made slow progress, so much so that we altered our compass bearing and headed south-east, trying to find easier going. After about two hours we cleared the woods and were able to trek across country at a good speed, aiming at a chosen star which we checked by the compass as being in our line. It was then only necessary to look at the compass every hour or so and change our guiding star as the constellations moved in the sky.

Walking at night straight across country is an eerie experience. Only the actual ground for a few yards around is real, be it long grass, corn stubble, potato field, or moorland. Beyond this island lies an ocean composed entirely of shadows, unreal and mysterious. Into this outer world one gropes with the eyes, peering and straining all the time, seeking to solve its mysteries. Shadows of every shape, some grotesque, some frightening, varying infinitesimally and subtly in depth from the deepest black, through blues and greens to the patchy greys and whiteness of the ground mist. One walks into the unknown; one might be walking on the moon. Shadows are deceptive things. A little copse seems like an impenetrable forest. A field of hay may turn into a discouraging reedy marsh. A stook of corn suddenly takes on a fantastic resemblance to a silent listening man. A sheet-white ghost looms out of the mist. It moves – a stray cow shies off, as frightened as ourselves by the encounter. Stately mansions turn into derelict barns, and a distant hedge becomes a deep cutting with a railway line at the bottom. On this unreal planet one walks with every sense alert to the 'sticking-point.'

We went in single file spaced as far apart as possible, taking turns at leading with a white handkerchief draped over our backs. We would jollow the leader, listening for the muttered warnings: 'ware wire, brambles, a ditch, marsh, and so on. We often stumbled. We avoided buildings, but even so, in the silence of the night, our progress would be heard by dogs and they would start barking as we hurried off into the shadows. We knew there was no big river in our path but we had to ford several streams, sometimes taking off boots and stockings and wading knee-deep to do so. We stopped to rest occasionally, and had a meal under a haystack at about 1 am.

As dawn approached, we searched for a hiding-place for the day and found one in a grove of trees far away from any buildings. We had done only thirteen miles, and were rather disappointed. We did not sleep much and were anxious to move on. The first part of our next night's march lay across a wide valley. Noting landmarks on our line, we set off a little before nightfall. Our feet were sore and blisters were appearing. Peter had borrowed a pair of suitable-looking boots which, however, did not fit him too well, and he developed enormous blisters on his heels. I had warned him what to expect. He stuck it well.

Later we found ourselves in mountainous country with occasional rushing torrents, waterfalls, and deep gorges, and mostly wooded. Farms, surrounded by small patches of cultivation cleared out of the woods, were few and far between.

The weather held fine. On our third day of freedom we considered making a start in daylight. By the early afternoon our impatience got the better of us and we set off.

After some steep climbing, we found a sparkling stream where in the clearer pools basked mountain trout.

'Rupert,' I said, 'I can't resist this. My clothes are wringing wet; I'm perspiring like a pig. I'm going to have a bathe.'

I started to undress. Rupert bent over a rock to feel the water.

'Ye gods!' he shouted, withdrawing his hand as if he had been scalded. 'This water comes straight from the North Pole.'

'Just what you need to freshen you up.' I thought of my long walking tours as a student, when I learnt the benefit of bathing my feet frequently in cold water.

'Peter,' I added, 'it'll do your blisters no end of good. I insist we all sit with our feet dangling in a pool for at least ten minutes.'

We all had a lightning dip, while our damp and sweaty clothes lay drying in the sun, and then we dangled our feet until we could not feel them any more. When we set off again, we were walking on air.

The going soon became so difficult that we took to paths and cattle tracks, and for the first time met another human being. Previously we had narrowly escaped being seen by some Hitler youths and girls whom we heard singing and laughing on our path close behind us. The new intruder was a woodman – we passed him with a casual 'Heil Hitler!' He took no notice of us.

Later we came upon a small farm and Peter made so bold as to ask the farmer the way. Although our survey map could hardly have been better, our route was strewn with deep narrow valleys and we became confused as to which one we were in.

As evening drew on we found another gurgling stream and, piling up some stones on its bank, we made a fire. We had hot soup from cubes and roasted some potatoes, which we had collected earlier from a potato patch. It was a heavenly meal. After a good rest and a doze, we pushed on again as night fell.

We tried to maintain our direction on the small mountain paths, but found ourselves more and more frequently consulting our map with the aid of matches. This was an unwelcome necessity, for we did not want a light to give us away, and, even in woods, shielded the matches with our capes. Eventually we found a minor road and embarked on it. Soon it started to wind downhill and in a general direction at right angles to ours. At the same time we became hemmed in with impenetrable-looking forest which we dared not enter. We did not want to go downhill; it was out of our way and, in any case, it is always an advantage when walking across country to keep high up; then, with a map, one's position can be checked by bearings taken on the surrounding country. At the rate we were going we would be in the main Salzburg (Salzach) valley by morning. Even from our map we could not be certain which road we were on. In fact, we were lost.

We decided to wait till dawn and retrace our steps until our position could be checked up. Penetrating about fifty yards into the woods, we lay down to sleep in a leafy hollow. It was bitterly cold and we huddled together for warmth, with our scanty coverings spread over all three of us. Our muscles ached and we spent a miserable few hours dozing fitfully. Just before daylight we could stand it no longer and were about to move off when Rupert suddenly declared in a horrified tone:

'The compass is gone, I can't find it!'

There was a long silence as we regarded each other. I broke the awkward spell.

'That's a nice kettle of fish! When do you last remember having it?'

'Miles away! Before we started coming downhill – the last time we lit those matches.'

We stared blankly at each other in the cold dawn, shivering miserably and depressed beyond description.

'Well! let's start searching,' I said. 'Be careful where we've been lying. Start from one end of the hollow and let's work on our hands and knees in line. Feel first for lumps and don't turn over more leaves than you can possibly help.'

We searched, carefully patting the leaves and moss, advancing slowly yard by yard over the whole area of our bivouac.

'I've got it!' said Peter in triumph suddenly, holding it up like a trophy.

We sighed our relief. In this country, without a compass we could not keep a consistent course for five minutes.

After about two hours' walking, as the dawn came up we were able to locate ourselves and once more set off in the right direction across meadows and along the edges of woods, following a mountain ridge while it ran more or less parallel with our course.

This was our fourth day of freedom and we had had no rain. We met nobody all day. By evening we had reached the main road which heads south-east from Golling to Radstadt and across the mountain hump by way of the Radstädter Tauern pass. From now on it was apparent we should have to follow the road, because the mountains were high and the valley was a gorge. We set off along the road in the cool of the evening. Within ten minutes several people passed us on foot or on bicycles, and a Jerry soldier ambled by with a 'Heil Hitler!' to which we replied with gusto. Although he had not appeared to see anything unusual in our now ragged and dirty clothing, we decided to retire into the woods and continue only after dark. This we did, and during the night we walked fast and with few stops, for the cold was becoming intense.

Our feet were at last becoming hardened. We made good going and by dawn had gone about twenty-four miles. There were two incidents during the night. At about 11 pm a girl on a bicycle caught us up and insisted on talking to us.

'*Guten Abend! wo gehen Sie hin?*' she volunteered, dismounting and walking along beside us.

'Forward hussy, what?' murmured Rupert under his breath.

'Peter, you're a lady-killer,' I whispered; 'go on, do your stuff.' Peter took over.

'We're going to Abtenau. We've got army leave and are hiking. And where might you be going?'

Peter's German was correct even to the Austrian accent. The girl was pleased.

'I live at Voglau. It's only two miles from here on the main road. You come from Salzburg?'

'No, from Saalfelden,' replied Peter, naming a place as far away from Salzburg as possible.

'I'll walk with you to my house. Father may offer you beer.'

I understood enough to know that the conversation was taking an unhappy turn. I promptly sat down on a grass bank at the edge of the road and, pulling Rupert by his sleeve, said in an undertone, hoping my indifferent German accent would not be noticed, '*Hans! Kommen Sie her. Ich gehe nicht weiter.*' Rupert took the hint and sat beside me. Peter and the girl were already some yards ahead. I heard her say: 'Your friends do not seem to like me. They will not speak. How rude they are.'

'They are not rude but very tired, *Fräulein*,' put in Peter. 'I am too tired to continue farther without a rest. *Auf Wiedersehen!* You must hurry home, for it is very late and your father will be worried. *Auf Wiedersehen!*'

With that Peter practically sat her on her bicycle and finally got rid of her. She left us a bit disgruntled and probably with some queer impressions. I doubt if she suspected us, though she was capable of talking to someone in a village who might. This was an added reason for our making good headway during the night and moving out of the district.

Occasionally a car passed with headlights blazing – no thought of blackout! – which gave us enough warning to take cover. We did not take cover for pedestrians who passed or for cyclists who, in any case, were liable to catch us up, unheard above the roar of a mountain river which the road now followed. We walked together, feeling that if we were accosted there was always one of us who could reply.

Approaching a small village beyond the junction town called Abtenau, we saw several lights and torches flickering. We hastily took to a field. The lights persisted for a long time – about two hours – and garrulous voices could be heard. Finally the episode wound up when a very drunken man passed down the road reeling from side to side, throwing and kicking his bicycle along in front of him. He was shouting and swearing and could be heard a mile away. Loud crashes punctuated his tirade, indicating that the bicycle was the victim of his rage and presumably the cause of it!

The lights were ominous. We continued when all was quiet and shortly afterwards encountered a small house with an army motor-cycle standing outside. Dogs barked as we passed, so we hurried on.

We were about three thousand feet above sea-level. The valley became narrower than ever and it was out of the question to travel other than on the road. In daylight we would be conspicuous walking through the small villages.

We rested during the fifth day (a Monday) on a promontory over-looking the road. Towards late afternoon a cold drizzle began to fall. We became restless and argued about going on. One by one we gave in and agreed to move. With our odd-looking capes and blankets over our shoulders, we trudged uphill along the now muddy road – passing a sawmill where a few men were working. They stared at us, and later a motor-lorry from the mill caught us up before we had time to take cover. As it passed, a youth leaned out and had a good stare at us.

This was disquieting. I insisted we should disappear again until nightfall. We found a resting-place beside the river among trees about fifteen yards from the road. The rain continued till nightfall and then ceased, leaving us cold, wet, and dispirited. I was nervous after the experience of the sawmill. We drank water copiously before starting. If a man drinks far more than he has the desire for, he can walk for eight hours without feeling unduly thirsty. We continued up the winding valley past straggling villages and small chalets. The night was pitch-dark and there were no stars. We were nearing the top of the pass and were only a few miles from Radstadt, which was the halfway point on our journey to Yugoslavia. We had walked about seventy-five miles.

We entered a small village at about 11.30 pm. It was called Lungötz. All was quiet. Suddenly the light of an electric torch was directed down at us from a window high above. After a few seconds it went out. Very suspicious! But there was nothing we could do about it in the middle of a village. We had been seen, so we had to bluff our way out. Coming to a fork in the road, we hesitated a moment while I peered at the signpost, and then took the left branch. After a couple of hundred yards we left the village behind and the road entered deep woods. We breathed more freely.

The next moment there was a loud crashing of branches and undergrowth. Beams from powerful torches flashed on us and we saw the gleam of rifle barrels. Men shouted 'Halt! Halt! Wer da?' We stopped, and Peter, a few steps ahead, answered 'Gut Freund.' Three men jumped down to the road from the banks on either side and approached, with their rifles aimed at us from the hip. At a few yards' distance they began shouting at Peter all together. I could see they were very nervous.

'Who are you? What are you doing in the woods at this hour? Where are you going? Produce your papers!'

'One at a time! One at a time!' shouted Peter. 'What is all this fuss? We are innocent people. We are soldiers on leave and we go to Radstadt.'

'Where are your papers? We do not believe you. Show us your papers.'

'We do not carry papers. We are on leave.'

One of them approached Rupert and me and knocked the sticks which we held out of our hands with his rifle, jabbering hysterically at us. We could not have answered him if we had wanted to.

'So you have no papers. Why are your two companions silent? We think you are spies, enemies of the Reich!'

There was a moment when Rupert and I might have run for it – back down the road, zigzagging – leaving Peter. But the opportunity passed before we had time to pull our wits together. We might have got away with it if there were no patrols behind us.

Then the men were all shouting, *'Hände hoch! Hände hoch!'* and we put up our hands, Peter still protesting we were innocent and anxious to get on to Radstadt. It was no use. If Peter had been alone he might have deceived them, but we two were just so much dead weight and our dumbness or sullenness was the last straw.

We were marched back at the bayonet point to a small inn in the village. Several windows in a house opposite were lit up. I recognized it as the house from which the torchlight had first been flashed at us. The owner of the torch had probably been in touch with the ambush party by signal. In the *Gaststube* (dining-room) of the inn, we were lined against a wall and ordered by one of the three policemen, more ferocious and nervous than the rest, to keep our arms stretched upwards. We were then left with two guards until about 1.30 am, when the third guard returned. We were marched out and put in the back of an open lorry, which I recognized as the one which had passed us, and were driven off down the road along which we had come. It was heartbreaking to see the landmarks we had passed only a few hours before as free men. The two guards sat facing us with their rifles at the ready. Since our capture there had not been the faintest chance of a getaway. The remainder of the night was spent at the police-station at Abtenau, then two hours' drive under armed guard, and we were back in the German *Kommandantur* at Oflag VII C, a depressed and sorry-looking trio.

A German under-officer approached us and we were 'for it'. He was the one who checked numbers at *Appells*, and he knew Peter well, since Peter had acted as camp interpreter on many occasions. He roared at us, forcing us to stand rigidly to attention while he tore off pieces of our clothing. He shook Peter wildly by the shoulders, spluttering into his face. It was a wonderful exhibition. He had obviously had a bad time since our absence was discovered.

After working off his revenge he led us to the German Camp

Adjutant, who took us one by one into his office and questioned us. He began with me.

'It was useless to try to escape. You were warned. Now it is proved. You were fortunate not to have been shot. When did you leave?'

'I cannot say.'

'But what difference does it make? We know everything. Six of you escaped. You left on Saturday, did you not?'

'I don't know.'

'Herr Hauptmann, you are an officer and I understand your point of view, but when the whole matter is closed and finished, surely we can talk together freely?'

'Of course, Herr Oberst, I understand. I did not know you had recaptured three more officers.'

'That is a leading question. Please remember I am questioning you – and that you are not here to question me. You had money, of course?'

'Money? No.'

'Then how have you travelled so far in such a short time?'

'There are ways of travelling, Herr Oberst.'

'Ha! So you stole bicycles?'

I was becoming involved. My 'No' to the question concerning money was not a good answer. I fell back upon 'I cannot reply to your questions.'

'Unless you tell me the day you escaped, I shall have to assume you have stolen bicycles. This is a very serious charge.'

'I cannot help it.'

'You have concealed your absence at one *Appell*. How did you do it?'

'I did not do it.'

'You did not, but others did. You see, your absence was known at evening *Appell* on Saturday. Your escape was made at night. Therefore at the morning *Appell* your absence was concealed. You admit it was at night, do you not?'

'I admit nothing.'

'Do not be so silly. It was, of course, clever of you to hide in the grass compound. We are building a guard ring of barbed wire two yards from the fences now. You will not be able to repeat your escape. Did you hide near the river or high up?'

'I just concealed myself.'

'But where?'

'I cannot say.'

'I know that soldiers concealed your *Appell*. Unless you tell me their names, I shall be compelled to have them all punished. That is not fair, to punish all for the offence of six. What were their names?'

'I do not know.'

'You know well. If you do not give the names, it will be bad for all. You can save much hardship by a simple answer.'

'I am sorry, Herr Oberst.'

'Well then! You have either stolen bicycles or you have had assistance from outside the camp. For a prisoner to steal a bicycle is punishable with death. If you have received help, you can say so. I shall not ask the names and shall not charge you with theft of German private property. Come now, that is fair.'

'Your answer is so fair, Herr Oberst, that I know you will understand my inability to answer you.'

'You are a fool,' he answered, becoming angry. 'I have given you enough chances. You will suffer for your silence. Do you like concentration camps? Do you like to starve? Do you like to die? I give you one more chance. Your obstinacy is madness – it has no reason. Did you receive any help?'

I did not answer.

'So you insult me. Very well. You will be punished for silent insolence as well. About turn! March!'

I left the room and the others were paraded in turn. The questioning and tactics were the same in each case, as I found out. Rupert and Peter gave nothing away. We had a pretty good idea by now of German bluff, and in our three months' imprisonment we were beginning to learn that even a POW had rights and that a document known as the 'Geneva Convention' existed.

I learnt in time to bless this International Convention for the Treatment of Prisoners-of-War and must record here my gratitude to its authors. This product of the League of Nations stands as a testimony to our civilization. Its use in World War II demonstrated the force of that civilization amidst the threat of its ruin.

Our questioning ended, we were marched off to the town jail, which was close by, and each locked in a separate cell. For several days we languished in our dungeons like forgotten men. My cell was empty except for an unused heating stove, a bucket, and a jug of water. Wood floor, stone walls, and a tiny window just below a high ceiling made up my surroundings. There was no bed or bedding. At night the cold was intense, though it was only September.

During the day we walked our rooms or sat on the floor. We tried knocking to each other through the walls, which annoyed the guards, who cursed and threatened us if we continued. This depressing period was no doubt intended to demoralize us, for we were again taken individually and questioned, and when we refused to speak we were informed that we would be held for court martial.

When an officer is recaptured after an escape, the same principle holds good as when he is first taken prisoner – namely, that it is better to say nothing than tell lies. Lies may temporarily deceive the enemy in one direction, but they often lead him to unearth something which was never intended to be discovered. If I had replied to the question 'How did you escape?' by saying we escaped over the roofs, it was quite liable to upset a plan being prepared by other officers in the camp unknown to us.

If to the question 'When did you escape?' I gave a date several days before the actual event, I ran a good risk of being found out in a lie through a chance identification, or I might make the Germans so aghast at the length of my absence that the repercussion on future *Appell* precautions might be disastrous. If I named a date some time after the actual event, I immediately gave the Jerries false ideas as to how far I could travel in a given time and thereby enlarged the circumference of cordons for future escapers. I found also that Jerry quickly lost respect for an enemy who talked. He expects silence. It is in accord with his own rules.

We returned, to languish in our jail. Every second day we were thrown a slab of brown bread in the morning and given a bowl of soup at midday.

On the fourth day there was a loud commotion and we heard the voices of Dick Howe, Harry Elliott, and Kenneth Lockwood! They were locked in neighbouring cells. Their arrival was further cause for depression.

We soon made complaints about the bucket sanitation and were eventually allowed to use a lavatory at the end of the corridor. Then we complained of lack of exercise and were allowed to walk for half an hour daily in single file at twenty-five paces from each other in a circle in the Oflag courtyard, the other officers being temporarily shut off from the area.

We established communications with the camp and among ourselves. With the aid of pencil butts dropped in the courtyard where we walked, notes were later written on pieces of lavatory paper, and left to be picked up by officers. The first Red Cross parcels had just arrived. We asked for food in our notes and were soon receiving it: chocolate, sugar, Ovo-sport, cheese!

We would enter the courtyard carrying our towels as sweat-rags. After a turn or two we would notice an inconspicuous pile of swept-up dust. This was the food done up in a small round parcel. A towel would be dropped carelessly in the corner over the rubbish and left until the end of the half-hour's exercise. The towel and the parcel would then be recovered in one movement and nonchalantly carried back to the cells to be divided later and left in the lavatory.

Gradually we learnt each other's stories. We found out also that no one else had escaped, and were aghast at this and extremely disappointed. Men could have been escaping every other day or so. We could not understand it.

Dick Howe, Harry Elliott, and Kenneth Lockwood had been recaught about sixty-three miles away, on the road to Switzerland, after eight days of freedom. Their escape worked to plan. Scarlet O'Hara closed up the hole. After two days' march the three of them jumped a goods train near Golling which took them to a place called Saalfelden. Although they gained about four days' march by this, they had to retrace their steps for some two days to regain their correct route. They had some bad going and bad weather, and had to lie up for a day or two in deserted mountain huts. Walking along a river bank close to a village, they were accosted by two women who appeared to suspect them. Harry's German passed. The women were looking for a man who had burgled their house. Farther on they were trapped by a policeman who conducted them to the village to question them concerning the burglary. Only when they were searched did the local bobby realize he had strained at a gnat and had narrowly missed swallowing a camel.

After ten days in the cells we were told that there would not be a court martial after all, but we were to await our sentences. In due course these were meted out, and to our surprise varied considerably. Peter got off with a fortnight, Rupert and I were the longest with a month each, without retroactive effect from our first day in cell. The differences were explained by minor offences, such as carrying a cut-up German blanket or being in possession of a compass or a map and so on. The sentences were 'bread and water and solitary'; that is to say, bread and water only and a board bed for three days out of every four. On the fourth day the prisoner was given a mattress and two meals of thick potato soup or other gruel. As sentences finished we were allowed to live together in one cell; a large one with mattresses, blankets, and German prison ration food. Thus it came to pass, after forty days, that all six of us were together again. We wondered what would happen to us next. We knew that escaped prisoners were usually moved to new camps.

One day a camp padre was allowed to visit us and give us spiritual comfort. We had complained repeatedly that we were not allowed to read books, not even a Bible. Padre Wynne Price Rees gave us the first news as to what had happened to our tunnel.

For some inexplicable reason Scarlet O'Hara and others had postponed using the tunnel, at first for a week and then, upon our recapture, indefinitely. Finally, questions having been asked in the town as to whether any suspicious individuals had been seen between certain dates, a little girl was brought by her mother to the Camp Commandant. She reported having seen one morning, in a wood-shed near the camp walls, a man in pyjamas whom she did not recognize as being anyone belonging to the household of the wood-shed owner. A stranger in pyjamas in the woodshed of a house in the early morning – wonderful food for gossip in Laufen! This event occurred about three weeks after our escape. Little notice was taken of the child's story by anyone except an elderly *Feldwebel* who had been a POW in England during the First World War and who had helped German officers to build a tunnel. He went 'snooping' in the part of the camp near the woodshed, sounding the walls and floors.

Eventually he arrived at the little locked room, where he came upon the hidden piles of earth and finally our tunnel entrance in the darkest corner under a table. It was camouflaged against casual observation by a large piece of painted cardboard made to fit the hole.

We could pride ourselves on the fact that the camouflage of the tunnel exit had held out. I felt a little ashamed that our entrance had not been better finished. My excuse was that I had never meant it to last three weeks and, moreover, we found from later experience that it was difficult under any circumstances to keep an escape-hole concealed for long after prisoners were known to have escaped.

The figure in pyjamas turned out to be Scarlet O'Hara, who was feverishly screwing up the woodshed door-bolt when he looked up to see the face and startled eyes of the little girl peering at him through the slats of the door. She bolted in terror, and Scarlet, equally frightened, disappeared backwards down our rabbit burrow at high speed. Scarlet's face was at no time beautiful, and I am sure the little girl had nightmares for weeks afterwards.

A few days after the padre's visit we were summoned and, to our utter astonishment, sent back to the camp. We became once more normal prisoners-of-war. It was not to be for long. A week later we were given an hour's notice to assemble for departure to an unknown destination.

The six of us had profited by our week to pass on what information and experience we had gained to the others, and we could not understand why the Germans had given us the opportunity. They had no microphones in Laufen; of that we were certain. Before we departed, our Senior British Officer (always known as the SBO) insisted on being told our destination. I believe he also insisted on this information being cabled to the International Red Cross. We packed our meagre belongings and, with a large five-gallon drum filled with cooked potatoes which we took it in turn to carry, two at a time, we set off on foot for the station under heavy guard. Our destination was Oflag IV C, Colditz, Saxony.

PART TWO
Escape Officer

PART TWO
Escape Officer

4

The Fortress Prison

WE LEFT LAUFEN on November 7th, 1940, and arrived three days later in Colditz, Oflag IV C.

There was little or no chance of escape on the journey. Moreover, we had no escape material or reserve food (except potatoes!). The guards were watchful; we were always accompanied to the lavatory. We travelled sometimes in second class, sometimes in third, at all hours of the day and night. There were many changes and long waits, usually in the military waiting-rooms of stations. Passers-by eyed us curiously but without, I thought, great animosity. Those who made closer contact by speaking with our guards were concerned at our carrying potatoes with us. We, who had had three months of starvation diet, followed by many weeks of bread and water, were taking no risks and would have fought for those cold scraggy balls of starch with desperation!

We arrived at the small town of Colditz early one afternoon. Almost upon leaving the station we saw looming above us our future prison: beautiful, serene, majestic, and yet forbidding enough to make our hearts sink into our boots. It towered above us, dominating the whole village: a magnificent castle built on the edge of a cliff. It was the real fairy castle of childhood's story-books. What ogres there might live within! I thought of the dungeons and of all the stories I had ever heard of prisoners in chains, pining away their lives, of rats and tortures, and of unspeakable cruelties and abominations.

In such a castle, through the centuries, everything had happened and anything might happen again. To friendly peasants and trades-people in the houses nestling beneath its shadows it may have signified protection and home, but to enemies from a distant country such a castle struck the note of doom and was a sight to make the bravest quail. Indeed, it was built with this end in view. Being about one thousand years old, although partly ruined, built over and altered many times, its inherent strength had preserved it from destruction through the stormy centuries.

It was built on the top of a high cliff promontory that jutted out over the River Mulde at a confluence with a tributary stream. The outside walls were on an average seven feet thick, and the inner courtyard of the Castle was about two hundred and fifty feet above the river-level. The Castle rooms in which we were to live were about another sixty feet above the courtyard. The Castle was built by Augustus the Strong, King of Poland and Elector of Saxony from 1694 to 1733, who was reputed to have had three hundred and sixty-five children, one for every day of the year. He built it upon ruins left by the Hussite wars of the fifteenth century. It had seen many battles and sieges in a long history, and the present name, Schloss Colditz, testified, not to its origin, but to a time when it was under Polish domination. The 'itz' is a Slavonic not a Teutonic or Saxon ending. The original spelling was Koldyeze.

The River Mulde, we later learned, was a tributary of the Elbe, into which it flowed forty miles to the north. Colditz was situated in the middle of the triangle formed by the three great cities of Leipzig, Dresden, and Chemnitz, in the heart of the German Reich and four hundred miles from any frontier not directly under the Nazi heel. What a hope for would-be escapers!

We marched slowly up the steep and narrow cobbled streets from the station towards the Castle, eventually approaching it from the rear, that is to say, from the mainland out of which the promontory protruded. Entering the main arched gateway, we crossed a causeway astride what had once been a deep, wide moat and passed under a second cavernous archway whose oaken doors swung open and closed ominously behind us with the clanging of heavy iron bars in true medieval fashion. We were then in a courtyard about forty-five yards square, with some grass lawn and flower-beds and surrounded on all four sides with buildings six stories high. This was the *Kommandantur* or garrison area. We were escorted farther; through a third cavernous archway with formidable doors, up an inclined cobbled coach way for about fifty yards, then turning sharp right, through a fourth and last archway with its normal complement of heavy oak and iron work into the 'Sanctum Sanctorum', the inner courtyard. This was a cobbled space about thirty yards by forty yards, surrounded on its four sides by buildings whose roof ridges must have been ninety feet above the cobbles. Little sun could ever penetrate here! It was an unspeakably grisly place, made none the less so by the pallid faces which we noticed peering at us through bars. There was not a sound in the courtyard. It was as if we were entering some ghostly ruin. Footsteps echoed and the German words of command seemed distorted out of reality. I had reached the stage of commending my soul to the Almighty when the faces behind the bars suddenly took on life; eyes shone, teeth flashed from behind unkempt beards and words passed backwards into the inner depths:

'Anglicy! Anglicy!'

Heads crowded each other out behind tiny barred windows, and in less time than it took us to walk thirty yards there was a cheering mob at every window; not only at the small ones which we had first seen and which we were to come to know so well, but from every other window that we could see there were jostling heads, laughing and cheering. Welcome was written on every face. We breathed again as we realized we were among friends. They were Polish officers.

Relief was quickly followed by amazement as we heard the men behind the bars shout insults at the Germans in their own language, at the same time making violent gestures indicating throat-cutting of the unmistakable ear-to-ear variety. The Jerries were angry. They threatened reprisals, and quickly hustled us away to a building and up many flights of stairs into a couple of attic rooms, where they left us under lock and key behind a wooden grill.

We were not the first arrivals: three RAF officers were there to greet us! They were Flying Officers Howard D. Wardle, Keith Milne, and Donald Middleton.

Wardle, or 'Hank' as he was called, was a Canadian who had joined the RAF shortly before the war. He was dropping propaganda leaflets over Germany in April 1940, when his bomber was shot down. He parachuted and landed in trees as his parachute opened. He was one of the earliest British POWs of the war. He had escaped from the Schloss camp of Spangenburg, about twenty miles from Kassel, by climbing a high barricade on the way to a gymnasium just outside the camp precincts. The other two, also Canadians, had escaped dressed as painters complete with buckets of whitewash and a long ladder, which they carried between them. They had waited for a suitable moment when there appeared to be a particularly dumb Jerry on guard at the gate, marched up briskly, shouted the only words they knew in German and filed out. Having passed the gate, they continued jauntily until they were half-way down the hill on which the Schloss reposed. They then jettisoned ladder and buckets and made a bolt for the woods.

These escapes were in August 1940, and were probably the first escapes of the war from regular camps. None of the three travelled very far before recapture and it was, alas, only a matter of hours before they were back behind the bars. They suffered badly at the hands of their captors, being severely kicked and battered with rifle-butts. The local population were bitter and revengeful.

The three RAF officers had arrived a couple of days before us at night and had seen no one. They were told that sentences awaited them and that they would probably be shot. On the first morning at dawn they had been marched out to some woods in a deep valley flanking one side of the Castle and halted beside a high granite wall . . . They had then been told to exercise themselves for half an hour! The Germans took a sadistic pleasure in putting the complete wind up the three of them. By the time they reached the high wall in the early half-light they had given up hope of ever seeing another sunrise. This joke over, the Jerries took them back to the rooms in which we found them.

Later that evening we made our first acquaintance with the Poles. There were hushed voices on the staircase, then four of them appeared beyond the grill. They unlocked the door with ease and advanced to greet us. We were the first English they had seen in the war, and the warmth of their welcome, coupled with their natural dignity of bearing, was touching. Each one of us might have been a hero, for to them we represented the friend who had come to their aid when in dire need, who had been prepared to fight in their cause. The Polish people are above all loyal, and they have long memories too – a capacity worth noting in our present times.

They brought food and some beer. Two of the four could speak English and the remainder French. They all spoke German. The meeting soon became noisy and there was much laughter, which the Poles love. Suddenly there was a warning signal from a Pole on the look-out by the stairs, and in less than no time they were all distributed under beds in the corners of our two rooms, where suppressed laughter continued up to the instant of the entry of a German officer with his *Feldwebel*.

The attic door, and others below, had, of course, been locked by the Poles, so that there was nothing to cause suspicion other than our laughter, which the Germans had overheard and had come to investigate. The officer was shocked that we, reviled prisoners, whose right to live depended on a word from him, should find occasion to laugh. It was like laughing in church, and he implied as much to us. He noticed we had shifted all the bunks to make more floor space and promptly made the *Feldwebel* move them back again into orderly rows. The Poles moved with the beds. No sooner had they departed than the Poles, like truant schoolboys, reappeared, laughing louder than ever at the joke. They called the sergeant '*La Fouine*', the French for a marten, which has also a figurative meaning, namely 'a wily person', whose propensities have been translated into English as 'ferreting'. The merriment continued for a while, then they departed as they had come, leaving us to marvel at the facility with which they manipulated locks. In order to visit us they had unlocked no fewer than five doors with a couple of instruments that looked like a pair of button-hooks. Such was our introduction to Colditz, which was to be our prison house for several years.

There were about eighty Polish army officers in the camp when we arrived. They were among the cream of the Polish army and some had undoubtedly charged tanks at the head of their troop of horse. Although stripped of much of their military attire, they were always smartly turned out on parade. They wore black riding-boots which they kept in beautiful condition. Their Senior Officer was General Tadensz Piskor, and there was also an Admiral named Joseph Unrug.

The officers had all committed offences against the German Reich and the majority had escaped unsuccessfully at least once. They had been prisoners, of course, since the end of September 1939. So many of them had prison sentences outstanding against them that the half-dozen cells normally set apart for solitary confinement housed about six officers each. The cells were about three yards square and each had one small, heavily barred window. These were the windows we saw, crammed with grimy faces, immediately on entering the prison upon our arrival. Thus nearly half of their contingent was officially in solitary confinement!

Time passed more quickly in the new surroundings and in making new friends. The Germans, after a week or so, gave us permanent quarters: a dormitory with two-tier bunks, a washroom, a kitchen, and a day-room in a wing of the Castle separated from the Poles. The courtyard was the exercise area. At first we were given different hours to exercise, but the Jerries eventually gave up trying to keep us apart. To do so would have meant a sentry at every courtyard door, and there were half a dozen of these. Moreover, the Castle was a maze of staircases and intercommunicating doors, and the latter merely provided lock-picking practice for the Poles. We were so often found in each other's quarters that the Germans would have had to put the whole camp into 'solitary' to carry out their intentions, so they gave it up as a bad job.

A trickle of new arrivals increased the British contingent, until by Christmas we numbered sixteen officers. A few French and Belgian officers appeared. All the newcomers were offenders, mostly escapers, and it was impressed upon us that our Castle was 'the bad boys' camp', the 'Straflager' or 'Sonderlager' as the Germans called it. At the same time we also began to appreciate its impregnability from the escape point of view. This was to be the German fortress from which there was no escape, and it certainly looked for a long time as if it would live up to that reputation. As I said in my Prologue, the garrison manning the camp outnumbered the prisoners at all times; the Castle was floodlit at night from every angle despite the blackout, and notwithstanding the sheer drop of a hundred feet or so on the outside from barred windows, sentries surrounded the camp within a palisade of barbed wire. The enemy seemed to have everything in his favour. Escape would be a formidable proposition indeed.

★ ★ ★

The Poles entertained us magnificently over the Christmas period. They had food parcels from their homes in Poland. We had nothing until, lo and behold, on Christmas Eve Red Cross parcels arrived!

The excitement had to be seen to be believed. They were bulk parcels; that is to say, they were not addressed individually, nor did each parcel contain an assortment of food. There were parcels of tinned meat, of tea, of cocoa, and so on. Apart from a bulk consignment which reached Laufen the previous August, these were our first parcels of food from England and we felt a surge of gratitude for this gift, without which our Christmas would have been a pathetic affair. We were also able to return, at least to a limited extent, the hospitality of the Poles, whose generosity was unbounded. We had to ration severely, for we could not count on a regular supply, and we made this first consignment, which we could have eaten in a few days, last for about two months. Our estimate was not far wrong.

Throughout the whole war, in fact, supplies of Red Cross parcels to Colditz were never regular and a reserve had always to be stocked. Parcels were despatched from England at the rate of one per week per person. In Colditz we received normally one, on rare occasions two, parcels per person in three weeks. The parcels both from the United Kingdom and from Canada were excellent in quality and variety. The 'individual' as opposed to the 'bulk' parcels weighed ten and a half pounds each and contained a selection of the following: tinned meat, vegetables, cheese, jam and butter, powdered egg, powdered milk, tea or cocoa, chocolate, sugar, and cooking-fat. These parcels were paid for to a large extent by a prisoner's relatives, but it became almost a universal rule at all camps that 'individual' parcels were put into a pool and everybody shared equally.

The Poles prepared a marionette show for Christmas. It was 'Snow-White and the Seven Dwarfs'. They had the full text of the story, and the characters were taken by persons behind the screen. It was a picturesque show, professionally produced both as to the acting and the décor. The marionettes were beautifully dressed and the frequently changing scenery was well painted. It lasted about two hours and was a great success. During the interval, sandwiches and beer were served and afterwards a feast was offered. The Poles had saved everything for months for this occasion. The beer was a ration, also saved. It was bottled lager which was handed out by the Jerries against prison money on spasmodic occasions. To begin with, in Colditz, it was not too scarce, but by the middle of 1941 it had disappeared completely.

5
Routine

PRISONERS WERE NOT allowed so much as to look at a real
Reichsmark; instead, the special paper money known as *Lagergeld*
was issued. *Lagergeld* did not go far. The canteen offered for sale the
usual razor-blades, toothpaste, shaving soap, and occasionally some
turnip jam or beetroots in vinegar, and saccharine tablets. We could
also buy musical instruments by order. They were very expensive –
in fact, the prices were downright robbery – but they gave satisfaction
to many amateur musicians.

During my sojourn in prison I bought two guitars, one for about
£10 and the other for about £25, and a brass cornet for about £30.
I must admit that the cornet was of good quality and the more
expensive guitar was a beauty. The instruments came from a well-
known firm in Leipzig. I studied the guitar for a year and a half,
becoming fairly proficient. I could read music slowly and could play
some classical pieces by heart. The cornet provided me with a means
of letting off steam when I had nothing better to do. My colleagues
limited the use of it to the washroom, with the door closed, in fine
weather, at hours when they were normally out in the courtyard.

The German food was cooked in a large, well-equipped, and
clean kitchen off the prison courtyard. Private cooking by the prisoners could also be done in our small kitchen provided with a
cooking-stove and a hopelessly inadequate supply of coal. All loose
and unessential items made of wood, together with large numbers of
fixtures, partitions, floorboards, beds and the like, quickly disappeared into the greedy mouth of our grubby little pot-boiler and
frying-pan heater. However, the smells which exuded from that
murky room invariably outweighed any pangs of conscience, not to
mention fears of reprisals, on account of the dubious origin of most

of our fuel. My favourite meal was corned beef fried with dried currants or sultanas. Even today my mouth waters in grateful memory of the delectable dish which warded off many an incipient depression. Rupert Barry was the *chef par excellence* for this *spécialité de la maison*. It was not an everyday meal – indeed, it was a rarity – which perhaps accounts for the poignant memories I still have of it.

The daily course of life, as may be expected, did not vary much. We awoke in the morning at 7.30 am to shouts of '*Aufstehen*' or 'get up' from a couple of German non-commissioned officers who passed through the dormitories. At 8 am, breakfast orderlies (our own troops), helped by officers, carried up from the German kitchen a large cauldron of 'ersatz' coffee (made from acorns), a certain number of loaves of bread, a small quantity of margarine, and on certain days a little sugar. At 8.30 am there was *Appell*. All ranks formed up in the courtyard, the Poles in one contingent, the British in another, with their respective senior officers in front. A German officer would appear. Everybody would salute everybody else and the German non-commissioned officers would go through a painstaking count of the bodies. When all was found correct there would be more saluting and the parade would break up. As time went on, the first of four daily *Appells* was sounded at 7 am by means of a factory hooter. By 9 am we were free to carry on any lawful pursuit such as reading, studying, language lessons, music lessons, or exercise. The Poles knew every language imaginable between them, and most Englishmen took up a foreign language with a Polish teacher in exchange for English lessons.

Teachers and pupils paired off and sought out quiet corners all over the Castle, where they would settle down to explain to each other the intricacies of the various European languages. Our living-room became a hive of industry and the low murmur of voices continued unabated throughout the morning hours. Those who sought more privacy chose to sit on the staircase or on blankets in the lobbies or out in the courtyard, if it was fine. Here, voices did not have to be hushed and temperament could be indulged in. I remember passing a couple once, deep in the throes of an English lesson, and I overheard the following instruction:

TEACHER: 'Now we shall read. Start where we left off yesterday.'

PUPIL (*reading*): 'Thee leetle sheep—'

TEACHER: 'Not "thee", say "the".'

PUPIL: 'The leetle sheep—'

TEACHER: 'No! "The little ship!" '

PUPIL: 'The little sheep—'

TEACHER: '*Not* "sheep", you ass, but "ship".'

PUPIL: 'The leetle ship—'

TEACHER: 'Damn it: Are you deaf? I've already said "little ship", not "leetle ship". Start all over again.'

PUPIL: 'Thee little ship—' and so on.

When books started to arrive from the UK, study courses began. Later, a prison theatre was opened and plays, varieties, and concerts occupied much of the time of officers with any talent for amateur theatricals or musicals.

One variety concert, arranged by Lieutenant Teddy Barton, RASC, played to packed houses for several nights. It was called *Ballet Nonsense*. Costumes were made mostly out of crêpe paper, which served the purpose well. The orchestra was of surprisingly high quality and the airs and lyrics, composed by 'Jimmy' Yule (Lieutenant J. Yule, RCS) and Teddy Barton, gave the show a professional touch which savoured poignantly of Drury Lane and the Hippodrome. The orchestral talent was provided by a mixture of all the nationalities under the able band leadership of John Wilkins, a naval (submarine) Leading Telegraphist who had a fantastic aptitude for playing any wind instrument he chose to pick up, in a matter of days. The underlying theme of *Ballet Nonsense* was provided by a *corps de ballet* consisting of the toughest-looking, heaviest-moustached officers available, who performed miracles of energetic grace and unsophisticated elegance upon the resounding boards of the Colditz theatre stage attired in frilly crêpe paper ballet skirts and brassières.

Ballet Nonsense very nearly never came off! A grand piano was to be installed for the occasion. When it arrived in the courtyard, the workmen engaged in hauling it up the narrow stairs took off their jackets and waistcoats for the job. These, of course, quickly disappeared. The contents of pockets were left intact, but the civilian clothing was considered by the vast majority of the camp to be fair game!

The Commandant promptly closed the theatre and demanded the return of the clothing. Monetary compensation was offered by the POWs, but the return of the clothes – no! It was all very upsetting for the Management, who had gone to endless trouble over advertisement with decorative posters spread about the Castle. They, the Management, were in the throes of preparing postponement strips beginning with 'The Management regrets . . .' and were haggling over the phrases to follow, which were quite likely to put the author in 'solitary' for a month if he was not tactful as to their content, when their worries were dispelled in an unforeseen manner. The French, true to a Riviera tradition, solved the problem in their own way. When the morning after the piano incident dawned, a second poster had been superimposed over the *Ballet Nonsense* Folly Girls. It read:

For Sunshine Holidays visit
Sunny Colditz
Holiday Hotel
500 beds, one bath
Cuisine
by French chef
Large staff
always attentive and vigilant
Once visited, never left

(The camp cook was a French chef, though he had no scope for his talent.)

After a month of futile searching for the clothes by the Jerries, the money was accepted and the theatre reopened. *Ballet Nonsense* was a far greater success, due to a month of extra rehearsals!

* * *

The midday meal at Colditz was sounded at 12.30 pm and consisted of thick barley gruel. Occasionally, pieces of hog's hide were cut up and put into the soup, which gave it a delicious odour of pork and that was about all. On such days the German menu on the blackboard outside the kitchen triumphantly announced '*Speck*' – in other words, Bacon. It deceived nobody but the far-away 'Protecting Power' who read the menus, sent by the German *Kommandantur* in answer to questionaires. Nor did it deceive the 'Protecting Power' for long either; the latter was quickly disillusioned on its representatives' first visit to the camp. The 'Protecting Power' is a neutral Government which represents the interests of one belligerent Power in the territories of the other. In the case of the UK the Government was Switzerland's, and unstinted praise is due for its good work on behalf of British prisoners throughout the war.

The rations deteriorated as the war progressed. An idea of the German ration of food provided from about 1942 onwards is given by the table below, which has been taken from a 'Protecting Power' report on Colditz.

It was inevitable that the camp should possess a cat. It arrived, of course, as a kitten and in time grew up into a fine brindled specimen through the undisputed and indulgent care of a rather fat Belgian officer. The two were inseparable, for the Belgian never stinted the cat's rations and the latter grew fat while the Belgian grew thin. One day the cat disappeared. His absence was mourned by all, while his master, though visibly moved, bore the loss with a smile. As the days passed it was assumed that the cat, tiring of monastic life, had gone a-roaming to find a mate; and the affair was forgotten. Then, a British orderly, while emptying the camp dustbins, came across a brown-paper parcel. Curiosity led him to open it and, as the layers of paper were unfolded, out fell an unmistakable brindled pelt. The cat was out of the bag; the smile had been on the face of the tiger.

(One English pound equals 454 grammes)

Day	Breakfast	Lunch	Dinner
Monday	Coffee-subst. 4 gr.	Potatoes 400 gr.	Jam-subst. 20 gr.
		Turnips 500 gr.	Bread 300 gr.
Tuesday	Coffee-subst. 4 gr.	Potatoes 400 gr.	Jam-subst. 20 gr.
		Turnips 600 gr.	Bread 300 gr.
Wednesday	Coffee-subst. 4 gr.	Potatoes 400 gr.	Jam-subst. 20 gr.
		Turnips 500 gr.	Bread 300 gr.

Thursday	Coffee-subst. 4 gr.	Potatoes 400 gr.	Jam-subst. 20 gr.
		Turnips 600 gr.	Bread 300 gr.
Friday	Coffee-subst. 4 gr.	Potatoes 400 gr.	Jam-subst. 20 gr.
		Turnips 600 gr.	Bread 300 gr.
			Cheese 31·25 gr.
Saturday	Coffee-subst. 4 gr.	Potatoes 400 gr.	Jam-subst. 20 gr.
		Peas 112·5 gr.	Sugar 175 gr.
		Millet 75 gr.	Jam 175 gr.
		Oats 62·5 gr.	Bread 300 gr.
		Cooking-fat 68 gr.	
		Barley 37·5 gr.	
Sunday	Coffee-subst. 3·5 gr.	Potatoes 350 gr.	Jam-subst. 30 gr.
		Fresh meat 250 gr.	Bread 425 gr.
		Turnips 600 gr.	

* * *

In the afternoon, sport came to the fore. Foils made their appearance at one time and many took up fencing. The little courtyard only lent itself to games such as volleyball; that is to say, a football pushed backwards and forwards over a high badminton net with about three players on each side. Boxing was another favourite pastime.

There was one game which deserves special mention. It was invented by the British and belonged to that category of local school game devised in almost every public school of England. The wall game at Eton is an example. The rules soon become a matter of tradition and depend on the surface and shape of the ground, the buildings round it, and various hazards such as jutting corners or stone steps. The Colditz variety, which we called 'stoolball', was played, of course, in the granite cobbled courtyard. It is the roughest game I have ever played, putting games like rugby football in the shade. The rules were simple. Two sides, consisting of any number of players and often as many as thirty a side, fought for possession of the football by any means. A player having the ball could run with it but could not hold it indefinitely; he had to bounce it occasionally while on the move. When tackled, he could do whatever he liked with it. A 'goalie' at each end of the yard sat on a stool – hence the name – and a goal was scored by touching the opponent's stool with the ball. Goal defence was by any means, including strangulation of the ball-holder, if necessary. There was a half-time when everybody was too tired to continue. There was no referee and there were, of course, no touchlines.

The game proceeded as a series of lightning dashes, appalling crashes, deafening shouts, formidable scrums – generally involving the whole side – rapid passing movements, as in a rugby three-quarter line, and with a cheering knot of spectators at every window. Nobody was ever seriously hurt, in spite of the fury and the pace at which the game was played. Clothing was ripped to pieces, while mass wrestling and throwing of bodies was the order of the day. To extract an opponent from a scrum it was recommendable to grab him by the scalp and one leg. I never saw any 'tripping'. This was probably due to the instinctive reaction of players to long schooling in our various ball games where tripping is forbidden. I realize now that this game was a manifestation of our suppressed desire for freedom. While the game was in action we were free. The surrounding walls were no longer a prison, but the confines of the game we played, and there were no constraining rules to curtail our freedom of action. I always felt much better after a game. Followed by a cold bath it put me on top of the world.

The Poles, and later the French when they arrived, were always interested spectators. Although we had no monopoly of the courtyard, they naturally took to their rooms and watched the game from windows. They eventually put up sides against the British and games were played against them, but these were not a success. Tempers were lost and the score became a matter of importance, which it never did in an 'all-British' game.

As time went on, the Jerries allowed us a couple of hours' exercise three times a week in a barbed-wire pen in the wooded grounds below the Castle, but within the external Castle walls. Here we played something resembling soccer – the hazards were the trees amongst which the game surged backwards and forwards. Our ball games amused the Jerries. Officers and NCOs were occasionally caught watching them surreptitiously – not because they were afraid of being seen as spectators, but because their vantage-points were supposed to be secret and were used for spying upon us.

Towards the afternoon musical instruments could be heard tuning up on all sides. As soon as they could be purchased, many officers started practising one type or another. In the late afternoon, too, we could usually rely upon a *Sondermeldung* – which was always a good diversion.

What happened was that the Germans, who had placed loud-speakers at strategic points throughout the Castle, would switch on the power when a German *Sondermeldung* or Special War Progress bulletin was announced. These were calculated to raise German morale through the Reich to incredible heights and correspond-ingly to demoralize Germany's enemies to the point of throwing in the sponge.

Anyway – in the camp – the power would suddenly be switched on with unmistakable crackling noises as the loudspeakers heated up. First a fanfare of trumpets sounded. Then, the strains of Listz's preludes would come over the air, followed after a few moments by the announcer's proclamation in solemn and sonorous tones:

Das Oberkommando der Wehrmacht gibt bekannt! In tagelangen schweren Kämpfen gegen einen stark gesicherten Geleitzug im Atlantik haben unsere Unterseeboote sechzehn Schiffe mit ingesamt hundertfünfzigtausend Bruttoregis-tertonnen versenkt. Ferner wurden zwei Zerstörer schwer beschädigt.

As soon as the announcer had ceased, German brass bands would strike up *Wir fahren gegen Engeland*, and to the additional accompani-ment of the whine of descending bombs, the crackle of machine-guns and the bursting of shells the act would attain a crescendo of power and then end with trumpets heralding victory.

The show was intended to make the bravest quail. It regularly produced pandemonium in the camp. No sooner had the ominous crackle of the loudspeakers started than windows all over the Castle would open, heads would reach out to the bars and every musical instrument that could be mustered was automatically requisitioned for the coming spectacle. As Liszt's preludes softened to give way to the announcer, this was the signal: drums, cymbals, clarinets, cornets, trombones and accordions, all gave voice at once in a cacophony that could be heard re-echoing from distant hills. The German *Kommandantur* shook with the reverberations.

But the Germans persevered and the war went on in earnest for several months, until eventually they gave in and the loudspeakers were for ever silenced.

Of course they tried all means at first to stop our counter-attack – but that was not easy. What broke the German morale, in the end, over the battle, was not so much the opposition we put up, as the insidious counter-propaganda we produced. For we recorded regularly the numbers of *Bruttoregistertonnen* involved, until we could show the Germans in the camp that there could not be a British ship left afloat, according to their figures.

In our less energetic moments, especially in the evenings, we played bridge and chess. Chess games, in a community where the passage of time was of no importance, went on for days. Players were known to sit up all night with a home-made, foul-smelling oil-lamp (for the electricity was turned off). The light had to be shaded so as not to show through the windows and bring the Jerries in.

There was also a card game for two players which we learnt from the Poles, called 'Gapin', which means, in Polish, 'a person who looks but does not see'! The term applied well to the game, for it was one in which many cards lay face upwards on the table. These cards could be made use of, provided a player held certain corresponding cards in his hand. The open cards were continually changing, so that concentration and quick thinking were necessary. The game was aggravating, for after finishing a turn an opponent could promptly make good use of a card overlooked. It was so exasperating a game that I have known friends not to be on speaking terms for days because of humiliation and wounded pride involved in the showing up of an opponent's obtuseness. Rupert Barry and I had a running 'Gapin Contest' with high stakes in *Lagergeld* which ended with the payment, after the war, of a fat cheque – to Rupert!

The last roll-call of the day occurred usually at 9 pm, after which soon came 'lights out'. At this 'witching hour' many of the nefarious escape activities of the camp started up. They were lumped together under the general heading of 'night shift'.

6

The Second Tunnel

WITH CHRISTMAS FARE inside us, optimism returned, and we began to wonder how the walls of our unbreachable fortress could be pierced. Tunnelling seemed to be the only solution, and we (the British) were such a small number, and so united in our resolution to escape, that we worked as one team. Lieutenant-Colonel Guy German (Royal Leicestershire Regiment), our senior officer, placed me in charge of operations, and kept aloof from them himself so as to be in a strong position *vis-à-vis* the Jerries. Nevertheless, he was keen to take part in any escape into which he could be fitted.

As at Laufen, we concentrated on parts of the Castle not used by ourselves. Our début was made early in January 1941 in a room on the ground floor under German lock and key. We were learning from the Poles their art of picking locks, and in this empty room, with our usual guards on the look-out for alarms, we started work. Unloosening floor boards, we came on loose rubble and in a short time had a hole big enough for a man to work in, with the floorboards replaced over him.

I was dissatisfied with this tunnel entrance before long, because the boards were very old and one of them could be lifted easily; moreover, they sounded ominously hollow underfoot. I made a sliding trap-door out of bed boards, which fitted between the floor supporting-beams. The trap-door itself was a long, open-topped box which slid horizontally on wooden runners. The box was filled with the under-floor rubble. When the trap-door was closed, a German could lift the floorboards and see nothing suspicious; he could even stand on the trap-door. At the same time, the rubble filling damped out the hollow sound. Without any discussion, the trap-door became known as 'Shovewood II'!

PLAN OF

COLDITZ CASTLE

OFLAG IVC 1939~45

NOTE: The plan of the older Northern part
of the Castle is copied from an MS of
the Seventeenth Century

ESCAPE ROUTES SHOWN THUS: ———

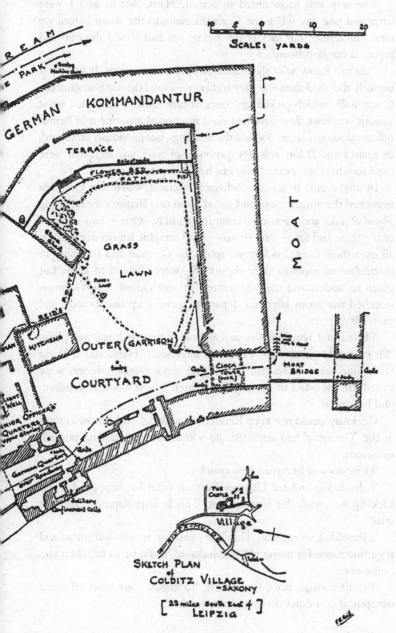

SCALE: YARDS

GERMAN KOMMANDANTUR

TERRACE

FLOWER BED

PATH

GRASS

LAWN

MOAT

OUTER (GARRISON)

COURTYARD

KITCHENS

REID'S ROUTE

MOAT BRIDGE

CLOCK TOWER (oven)

SENIOR OFFICERS' QUARTERS

German Quarters

Solitary Confinement Cells

THE CASTLE

Village

SKETCH PLAN
of
COLDITZ VILLAGE
—SAXONY

[22 miles South East of
LEIPZIG]

The trap was soon tested in action. Hank Wardle and I were surprised one day when the Germans came to the room before we could disappear, but luckily not before we had closed the trap and replaced the floorboards.

I do not know why they came directly to this room. It was most unlikely they had then – as they had later – sound detectors around the Castle walls, which picked up noises of tunnelling. Their spies, set at various windows, may have remarked an unusual movement of British officers through certain doors in the buildings, not previously employed, or again some Polish orderlies (prisoners-of-war), whose rooms were close to where we worked may not have been trustworthy.

In any event, it was an awkward moment when the Germans unlocked the empty room and gazed upon two British officers doing physical jerks and press-ups, counting audibly, 'One – two – one – two – three and four – one – two—' with seraphic innocence written all over their faces. Luckily we spoke no German and had only to gesticulate in reply to their shouts. We were allowed to leave, but given to understand that the matter was not closed. The Germans searched the room after our departure, prising up floorboards, and then left.

The tunnel would never succeed now; that, at least, was plain. We promptly gave it up. The same afternoon, Hank and I, along with four others who had committed some minor offence, were called for, escorted to the room in which 'Shovewood II' reposed, and locked in.

Curiosity could not keep Kenneth away long, and almost as soon as the 'Goonery' had departed, he was at the door asking puckish questions.

'How do you like your new quarters?'

'I don't. Go and tell Colonel German what has happened. He'll kick up hell with the *Kommandant*. This is imprisonment without trial!'

'I shouldn't worry, Pat. They'll let you out in a month or so and it's a fine room for doing physical jerks in! You'll be so fit when you come out.'

'I'm fit enough now,' I answered, 'to knock your head off like a ninepin, if you don't do something quickly.'

'But there's the tunnel to get on with! No need to bother about shifts – you can just go on and on. Maybe you'll be out in a month by the tunnel instead of by the door!'

'Kenneth,' I shouted, exasperated, 'I'm getting out of this today. Go and fetch my "Universal".'

He went, and a few moments later returned with it.

'What do you want me to do with it?' he said.

'Open the door, you idiot; what else do you think?'

'But why? It's such a lovely opportunity to go ahead with the tunnel, I think I'll leave you there.'

'Open up!' I yelled.

Inside, the six of us were champing at the bit over the curtailment of our liberties. Hank, tall six-foot length of loose-limbed Canadian, with freckles and curly hair, and handsome withal, suggested:

'Let's take the ruddy door off its hinges and drop it over a cliff somewhere.'

'Good idea,' I said, 'if you'll hack the bars away from a window first. I propose we carry the door in procession round the camp in protest and then dump it at the top of the Castle.'

Kenneth opened the door.

'Kenneth,' I said, 'go and get someone upstairs to play the Dead March!'

We had the door off its hinges in no time. The six of us then carried it solemnly like a coffin – marching in slow time – around the courtyard. In a few minutes the Dead March started up. After three turns of the courtyard, by which time a crowd of mourners had fallen in behind the cortège, we started to mount the winding stairs slowly.

The staircases, of which there were three in the Castle, though of simple design, were beautiful, consisting of flat stone steps about two yards wide, winding upwards in a perfect spiral around a central column. Each staircase formed a round tower built into the corners of the Castle, and the doors to all rooms opened outwards from the towers at various levels. At one period of our imprisonment, the British contingent were housed eighty steps above ground-level! To the top was a matter of about a hundred steps.

By the time our procession with the door was halfway up the

stairs, a German officer and two corporals, all panting hard, caught us up and joined in behind us. The officer, who was known as Hauptmann Priem, possessed a rare quality among Germans – a sense of humour. An interpreter was demanded.

'Herr Hauptmann Reid, what does this mean? A few moments ago I locked you all into close confinement.'

'That is exactly why we are here now,' I replied.

'Not at all, Herr Hauptmann, you are here now because you have unlocked and removed the door of your prison cell. Why have you done so? – and how have you done so?'

'We protest at being imprisoned without sentence and pending fair trial. We are prisoners-of-war, and you should treat us according to the German Army Code and the Geneva Convention.'

Priem smiled broadly and said:

'Very well! If you will return the door to its hinges, you shall go free, pending trial!'

I agreed, and the whole solemn procession wended its way downstairs again. The door was replaced ceremoniously with saluting and heel-clicking.

Priem was intrigued to know how we unhinged a locked door, so I gave him a short piece of twisted wire, which I had obtained specially for the eventuality of a search. This may seem an unwise thing to have done, but by now the Germans knew well that we could pass through a simply locked door. They had given up separating the different nationalities for that reason among others, and a piece of useless wire gave nothing away. We heard no more of the incident.

We continued our search for the weak spots in the Castle's armour. I was next attracted by the drains, and a trusted Polish orderly told me that once, when a certain manhole cover in the yard had been raised, he had seen small brick tunnels running in various directions. This sounded promising. There were two round manhole covers in the courtyard, but alas! they were in full view of spy windows and of the spyhole in the main courtyard gate.

I decided to make a reconnaissance by night. In the darkness we could unlock our staircase door into the courtyard – we were always locked into our quarters at night – and provided the guard outside the gate was not disturbed or tempted to switch on the courtyard lights, we could proceed with our examination. The moon was not up. It was February and bitterly cold. We knew the manhole covers were frozen solid to their bases, but we had prepared boiling water in our blackout kitchen. With Kenneth acting as doorkeeper with the key, Rupert made sorties at ten-minute intervals and poured the boiling contents of a kettle around the nearest cover. Then we both sortied, I with a stout piece of iron unscrewed from a door support, and together we managed to loosen and lift up the cover. The hole was not deep and there were tunnels as the orderly had said. I jumped in and Rupert replaced the lid and disappeared. He was to return in half an hour.

My reconnaissance along the slimy tunnels, which were about three feet by two feet in section, arched and flat-bottomed, revealed one leading up to the camp building in which the canteen was housed. This was bricked up at the canteen entrance, but obviously continued inside. Another led to the kitchens, which accounted for the slime. A third was the outfall sewer and ran under the courtyard to another manhole. It looked promising and I followed it, but a couple of yards beyond the second manhole it, also, was bricked up with a small pipe at the bottom serving to drain the system. The pipe headed out under the courtyard gateway. I had my iron tool, a cigarette-lighter, and one of our home-made lamps. I tackled the brick; the joints were very tough indeed, and I made little impression. The wall had been recently built and obviously with special attention to strength.

Rupert returned on time and the two of us – myself pushing upwards from within – managed to remove the heavy cover. I was filthy and smelling badly, but there was hope in two directions!

During several nights following I took turns with Rupert and Dick Howe in attacking the brick wall in the tunnel with an assortment of steel bits and nails which we 'won' by various means.

The task proved hopeless, especially as we dare make very little noise. In the silence of the night, the sound of hammering could be plainly heard in the courtyard even from below ground. The tunnels and pipes echoed the sound and carried it a long way.

We thought of doing the job in daylight and I actually descended two days running in full view of those officers who happened to be exercising in the yard, but protected from the direction of the main gate by a small knot of Britishers while the manhole cover was being removed. Although I hammered loudly enough to wake the dead, I made little impression. The joints in the brickwork were made with '*ciment fondu*' – a specially tough cement.

We tried the second direction. Inside the canteen, where we bought our razor-blades and suchlike, in front of the counter on the buyers' side was a manhole cover. I had not far to seek for assistance in opening up this manhole, for Kenneth had already provided the solution. Some weeks before he had had himself appointed assistant manager and accountant of the canteen!

Kenneth was a London Stock Exchange man and the idea of keeping even the meagre canteen accounts evidently made him feel a little nearer home. He had been educated at Whitgift School and was by nature a tidy person, meticulous in his ways and in his speech. He made a point of buckling the nib of the pen used by the German *Feldwebel* (sergeant) in charge of the canteen so that that unfortunate man invariably started his day's accounts with a large blot at the top of his page. Kenneth explained to the *Feldwebel* on the first occasion that nibs made with poor wartime steel always buckled if used with bad wartime ink owing to the 'springiness' of the nib being affected by a film of corrosion. Thereafter he consoled the *Feldwebel* whenever the latter fell into his trap. He always added a titbit of demoralizing propaganda such as that the whole war was a shame and he was sure the Germans didn't want it any more than the English. Within a few months he had broken down the morale of the *Feldwebel* to such an extent that the latter was preaching sedition to his colleagues and had to be removed.

The table which Kenneth and the *Feldwebel* used for writing was situated under the only window in the room, at some distance from the counter. While a few people stood at the counter, and Kenneth distracted the German's attention with some accounting matter at the table, it was comparatively simple to tackle the manhole cover.

Incidentally, Kenneth in his position as canteen accountant had also to deal with the mail. This brought him into contact with the German camp interpreter, who was responsible for censoring our letters home. His name was Pfeiffer – in English 'Whistler' – and to suit his name his voice never descended below the treble clef.

Our group were leaning over the counter preparatory to dealing with the manhole when Pfeiffer entered the canteen and demanded to see Kenneth. I should say, in parenthesis, that we had been allowed, on rare occasions, to send home with our mail photographs taken by a German civilian photographer.

Pfeiffer addressed Kenneth:

'Herr Hauptmann, once again must I not tell you that officers on the backside of photographs to write forbidden are. Will you please foresee that my instructions be carried out?'

Before Kenneth had time to make any retort, a Polish officer, Felix Jablonowki, rushed into the canteen, beaming all over, and shouted:

'Have you heard the news? Benghazi has fallen down!' (It was early February 1941.)

We forgot the manhole and started cheering. Pfeiffer's brain must have been working at top pressure conjuring up a sarcastic retort to combat this exhibition of non-defeatist morale. There was a moment's lull in the cheering and he piped up shrilly:

'All that you too to the Marines can tell.'

The cheering redoubled in intensity.

When the excitement had died down, we continued our work. The manhole came away after some persuasion. Sure enough, there were tunnels leading in two directions, one connecting with the tunnel already noticed from the yard, and the other leading out under the window beside which Kenneth and the German worked. A second reconnaissance in more detail showed this latter to be about eighteen yards long and built on a curve. Under the window it was blocked up with large hewn stones and mortar. Outside the shop window and at the level of the canteen floor was a grass lawn, which also abutted the German section of the Castle. At the outer edge of this lawn was a stone balustrade, and then a forty-foot drop over a retaining wall to the level of the roadway which led down to the valley in which our football ground was situated. Maybe the tunnel led out to this wall. We had to find out.

A few days later we had made out of an iron bedpiece a key which opened the canteen door. Working at night as before, we would open our staircase entrance door and cross about ten yards of the courtyard to the canteen door. This opened, we would enter and lock it behind us. We then had to climb a high wooden partition in order to enter the canteen proper, as the door in this partition had a German-type Yale lock which foiled us. The partition separated the canteen from the camp office: a room in which all the haggling took place between our Commanding Officer and the German Camp Commandant on his periodic visits. The partition was surmounted with the aid of a couple of sheets used as ropes.

Entering our tunnel, we tackled the wall at the end. This time we were lucky. The mortar gave way easily and we were soon loosening huge stones which we removed to the other tunnel (the one leading back to the courtyard). Although the wall was four feet thick we were through it in a week of night shifts. Alas! the tunnel did not continue on the other side. Beyond the wall, under the grass, was sticky yellow clay.

My next idea was to make a vertical shaft which would bring the tunnel up to the grass. I would construct a trap-door which would be covered with grass and yet would open when required, thus repeating my Laufen idea of having the escape tunnel intact for further use. Escapes involved such an immense amount of labour, sometimes only to serve in the escape of one or two men, that it was always worth while attempting to leave the escape exit ready for future use.

Once out on the grass patch we could creep along under the Castle walls in the dark; descend the retaining wall with sheets; then continue past the guards' sleeping-quarters to the last defence – the twelve-foot wall of the Castle park surmounted for much of its length with barbed wire. This obstacle would not be difficult provided there was complete concealment, which was possible at night, and provided there was plenty of time to deal with the barbed wire. We had to pass in full view of a sentry at one point. He was only forty yards away, but as there were Germans who frequently passed the same point, this was not a serious difficulty.

I constructed out of bed-boards and stolen screws a trap which looked like a small table with collapsible legs – collapsible so as to enter the tunnel. The legs were also telescopic; that is to say, they could be extended by degrees to five feet in length. The table-top was a tray with vertical sides four inches deep. It sat in a frame and had shutters so that I could excavate upwards from below, removing half the table area at a time. As soon as the edge of the tray came to within an inch of the surface of the lawn I merely had to close both shutters and cut the last inch of earth around the tray with a sharp knife. Then, pushing the tray up I could lift it clear, still full of undisturbed grass. The last man out would replace the tray in the frame and patch up carefully any telltale marks around the edge. The frame, supported on its extended legs, set on stones at the bottom of the tunnel, would take the weight of a man standing on the tray. The tunnel floor (in the clay) was just five feet below the lawn surface. I need hardly mention that the contraption was christened 'Shovewood III'!

Before all this happened, our plans were temporarily upset. Two Polish officers got into the canteen one night when we were not working and tried to cut the bars outside the window which I have mentioned before. Cutting bars cannot be done silently. They did not take the precaution of having their own stooges either to distract the attention of the nearby sentry or to give warning of his approach. Throughout our work on the tunnel we had a signalling system from our rooms above which gave warning of this sentry's approach. He was normally out of sight from where our tunnel exit was to be, but he only had to extend his beat a few yards in order to come into view.

The Poles were caught red-handed and within a few days a huge floodlight was installed in such a position as to light up the whole lawn and all the prison windows opening on to it.

This was a good example of what was bound to happen in a camp holding none but officers bent on escape. We had already asked the Poles for liaison on escape projects so that we would not tread on each other's toes all the time, and now Colonel German called a meeting with their Senior Officers, at which an agreement was reached. The Senior Polish Officer was in a difficult position because he frankly could not control his officers; he knew that they might attempt to escape without telling him or anybody else. However, after this meeting the liaison improved, and when we offered some Poles places in our tunnel escape, mutual confidence was established.

Shortly after this incident about two hundred and fifty French officers, led by General Le Bleu, arrived at Colditz. All of them were not escapers by any means, but about one hundred of them were. Among the remainder were many French Jews who were segregated from the rest by the Germans and given their own quarters on the top floor of the Castle.

We had to come to an arrangement with the French Senior Officer over escape projects similar to that agreed with the Poles, but unfortunately the French liaison system was also found wanting – at the expense of our tunnel – before a workable understanding was reached.

To return to the thread of my story: we were not allowed to store any tinned food, expressly because it was potential escape rations. Over a period of time we had all stinted ourselves to collect a reserve for distribution when our tunnel would be ready. It amounted to three heavy sack-loads. One night we were busy transporting the sacks into the tunnel from our quarters, where they were badly hidden. Rupert carried them one by one out of our courtyard door into the canteen. On the last trip all the courtyard lights were suddenly switched on from outside, and Rupert found himself between the doors, like Father Christmas caught *in flagrante delicto*! He made for the door of our quarters, which had to be unlocked again for him to re-enter. To our astonishment nothing further happened, so we completed our work for the night and returned to bed. Whether the Germans saw Rupert or not we shall never know, but since the Polish attempt they seemed to be more on the qui vive.

This incident was followed by a still more unfortunate one. Although the Germans often paid nocturnal visits to our quarters without warning, this did not seriously bother us. If we were in the tunnel, the doors were locked as usual, and pillows were placed in our beds to pass the casual inspection of a torch flashing along the rows of sleeping bodies.

One night, however, the Germans had been carousing – we could hear them. In fact, they kept our orderlies awake, and that was the start of the trouble. We had five staunch, 'game' orderlies, who had places reserved on our tunnel escape.

On this particular night, being unable to sleep for the Germans, one of the orderlies named Goldman, a Jew from Whitechapel, who had a sense of humour, started to barrack the German sentry outside the nearest window. Goldman had arrived at Colditz as Colonel German's orderly and was so voluble at their interrogation by the Camp Commandant that he was mistaken by him for our new SBO. The barracking must have been reported to the carousing Goons, for after some time, they arrived in the courtyard in force and headed for our quarters. Priem and another officer, the Regimental Sergeant-Major – Oberstabsfeldwebel Gephard – the corporal known as the *fouine* and half a dozen Goons entered and began shouting '*Aufstehen!*' They woke everyone up, poked the beds, and discovered that four officers were missing.

The Germans lost their heads. They had come upstairs drunk and disorderly, intent on having some fun at our expense, and had not expected this new turn of affairs. Gephard, who looked like the fat boy of Peckham, was wearing his dress parade uniform. He carried an enormous curved sword, which every now and then caught between his legs. He was despatched to count the orderlies.

'*Aufstehen! Aufstehen!*' he shouted. 'You English pig-dogs! I shall teach you—' Crash! – as he tripped up over his 'battle-axe'. Then, picking himself up he started again:

'You English pig-dogs! I shall teach you to laugh at German soldiers carrying out their duty! Tomorrow morning at dawn you shall be shot. All of you! I shall give the firing order myself.'

He strode up and down the room trying to increase his stature to cope with his sword which clattered and jangled along behind him. 'Goldman!' he screamed, 'what are you doing with those playing-cards?'

Goldman had quietly given each orderly a card face downwards.

'We are about to draw for places in the order of shooting,' he replied.

Gephard spluttered and drew his sword.

'Swine! You dare to insult me personally!' – still struggling with his sword, which was too long for him to extract comfortably from the scabbard – 'Put down those cards at once. You will be the first and I shall not wait longer. I shall remove your head.'

Finally unsheathing the sword by holding the blade with both hands, he advanced on Goldman, waving it wildly around his head. The latter disappeared under a bed. Gephard's dignity prevented him from following. Instead, he performed a dance of rage around the bed, hacking at the wooden supports. Having let off steam, he sheathed the 'battle-axe' once more, quickly counted the orderlies, noting significantly the presence of Goldman still underneath the bed, departed with much jingling and tripped up once more as he slammed the door behind him.

The confusion in the officers' dormitory became indescribable. The officers were paraded along the middle of the room while Goons turned every bed inside out, and emptied the contents of cupboards all over the floor.

Priem, with his face glistening and his nose distinctly showing signs of the bottle, was torn between rage at having his carousal upset for longer than he had anticipated, and high spirits which were his more natural reaction to alcohol. He compromised between the two moods by seizing a pick-axe from one of his soldiers, and started to hack up the floor.

With mighty swings, accompanied by gleeful war-cries, he smote the floorboards, wrenching off large pieces of timber. With each blow he shouted a name: 'Benghazi'; 'Derna'; 'Tobruk' (Rommel was advancing in Africa at the time). As he shouted 'Tobruk', a huge length of flooring came away on the end of his axe and impaled to it under the board was a brand-new civilian felt hat! It had been very carefully hidden there by Lieutenant Alan Orr Ewing, Argyll and Sutherland Highlanders, nicknamed 'Scruffy', who had only the day before paid a large sum in *Lagermarks* to a French orderly to smuggle it into the camp.

This gave Priem an idea. He sent out orders for the dogs to be summoned. They arrived; were led to the beds of the missing officers; encouraged to sniff; and then unleashed. They left the dormitory and made for the food-bin in the kitchen where Goldman was already pottering. Priem followed them. Spying Goldman, he seized him by the collar and demanded:

'What direction have the missing officers taken?' to which Goldman answered:

'That's right! Hauptmann Priem, pick on me! Every time an offi-cer wants to escape, he comes up to me and says: "Please, Goldman, may I go to Switzerland?" '

Priem saw the point, relaxed his grip, and shooed the dogs out of the food-bin. These promptly dashed out of the quarters and headed up the stairs, followed by Priem and Goldman's parting shot:

'That's right, Fido – they jumped off the bleedin' roof.'

When the dogs produced nothing, Priem sent out orders for the whole camp to be paraded. It was about 2 am by then. Suddenly, 'stooge' Wardle, a submarine officer lately arrived who was our look-out, shouted, 'They're heading for the canteen.' He had scarcely time to jump down into the tunnel, and I to pull the manhole cover over us, before the Jerries were in. They searched the canteen and tried hard to lift the manhole cover, but were unable to do so as I was hanging on to it for dear life from underneath, my fingers wedged in a protruding lip of the cover.

As soon as we noticed that a 'General *Appell*' had been called, I told Rupert and Dick (the others in the tunnel with me) to start at once building a false wall halfway up the tunnel, behind which they put our food store and other escape paraphernalia such as rucksacks, maps, compasses, and civilian clothing which we normally kept hidden there.

The hubbub continued in the courtyard for about an hour. The count was taken about half a dozen times amidst as much confusion as the prisoners could create without having themselves shot, and aided by the chaos caused by the Germans themselves, who were rushing all over the camp searching every room and turning all movable objects upside-down.

Rupert and Dick quietly continued their work and in a few hours had constructed a magnificent false wall with stones from the origi-nal wall which we had demolished, jointed with clay from under the lawn and coated with dust wherever the joints showed.

By 5 am all was quiet again. We departed as we had come and went to bed wondering how the Germans would react to our reap-pearance at morning *Appell*. We had apparently put them to a great deal of trouble, for we heard that, while the Jerries had had the whole camp on parade, they had carried out an individual identity check.

Every officer paraded in front of a table where he was identified against his photograph and duly registered as present. We were recorded as having escaped, and messages, flashed to the OKW (*Oberkommando der Wehrmacht*), brought into action a network of precautions taken all over the country as a matter of routine for the recapture of prisoners.

At the morning *Appell*, when we were all found present again, confusion reigned once more. The Goons decided to hold a second identification parade which they completed after about two and a half hours. They then called out our four names, which they had managed to segregate at last, and we were paraded in front of everybody. They dismissed the parade and led us to the little interview room, in which most of our fights with the *Kommandantur* took place. We refused to explain our disappearance and were remanded for sentence for causing a disturbance and being absent from *Appell*. The OKW orders had to be counter-manded and the Commandant, we heard, had a 'rap over the knuckles' for the incident.

The Goons were upset and watchful during the next few days. They again visited the canteen, and this time the manhole cover came away – too easily for our liking, of course! But they had done some scraping around the edges before trying it and were apparently satisfied it was the result of their own efforts. The dust and grit, inserted around the manhole cover, were placed there by us as a matter of routine after every working shift, so that the cover always looked as if it had not been touched for years. A Goon descended and, after an examination, declared 'nothing unusual' below. Kenneth, who was in the background of the shop, trying to appear occupied with his accounts, breathed an audible sigh of relief, which he quickly turned into a yawn for the benefit of his German colleague, busy at the same table.

The Germans were suspicious of this tunnel, either because they had seen Rupert doing Father Christmas in the courtyard or because they were warned by a spy in the camp. A third possibility would have been microphones, set to detect noises. Microphones were installed, to our knowledge, in many places later on, but it is doubtful whether the Jerries had them in Colditz at this period of the war. Microphones were installed in newly-built hutted camps for the

RAF, but their installation in an old Schloss would have left telltale marks which we could have traced.

The spy – that is to say, a 'stooge' or prisoner in the camp – set by the Germans to report on us was a definite possibility, and our suspicions were later proved correct. Suffice it to say that we repeatedly found the Goons very quick on the trail of our activities. We tried hard to make our actions look normal when among other prisoners, but it was not easy, especially on escapes such as tunnels, which involved preparation over a long period of time. Incidentally, we employed the term 'stooge' very loosely! Our 'stooge' Wardle was certainly no spy.

The Goons concreted four heavy clasps into the floor around the canteen manhole cover. However, we dealt with these forthwith by loosening them before the concrete was set, in such a way that they could be turned aside. This was done in daylight while Kenneth as usual occupied the Goon, and a few officers acted as cover at the counter. In their normal position the clasps still held the cover firmly.

This done, we decided to give the tunnel a rest, as things were becoming too hot for our liking.

7

The Community of Nations

IT WAS MARCH 1941. The camp was slowly filling up; the British contingent had increased by a steady trickle of new arrivals, escapers all, except for a sprinkling of 'Saboteurs of the Reich' – we had three Padres who were classed in the second category. One day about sixty Dutch officers arrived. Curiously enough, their Senior Officer was Major English, ours being Colonel German! The Dutchmen were a fine company of men and a credit to their country. They were all Netherlands East Indies officers. At the outbreak of war, they had sailed home with their troops to Holland in order to help the Mother Country. When Holland was occupied, the German High Command offered an amnesty to all those Dutch officers who would sign a certain document; this, if treated honourably, precluded an officer from acting in any way contrary to the wishes of the German Reich; it also laid down conditions relative to the maintenance of law, order, and subservience within the country. It was apparently a cleverly worded document and most Dutch officers of the home forces signed it.

The Colonials, on the other hand, refused to sign it almost to a man and were promptly marched off to prison in Germany. After many vicissitudes, including unending wordy battles with the Germans and numerous escape attempts, they finally ended up lock, stock, and barrel in Colditz. Since they all spoke German fluently, were as obstinate as mules and as brave as lions, heartily despised the Germans and showed it, they presented special difficulties as prisoners!

They were always impeccably turned out on parade and maintained a high standard of discipline among themselves. I regret to say that the French and ourselves were the black sheep in matters of parade 'turn out'. The French officer is never tidy at the best of

84

times. His uniform does not lend itself to smartness, and the French do not care about 'turn out' anyway.

The British were more unfortunate, and had an excuse for appearing a straggly-looking crowd. The British battle-dress is not particularly smart, and most of us had lost a part of it at our time of capture – a cap, or jacket, or gaiters – and many of us had to wear wooden-soled clogs, given us by the Germans. Occasionally a much-needed parcel came from home containing replacement for our worn-out kit, and the Red Cross once sent a bulk consignment of uniforms which were of great help. Still, we were a picturesque if not an unsightly company. The other nationalities had somehow succeeded in bringing much of their wardrobe with them, and, at any rate until time wore these out, they had a definite advantage over us. It was common for a Britisher to appear on parade, for instance, wearing a woollen balaclava or no cap at all, a khaki battledress blouse, blue RAF or red Czech trousers, home-knitted socks of any colour, and trailing a pair of clogs on his feet.

Speaking of the picturesque, colour was lent to our parades by two Yugoslav officers who had joined our happy throng. Their uniform, consisting of voluminous red trousers and sky-blue embroidered waistcoats, brought home to us what a Community of Nations we had become!

First, there was the Polish contingent. Then there were Englishmen, Irishmen, and Scotsmen. The Empire was represented by RAF officers from Canada, Australia, and New Zealand, and by an Army doctor, Captain Mazumdar, from India. The French included some officers from Algeria and the Jewish contingent. There were the two Yugoslavs and some Belgian officers. The Netherlands were represented by an aide-de-camp of Queen Wilhelmina and last, but not least, the Dutch East Indies Company completed this procession of nations.

Colditz was the only camp of this kind in Germany. The solidarity that existed among the various nationalities was always a matter of surprise to the Germans. The alliance amongst us was not fostered by any artificial means. It was natural, springing from something deep within us, and it withstood many tests. It was a sufficiently strong link to withstand any attempt by the Germans to alienate one nationality from another.

A favourite communal punishment meted out to any particular contingent was the curtailment of the hours of recreation allowed in the wooded park of the Castle. When this happened, the recreation parade was ostracized by all until the Germans withdrew the ban. If an officer of any one nationality was unfairly treated, the whole camp would go on strike without hesitation, the only condition agreed between us being the form of the strike! On one occasion, Captain Mazumdar, true to a noble tradition, went on hunger strike. I regret to say the whole camp did not follow suit! It was not easy to obtain unanimity and mutual sacrifice where such an elemental means of survival was concerned.

On another occasion the German camp doctor worked himself into a Polish 'hate' neurosis. He insisted that Poland no longer existed, and that in consequence every Polish officer, of whatever rank, should salute him smartly. He was a captain or *Stabsarzt*. When he tried to make the Polish General salute and went into a tantrum about it, this was too much for the Poles. The whole contingent went on hunger strike. The rest of the camp supported them in spirit! The SBOs of all the other nationalities sent parallel complaints concerning the doctor's attitude to the German commandant. After three days the commandant hauled his junior officer over the coals and the famished Polish officers, having registered a grudging salute from the *Stabsarzt*, took to their vittles again with ravenous ardour.

* * *

The German sentence upon the four of us who had disappeared for a night was a fortnight's solitary confinement. During this confinement a third unlucky incident occurred which piled up further difficulties in the way of our canteen tunnel escape. A Frenchman and a Pole managed to disappear one day, and were not missed until the evening *Appell*. The Goons suspected a getaway during the return of the prisoners from their recreation in the park, and searched all possible places of concealment in the proximity of the roadway leading down to it. The two officers were found, hiding up for nightfall, in the seldom-used basement of a house near the path (it was used as an air-raid shelter), into which they had slipped undetected. This operation was by no means easy. It had been done by split-second timing, with the assistance of officers who had successfully distracted the attention of the guards accompanying the parade on the march. The assisting officers placed themselves in the ranks so as to be near the guards who walked at intervals on either side. When the officers who were to escape reached a predetermined spot on the march, the others made gestures or remarks calculated to draw the attention of their nearby guards away from the scene of action. Three seconds after the predetermined spot was reached, the escaping officers bolted. In five more seconds they were behind a concealing wall. During these five seconds some eight guards in view had to be made to 'look the other way'! The chances of success were very slight, but the trick worked. When the count was taken after the recreation period outside the courtyard gate, the assisting officers created confusion and a German-speaking officer browbeat the sergeant in charge into thinking he had made a wrong count to start with, and bluffed out the discrepancy in numbers.

It was a pity that in this case a brilliant beginning was not carried through to a successful end, and that the concealment of the count was not maintained at the later general *Appell*. The *Appell* normally called after dark in the lighted courtyard was, on this day, called in daylight, possibly due to the German sergeant's suspicions getting the better of him. *Appell* times were often changed without warning, especially to catch prisoners out, and this should not have been overlooked.

Be that as it may, the officers, when caught, made up a story concealing their real method of escape and leading the Germans to suspect a rope-descent from an attic skylight on to the grass lawn under which our tunnel exit lay hidden. A sentry was now placed with a beat which brought him in full view of our projected tunnel exit at intervals of one minute both day and night.

This incident led me to make a complaint through Colonel German and to request closer liaison and more co-operation among the various nationalities so that we did not continually trip over each other in our hurry to leave the camp! Common sense prevailed, and from this date I can record no further serious instances of overlapping in escape plans.

Our tunnel was, nevertheless, in 'Queer Street'. I disliked the idea of lengthening it and making a long-term job of it, as any prolonged lapse of time worked against the success of the venture. The Germans also started gradually to install new locks on certain doors at key-points throughout the camp. They began with the lock of the canteen, thereby foiling us temporarily in any attempt to spend long hours at work in the tunnel underneath.

We called the new locks 'cruciform' locks. The simplest description I can give of them is to compare them to four different Yale locks rolled into one. Kenneth Lockwood obtained an impression in candle-wax of the four arms of the cruciform key to the canteen. I worked for a long time on the manufacture of a false key. There was a dentist's room in the camp which was normally locked, as was also the dentist's cupboard of instruments, but these had presented little difficulty to budding burglars like ourselves. I wore out many of the bits of the dentist's electric drill in the process of making my key, but all my efforts were in vain. I am afraid the drills after I had finished with them were very blunt. Ever afterwards when I heard the agonizing shrieks of sufferers in the dentist's chair I felt a twinge of remorse that I should have been the cause of so much fruitless pain! I often wonder what would have been my fate if all the dentist's visitors had known my secret sin. Luckily for me, only one or two of my trusted confederates knew, and they kept the secret. The dentist, who was a French officer and fellow-prisoner, must have thought little of German tool-steel! He filled one of my teeth excellently before I had ruined his drills, using I do not know what kind of rubbish as filling. I cannot explain the exis-tence of the up-to-date dentist's chair and equipment. The Poles said it was there when they arrived. Before the war the Castle had been used, among other things, as a lunatic asylum. Maybe it was thought too risky to allow lunatics to visit a dentist in the town!

At this unhappy stage, when we were casting around to decide what to do with our tunnel, Peter Allan and Howard Gee (a newcomer), both excellent German speakers, reported the existence of a helpful Goon sentry. He was a sympathetic type, and he started smuggling for us on a small scale; a fresh egg here and there in return for English chocolate, or a pound of real coffee in exchange for a tin of cocoa, and so on. He ran a terrific risk, but seemed to do it with equanimity – perhaps too much equanimity – and we decided also to take a risk and plunge. At several clandestine meetings, in doorways and behind angles in the courtyard walls, Peter and Howard Gee primed the sentry and eventually suggested that he might earn some 'big' money if he once 'looked the other way' for ten minutes while on sentry duty.

The sentry fell for the idea. He was told that we would have to arrange matters so that he did a tour of sentry duty for a given two-hour period, on a given day, on a certain beat, and that in the ten-minute interval, between two predetermined signals, he was to stand (which was permitted) at one particular end of his beat. He was to receive an advance of one hundred Reichmarks as his reward, which was settled at five hundred Reichsmarks (about £34), and the remainder would be dropped out of a convenient window one hour after the ten-minute interval. The sentry was told also that no traces would be left which could lead to suspicion or involve him in accusations of neglect of duty. To all this he listened and finally agreed. The escape was on!

The first escape party consisted of twelve officers, including four Poles. The French and Dutch were as yet newcomers, whereas the Poles were by now old and trusted comrades, which accounted for their inclusion. Further, the participation of officers of another nationality was decided upon for reasons of language facilities offered, and for camp morale. The Poles had been most helpful since our arrival; the majority of them spoke German fluently, some of them knew Germany well, and those of us who thought of aiming for the North Sea or Poland took Poles as travelling companions. A few decided to travel alone.

My mind was occupied with another problem – how to arrange for the entry of thirteen officers, twelve escaping and one sealing up the entry, into the canteen? During opening hours I examined the cruciform lock closely and came to the conclusion that, from the inside, I could dismount the lock almost completely, allowing the door to open.

The escape would have to be done after the evening roll-call and in darkness.

The fateful day was decided upon – May 29th. I arranged to knock down the false wall the day before and extricate all our provisions and escape material. This was comparatively simple. During the two-hour lunch interval the canteen was locked. Before it was locked, however, I hid in a triangular recess which was used as a store cupboard and to which I had the key. When the canteen was locked up I had two clear hours to prepare everything. I removed the false wall, took out all our escape paraphernalia, hiding it in the cupboard, and prepared the tunnel exit so as to give the minimum amount of work for the final opening. After 2 o'clock, with a suitable screen of officers, I came out of the cupboard and all the stores were carried to our quarters.

The arrangements for the escape were as follows: Howard Gee, who was not in the first party, was to deal with the sentry. He would pass him the first signal on receipt of a sign from us in the tunnel. This was to be given by myself in the first instance at the opening end of the tunnel, passed to our thirteenth man on watch at the canteen window in the courtyard, who would then transmit it to our quarters by means of a shaded light. Gee could then signal to the sentry from an outside window. The 'all clear' was to be given in the same way, except that our thirteenth man had to come to the tunnel exit and receive the word from me when I had properly sealed up the exit after all were out. A piece of string pulled out through the earth served the purpose. I would be over the wall at the far end of the lawn before the signal would be transferred to the sentry.

May 29th loomed overcast and it soon began to rain. It rained all day in torrents, the heaviest rainfall we had ever had, but this would mean a dark night and it did not upset our plans. The sentry was told during the course of the afternoon what post he was to occupy. He was given his advance in cash and instructed to avoid the end of his beat nearest to the canteen on receipt of an agreed signal from a certain window, and to remain away from that end until another signal was given.

As the evening approached, the excitement grew. The lucky twelve dressed themselves in kit prepared during many months of patient work. From out of astonishing hiding-places came trousers and slouch caps made of grey German blankets, multicoloured knitted pullovers, transformed and dyed army overcoats, windjackets and mackintoshes, dyed khaki shirts and home-knitted ties. These were donned and covered with army apparel. Maps and home-made compasses appeared, and subdued last-minute discussions took place concerning routes and escape instructions. As the time passed, impatience for the 'off' increased. I became alternately hot and cold, and my hands were clammy and my mouth was dry. We all felt the same, as I could tell by the forced laughs and the nervous jokes and banter which passed around.

I remained hidden in the canteen when it was locked up for the night, and dismounted the lock. When the evening *Appell* sounded, I slipped out of the door behind a well-placed crowd of officers. If a Goon pushed the door for any reason whatever we were finished. A wedge of paper alone held it. Sentries were posted for the *Appell* at all vantage-points, and one stood very close to the canteen. Immediately after the *Appell* we had to work fast, for all the prisoners then had to disperse to their rooms, the courtyard doors were locked, and every door tried by the German duty officer. All thirteen of us had to slip into the canteen behind the screen of assisting officers while German officers and NCOs were in the courtyard, and the lock had then to be remounted on the canteen door in double-quick time. The twelve escapers had to appear on parade dressed ready in their escape attire suitably covered with army overcoats and trousers. Assembled rucksacks had been placed in order in the tunnel during the lunch-time closing hours in the same way as before.

The *Appell* went off without a hitch. Colonel German, who had to stand alone in front, was looking remarkably fat, for he was escaping with us. He aroused no comment. Immediately after the 'dismiss' was given, and almost in front of the eyes of the sentry nearby, the thirteen chosen ones slipped silently through the door until all were in.

'Where do we go from here?' asked one of the Polish officers who had not worked on the tunnel.

'Over the palisades!' I replied, pointing to the high wooden partition, over which sheets had already been thrown.

He grabbed them and started to climb, making a noise like a bass drum on the partition door. A loud 'Sh! Sh!' as if a lavatory cistern was emptying greeted his effort.

'For God's sake!' I said, 'you're not in Paderewski's orchestra now.'

'No,' replied the Pole dramatically from the top of the partition, 'but his spirit is living with me, this night!'

Luckily the din in the courtyard covered any noise we made at this juncture.

While the lock was remounted on the door, I removed my army uniform and handed it to our thirteenth man. He was to collect all discarded clothes, conceal them in the cupboard, and remove them with assistance next day. I went straight away to the end of the tunnel, closely followed by Rupert Barry, for we were going together, and started work on the last few inches of earth beneath the surface of the opening. It was dark by now outside, and the rain was still pelting down. It began pouring through the earth covering the exit, and within five minutes I was drenched to the skin with muddy water. The lock-testing patrol tried the canteen door and passed. Soon all was quiet in the camp. Within an hour the sentry was reported by light flashes to be at his post. I gave the signal for him to keep away from the canteen window.

I worked frenziedly at the surface of grass, cutting out my square, and then slowly heaved the tray of the exit upwards. It came away, and as it did so a shaft of brilliant light shot down the tunnel For a second I was bewildered and blinded. It was, of course, the light of the projector situated ten yards away from the opening, which lit up the whole of the wall-face on that particular side of the Castle. I lifted the tray clear. Streams of muddy water trickled into the tunnel around me. I pushed myself upwards, and with Rupert's assistance from behind, scrambled out.

Once out, I looked around. I was like an actor upon a stage. The floodlight made a huge grotesque image of my figure against the white wall. Row upon row of unfriendly windows, those of the German *Kommandantur*, frowned down upon me. The windows had no blackout curtains and a wandering inquisitive eye from within might easily turn my way. It was an unavoidable risk. Rupert began to climb out as I put the finishing touch to the tray for closing the hole. He was having some difficulty. He had handed up my rucksack and was levering himself upwards when I happened to look from my work at the wall in front of me, there to see a second giant shadow outlined beside my own crouching figure. The second shadow held a revolver in his hand.

'Get back! Get back!' I yelled to Rupert, as a guttural voice behind me shouted:

'*Hände hoch! Hände hoch!*'

I turned, to face a German officer levelling his pistol at my body, while another leaped for the hole. He was about to shoot down the opening.

'*Schiessen Sie nicht!*' I screamed several times.

A bullet or two down that stone- and brick-walled tunnel might have wrought considerable damage, filled as it was with human bodies. The officer at the hole did not shoot.

Germans suddenly appeared from everywhere, and all the officers were giving orders at once. I was led off to the *Kommandantur* and conducted to a bathroom where I was stripped completely and allowed to wash, and then to an office where I was confronted by Hauptmann Priem.

He was evidently pleased with his night's work and in high spirits.

'*Ah hah! Es ist Herr Hauptmann Reid. Das ist schön!*' he said as I walked in, and continued:

'Nobody could recognize who the nigger was until he was washed! And now that we have the nigger out of the woodpile, what has he got to say for himself?'

'I think the nigger in the woodpile was a certain German sentry, was he not?' I questioned in reply.

'Yes, indeed, Herr Hauptmann, German sentries know their duty. The whole matter has been reported to me from the start.'

'From before the start maybe?'

'Herr Hauptmann Reid, that is not the point. Where does your tunnel come from?'

'That is obvious,' I replied.

'From the canteen, then?'

'Yes.'

'But you have been locked into your quarters. You have a tunnel from your rooms to the canteen?'

'No!'

'But yes! You have just been counted on *Appell*. The canteen has been locked many hours ago. You have a tunnel?'

'No!'

'We shall see. How many of you are there?'

'So many I have never been able to count them properly!'

'Come now, Herr Hauptmann, the whole camp or just a few?'

'Just a few!'

'Good, then I hope our solitary confinement accommodation will not be too overcrowded!' said Priem, grinning broadly. He added:

'I was perturbed when first I saw you. I gave orders at once not to shoot. You see I had my men posted at all windows and beneath on the road. They were to shoot if any prisoners ran or struggled. I saw this figure which was you, writhing upon the ground. I thought you had fallen from the roof and that you were in great pain!'

While this was going on, hell had broken loose inside the prison. The courtyard was filled with troops, while posses dashed around wildly trying to locate the inside end of our rat-hole. In our quarters there was the usual parade in the day-room while the Goons prodded beds and unearthed the customary thirteen inert corpses made of coats and blankets. At first they were convinced the tunnel started in our quarters on the first floor and they uprooted floorboards accordingly. Slowly it dawned upon them that it might be worth while to try the canteen.

Once there, as body after body issued from the manhole amidst shouts along the tunnel of 'Goonery ahoy!' mingled with shouts from above of '*Hände hoch! Hände hoch!*' the Goons started hopping with excitement and revolvers were waving in all directions. The Jerry officer-in-charge was an elderly 2nd Lieutenant. He was white to the lips and shaking all over. It was a miracle the weapons did not go off, for the Jerries were out of control. They practically stripped all the escapers naked in their anxiety not to miss any escape booty.

The escapers, on the contrary, appeared reasonably calm. When one of them lit a cigarette, it was the signal for an outbreak. The Goons turned on him in a fury. The German 2nd Lieutenant was near him and the two of them were penned in a corner surrounded by an angry armed mob. A further uproar occurred when Colonel German's face appeared at the tunnel entrance. Consternation was followed by action and our Colonel could hardly rise out of the tunnel on account of the number of Germans who pressed around him. This was 'big-game' hunting, they must have thought.

Eventually some semblance of order was established and each officer in turn, after a thorough inspection, was escorted back to our quarters in his underclothes.

The next day the usual inquiry took place. The Germans had overhauled the tunnel, but what puzzled them was how thirteen men could be inside the canteen, which was locked with their unbreakable cruciform lock, so soon after an *Appell*, and after having been apparently closed up in their quarters for the night.

Special attention was paid to Kenneth Lockwood, of course, as canteen assistant. He was made to sit in front of a table on which a solitary object reposed – the official key of the canteen. Two German officers faced him and repeated ominously in German the question:

'How did you get into the canteen?'

Kenneth ignored the hypnotic key and asked them in return:

'Have you ever read *Alice in Wonderland*?'

This was duly interpreted.

'No,' they said. 'Why?'

'Because Alice got through small doors and keyholes by eating something to make her smaller.'

The interpreter had difficulty in getting this over, but suddenly they broke into roars of laughter and Kenneth was dismissed without further questioning.

For a long time they searched for a tunnel connecting with our quarters, but eventually gave it up. I imagine that, after some time, they worked out the method used – this was not difficult.

In due course we were all sentenced to a fortnight's 'solitary', but as usual, the solitary cells were all occupied and, instead, we carried out the sentence in two small communal rooms. Funnily enough, one of the rooms was that in which we had started our first tunnel, and in which Hank and I had been caught.

'Shovewood II' was still in good working order, and as we had previously concealed some food reserves there, it at last came into its own – we were not short of extra rations during our term of 'solitary'! The 'solitary', in this case, with thirteen officers jammed into two small rooms, was of the 'Black Hole of Calcutta' variety.

Needless to say, we never saw 'our' sentry again! He did not receive his four hundred Reichsmarks, which was a good thing. It also puzzled the Jerries how we were getting supplies of German money.

8

The Heavy Palliasse

No SOONER WERE we all free again after our 'solitary', than a rare opportunity presented itself. One day, without warning, a large German lorry was driven into the courtyard under guard and stopped outside the doorway to our quarters. Some French troop prisoners descended. We knew a couple of them. They were not lodged in the camp but somewhere in the town where they worked, and they occasionally came into the camp to carry out odd jobs. We had naturally made contact to nose out particulars concerning the orientation of the village and the life of its inhabitants. Unfortunately, these Frenchmen appeared so rarely that they were useless as trafficking agents.

This time they had come to collect a large number of straw palliasses – the standard prison mattresses consisting of large canvas sacks filled with straw – which were stored on the floor above the Dutch quarters. The palliasses were needed for troops' quarters being prepared in the village to house, as it turned out afterwards, Russian prisoners-of-war. The French prisoners each collected a palliasse and, descending the winding staircase past our quarters, continued to the ground floor and then outside the main door swung the palliasses on to the lorry.

There was no time to waste. After hasty consultation, Peter Allan was selected for the attempt. He was small and light and could speak German fluently – so he was an ideal candidate for a one-man effort. We were prepared to try more, but Peter was to be the guinea-pig.

We rigged him out in what was left of our depleted stock of escape clothing, gave him money and packed him in one of our own palliasses, and then tackled the French.

On the stairway outside, I stopped our most likely Frenchman as he descended and pulled him into our quarters with his palliasse, saying:

'I want you to carry an officer downstairs inside a palliasse and load him on to the lorry.'

'*Mais c'est impossible*,' said the Frenchman.

'It is simple,' I assured him. 'It will be over in two minutes; nobody will notice it.'

'And if I am caught?'

'You will not be caught,' I argued, and pressed a tin of cigarettes into his hand.

'But the others?'

'They will not give you away. Give them some of the cigarettes.'

'I am not so sure,' was his reply. 'No! It is too dangerous. I shall be caught and flogged, or they may even shoot me.'

'You know you will not be shot. Courage! Would you not risk a flogging for the Allies, for France? We are all fighting this war together.'

'I would not risk much for many Frenchmen,' he said, cryptically, 'and France is no more!'

'Come now!' I cajoled, 'that is not a Frenchman speaking; that sounds like a collaborator. You are no collaborator. I know your reputation from Frenchmen in the camp who speak well of you. You have helped them. Can you not help us now?'

'Why should I suffer because a British officer wishes to be mad?'

'He is not mad. He is just like you and me. Remember, we officers are not able to move around like you. Why should he not want to escape?'

'*Eh bien!* I'll do it!' he consented, softening at last.

I breathed a sigh of relief and patted him on the shoulder. If he was caught, he was liable to suffer rough treatment.

Peter was already packed and waiting in another palliasse, which was propped over the Frenchman's shoulder. I never saw a bundle of canvas and straw looking less like a palliasse in my life, but the corners soon seemed to settle themselves out. By the time the Frenchman made his exit to the courtyard, he was looking much more as if he was carrying ten pounds than ten stones.

Alas! he could not off-load the mattress on to the high floor of the lorry alone, so he did the sensible thing; he dropped his load on the ground and looked around, pretending to wipe his brow. An opportune moment arrived almost immediately, as a couple of our stooges on 'attention distracting' duty promptly started to tinker with the front of the car. The Jerries on guard moved to the front, and our Frenchman asked for help from a compatriot just relieved of his mattress. The two of them swung Peter as if he were a feather on top of the rapidly growing pile.

That was enough for the morning. We had no intention of risking another body on that lorry. In due course it departed and was ineffectually prodded by guards at the various gates before trundling off down to the town below.

Peter was duly off-loaded by his guardian, although some of the French were becoming 'windy' as to the enormity of their crime. The guardian was subjected to a good deal of barracking and some threats from his compatriots about the loss of privileges, food and such-like, which was the usual whine of all prisoners who preferred the *status quo* to doing anything that might hurt the feelings of their captors.

Peter understood French well, and heard it all from his recumbent position as he busily imitated an inert mattress in a hurry to be put on a nice board bed in an empty room somewhere in the town of Colditz. He was eventually so deposited and the lorry team disappeared for the lunch interval. All was silent.

Peter extricated himself and found that he was on the ground floor of a deserted house in the town. He opened the window and climbed into a small garden and from there to a road. Our bird had flown!

Peter reached Stuttgart and then Vienna. His greatest thrill was when he was picked up by a senior German SS officer travelling in style in a large car, and accompanied him for about a hundred miles on his way. Only a man like Peter Allan, who had spent six months at school in Germany, could have got away with the conversation involved in a cheek-by-jowl car journey of such a kind.

Meanwhile, in the afternoon, work was resumed by the French on a second load of mattresses and we resumed work on the preparation of a second 'heavy' mattress. Peter had been instructed to make his getaway quickly for the reason that if we failed in the second attempt we did not want the Germans to find Peter quietly lying in his mattress awaiting nightfall!

By now, however, the Frenchmen were frightened and even our staunch French orderly wilted under the weight of the second mattress, duly prepared by us with Lieutenant J. Hyde-Thompson, MC (Durham Light Infantry), resting inside. Unfortunately Hyde-Thompson weighted nearly twelve and a half stone and was sufficiently tall to give the lie to the desired impression of a well-stuffed palliasse. In the courtyard he was dumped on the ground next to the lorry and the Frenchmen refused to load him. Our distraction stooges worked overtime, but the French strike continued and eventually the Jerries became suspicious. The non-commissioned officer-in-charge called for an officer, and by the time the latter arrived the lorry was loaded and our 'heavy' mattress still lay leadenly on the ground.

The officer prodded and then ordered the non-commissioned officer to investigate, while he held his revolver cocked, expecting the worst. Hyde-Thompson duly appeared covered in straw, and was ignominiously led off for examination and a month's cooling off in the cells.

Fourteen days later we heard the sad and discouraging news that Peter Allan had been recaught. His story was depressing.

He had reached Vienna and, having spent the last of his money, was looking around for ways and means to carry on to Poland. He thought of the American consulate – for the USA was still not at war. He went there and disclosed his identity. The Americans politely but firmly refused him any kind of help. After this he became despondent. He was worn out from long trekking, and the insidious loneliness of the solitary fleeing refugee in an enemy land descended on him. This curious sensation has to be lived through to be appreciated. It can lead a man to give himself up voluntarily, despite the consequences; to talk and mix with other human beings, be they even his jailers, means nothing to a hunted man, particularly in a city. He must have a strong inner fibre who can withstand the temptation for long. It was for this reason among others that escapers found it advisable to travel in pairs, where possible.

Peter Allan went into a park in Vienna and fell asleep on a bench.

In the morning he awoke and found his legs paralysed with cramp. He crawled to the nearest habitation and was taken to hospital, where his resistance broke down. He was quite well looked after and was soon fit to be escorted back to Colditz, where the greater despondency of failure was to hold sway over him during a month's lonely imprisonment.

Two questions, at least, arise concerning this escape. First, why was a tall and heavy person selected for the second attempt? The answer is the same as that which accounts for pure strategy so frequently becoming modified by paramount policy, often, as in this case, resulting in the failure of the project. Hyde-Thompson had arrived in Colditz with a considerable amount of German money in his possession, following an abortive escape attempt. Although the money was not officially his own, he had had the wit to save it through many searches and he had a justifiable lien on it. Officers were searched on departure from one camp and again on arrival at a new one. This consisted of being stripped naked and having each piece of clothing carefully examined, while luggage was gone through with a toothcomb. Hyde-Thompson had given a large proportion of the money to me with alacrity for the canteen tunnel attempt, and some more had gone with Peter Allan. It was time he should be rewarded, and the mattress escape was offered.

Secondly, one may wonder at the attitude of the Americans in Vienna. The explanation is probably twofold. The official one is that the Americans, though neutral, were having a hard time holding on to their Vienna Consulate, and were continually in danger of being ordered out of the country at a moment's notice. They were doing important work and could not risk their position officially. The other explanation, which is quite plausible, is that Peter did not succeed in convincing the Consulate that he was not a German 'agent provocateur'. He had nothing to prove his case and he spoke German perfectly. His English might have been sufficient proof to an Englishman if tested *in extenso*. Yet I dare any Englishman to accept in a similar situation, but with the nationalities reversed, the voice and accent of an alleged American as being that of a genuine American.

9

French Dash and Polish Temperament

LIEUTENANT MAIRESSE LEBRUN was a French cavalry officer, tall, handsome, and debonair, and a worthy compatriot of that famed cuirassier of Napoleon whose legendary escapades were so ably recounted by Conan Doyle in his book, *The Adventures of Brigadier Gerard*.

Lebrun had slipped the German leash from Colditz once already by what seems, in the telling, a simple ruse. In fact, it required quite expert handling. A very small Belgian officer was his confederate. On one of the 'Park' outings the Belgian officer concealed himself under the voluminous folds of a tall comrade's cloak at the outgoing 'numbering off' parade and was not counted. During the recreation period in the Park, Lebrun, with the aid of suitable diversions, climbed up among the rafters of an open-sided pavilion situated in the middle of the recreation pen. He was not missed because the Belgian provided the missing number, and the dogs did not get wind of him. Later he descended and, smartly dressed in a grey flannel suit sent by a friend from France, he walked to a local railway station and proffered a hundred-mark note at the booking-office in exchange for a ticket. Unfortunately, the note was an old one, no longer in circulation. The station-master became suspicious and finally locked Lebrun up in a cloakroom and telephoned the camp. The Camp Commandant replied that nothing was amiss and that his prisoner complement was complete. While he was phoning, Lebrun wrenched open a window and leaped out on top of an old woman, who naturally became upset and gave tongue. A chase ensued. He was finally cornered by the station personnel and recaptured. In due course he was returned to the Castle and handed over to the protesting Commandant.

This adventure lost Mairesse his fine suit and found him doing a month's 'solitary' confinement at the same time as Peter Allan.

One fine afternoon we heard many shots fired in the playground and rushed to the windows, but could see nothing because of the foliage. Terrific excitement followed in the German quarters and we saw posses of Goons with dogs descending at the double from the Castle and disappearing among the trees. Shouts and orders and the barking of dogs continued for some time and eventually faded away in the distance.

We heard by message from Peter Allan what had happened. The 'solitaries' – at the time a mere half a dozen – were having their daily exercise in the park, during which period they could mix freely. Being only a few, they were sparsely guarded, though confined to one end of the compound, where the prisoners played football among the trees. Lebrun was in the habit of doing exercises with two other Frenchmen, which included much leapfrogging. Now Lebrun was athletic. It was high summer and he was dressed in what remained to him of his former finery – shorts, a yellow cardigan, an open-necked shirt, and gym shoes – not good escaping clothes, but that was also what he reckoned the Germans would think. While a couple of the latter were lolling rather sleepily outside the wire and looking at anything but the prisoners, Lebrun innocently leapfrogged with the other Frenchmen.

It all happened in a flash. His French colleague stood near the wire and, forming with his two hands a stirrup into which Lebrun placed his foot, he catapulted him upwards. Acrobats can heave each other tremendous distances by this method. Precision of timing of muscular effort is its secret. Lebrun and his friend managed it, and the former sailed in a headlong dive over the nine-foot wire.

This was only half the battle. Lebrun ran twenty yards along the fence to the main wall of the park. He had to reclimb the wire, using it as a ladder, in order to hoist himself on to the top of the wall which was, at this point, about thirteen feet high. Rather than present a slowly moving target during this climb, Lebrun deliberately attracted the fire of the two nearest sentries by running backwards and forwards beside the wall. Their carbines once fired (and having missed), the reloading gave him the extra seconds he needed. He was on top of the wall by the time they fired again and dropped to the ground on the other side in a hail of bullets as the more distant sentries joined in the fusillade.

He disappeared and was never recaught. He certainly deserves the greatest credit for this escape, which was in the true French cavalry tradition and demanded the very quintessence of courage, remembering the effort was made in cold blood and with every opportunity for reflection on the consequences of a false step. A British officer, in a similar attempt a few years later, was shot dead. The escape savours of a generation of Frenchmen of whom the majority disappeared on the battlefields of the First World War and who, alas, never had the chance to sire and educate a generation like themselves to follow in their footsteps.

The loss, which was so deeply felt in the 'thirties and which found physical expression during the critical days of 1940, is happily in these days of the 'fifties fading like a bad dream. The young blood of France is quickening again and there is a new courage in the air.

I met Lebrun again long afterwards, when the war was over, and here is the end of his story.

Lebrun escaped on July 1st, 1941. Although he had the sleuth-hounds and a posse of Goons on his tail within ten minutes, he managed to hide in a field of wheat. (You must walk in backwards, rearranging the stalks as you go.) There he hid the whole afternoon with a search plane circling continuously above him. At 10 pm he set off. He had twenty German marks which were smuggled into his prison cell from the camp. He walked about fifty miles and then stole a bicycle and cycled between sixty and a hundred miles a day. He posed as an Italian officer and begged or bought food at lonely farm-houses, making sure, by a stealthy watch beforehand, that there were only women in the house. His bicycle 'sprang a leak', so he abandoned it and stole a second. On the journey to the Swiss frontier he was stopped twice by guards and ran for it each time. On the second occasion, about twenty-five miles from the frontier, he tripped the guard up with the aid of his bicycle and knocked him out with his bicycle pump. He took to the woods and crossed the frontier safely on July 8th.

Within a week he was in France. In December 1942 he crossed

the Pyrenees and was taken prisoner by the Spaniards, who locked him up in a castle. He jumped from a window into the moat and broke his spine on some rocks at the bottom, was removed, laid down on a mattress, and left to die. A local French consul, however, who had previously been endeavouring to extricate the incarcerated Lebrun, heard of the accident and insisted on an immediate operation. Lebrun's life was saved. He eventually reached Algeria to carry on the war. Today, though permanently crippled by his fall, he is a pillar in his own country.

If any German had examined Lebrun's cell at Colditz when he left for his daily exercise on July 1st, he might have nipped Lebrun's escape in the bud. Lebrun had packed up his belongings and addressed them to himself in France. Months later they arrived – forwarded by Oberstleutnant Prawitt, the Colditz Camp Commandant!

* * *

The most daredevil Polish officer at Colditz among a bunch of daredevils was 'Niki', 2nd Lieutenant (Ensign) N. Surmanowicz. He was a small weedy-looking young man with an untidy face made up of unequal-sided triangles. The fire that burnt in his soul showed only in his eyes, which glowed with fanatical ardour. He was a great friend of mine and we went on many marauding expeditions together through the forbidden parts of the camp. He taught me all I ever knew about lock-picking, at which he was an expert. It was Niki who had been one of our first visitors up in the loft on our arrival at Colditz. The manufacture of magnetic compasses was also a pastime of his. This he carried out with the aid of a home-made solenoid, employing the electric current of the main camp supply, which happened to be 'direct' current. The number of compasses fabricated by him alone, together with their pivots, compass cards, and glass-covered boxes, went into the fifties.

His schemes for escaping were, to my mind, mostly too wild to bear serious examination. He, on the other hand, thought my ideas were prosaic and I know he inwardly deprecated my painstaking way of setting about escape problems.

Like Lebrun, he relied on 'dash', to which he added a depth of cunning hardly to be equalled. In common with all the Poles, he despised the Germans, but, unfortunately also like many Poles, he underestimated his enemy; a form of conceit which, however, is not a monopoly of the Poles.

Niki spent as much time in solitary confinement as he spent with 'the common herd'. On one occasion, in the summer of 1941, he occupied a cell which had a small window, high up in the wall, opening on to our courtyard. Another Polish officer, Lieutenant Meitek Schmiel, a friend of Niki, occupied the cell next door. I received a message from him one day, saying that he and Schmiel were going to escape that night and would I join them!

I declined the invitation for two reasons; firstly, I thought Niki was crazy, and, secondly, I had given up the idea of escaping myself so long as I remained Escape Officer. With the British contingent on the increase rapidly, this latter course was the only one open to me if I wished to retain the confidence of our group as an impartial arbiter and helper.

I passed on Niki's invitation to a few of the most hare-brained among our company, but Niki's invitation was politely refused by all!

Nobody believed he was serious. Nobody believed he could ghost his way out of his heavily barred and padlocked cell, then open his friend's cell and then unlock the main door of the 'solitary' cell corridor which opened on to the courtyard. Having accomplished this feat he was inside the prison camp, the same as everyone else! Niki loved a challenge and he would chuckle with laughter for the rest of his life if he could show the Jerries once and for all that it took more than they could contrive to keep a Pole down.

He left the invitation open, giving a rendezvous in the courtyard outside the solitary confinement cells at 11 pm that night.

I was at my window watching as 11 pm struck, and on the minute I saw the door of the cells open slowly. All was dark and I could only faintly distinguish the two figures as they crept out. Then something dropped from a window high up in the Polish quarters. It was a rope made of sheets with a load strapped at the bottom – their escape kit, clothes and rucksacks. Next I saw the figures climb the rope one after the other to a ledge forty feet above the ground. What they were about to do was impossible, but they had achieved the impossible once already. I could no longer believe my eyes. The ledge they were on jutted four inches out from the sheer face of the wall of the building. They both held the rope, which was still suspended from the window above them. My heart pounded against my ribs as I saw them high above me with their backs against the wall moving along the ledge inch by inch a distance of ten yards before reaching the safety of a gutter on the eaves of the German guardhouse.

Once there, they were comparatively safe and out of sight if the courtyard lights were turned on. I then saw them climb up the roof to a skylight through which they disappeared, pulling the long rope of sheets, which was let loose by Polish confederates, after them.

Their next move, I knew, was to descend from a small window at the outer end of the attic of the German guard-house. The drop was about one hundred and twenty feet, continuing down the face of the cliff upon which the Castle was built.

I retired to my bunk, weak at the knees and shaking, as if I had done the climb myself.

The next morning the two of them were back in their cells! I find it hard to tell the end of the story. Niki wore plimsolls for the climb, but his colleague, with Niki's agreement, preferred to wear boots of the mountaineering type. As they both descended the long drop from the guard-house, the mountaineering boots made too much noise against the wall and awoke the German duty officer sleeping in the guardhouse. He opened the window, to see the rope dangling beside him and a body a few yards below him. He drew his revolver and, true to type, shouted '*Hände hoch!*' several times and called out the guard.

I spent a month in Niki's cell later on without being able to discover how he had opened the door!

After this episode the Germans placed a sentry in the courtyard. He remained all night with the lights full on, which was to prove a nuisance for later escape attempts.

10

Just Too Easy

THE SUMMER MONTHS were passing – slowly enough for us – yet too fast for all our plans. Winter, relatively speaking, is the escapers' 'close season', though the Second World War was to see many time-hallowed rules of this nature broken.

There was a long curved room over the canteen where a batch of our British contingent slept and passed much of their time. Roughly speaking, two sides of this room backed on to the German section of the Castle, and these two walls always attracted our attention as holding out possibilities. A door in the end wall, in the very early days, had been opened by Niki, who had been beyond into a deserted attic. He could describe no more than that. The doorway had promptly been walled up. Although efforts were made to break through the wall, this had been constructed with such tough cement that noise gave us away and the Germans calmly replastered our puny efforts. This is possibly where they planted one of their microphones, which they later had everywhere.

The second wall, according to the officers who slept near it, backed on to German lavatories.

Tommy Elliot (Lieutenant, Durham County Light Infantry) and Ted Barton announced to me one day that they had started a fair-sized hole which was making good progress. In a matter of a couple of days they were practically through. Listening carefully, they established by sounds from the other side that the hole was near floor-level and appeared to be close to a lavatory bowl. A pinhole was made through the plaster face from the inside, and it was confirmed that the opening would be just off centre and below the seat of a porcelain water-closet.

No time could be lost – the Germans appeared unconscionably

quiet and they might start a series of searches any day. The opening was not well concealed on our side and any search would have revealed it. I had my own misgivings, too, concerning the hole, but without evidence I could not withstand the enthusiasm of my fellow-officers for the venture.

The plan was simple. Towards late evening on the coming Sunday, when the German quarters would be at their quietest, the hole would be broken through and twelve officers at five-minute intervals between pairs or individuals would pass through in civilian attire and make their best way out. In effect, the entry into the German quarters would be only the beginning of their troubles, for they would still have to find their way to the exits of the German side of the Castle, then brave the various gates or, more probably, disappear into the wooded playground below the Castle and climb over the main wall under cover of trees.

Sunday arrived and the tension grew apace. The escapers appeared for a passing-out parade. Civilian attire was checked and in some cases altered or substituted by articles of civilian clothing supplied from the private hoards of willing helpers.

* * *

At this period of our captivity, escape equipment was becoming organized. Although every officer had not yet been equipped with identity papers, each had a home-made compass of one kind or another, a set of maps painfully traced over and over again from originals, and each was given some German money.

Every officer possessed his private escape kit, which he had ample time to devise during the long hours of enforced idleness – the devil indeed 'finds mischief still for idle hands to do' in a prison camp! And it was surprising what could be produced in the way of civilian clothing by dyeing and altering, by cutting up blankets, and by clever sewing and knitting. Many officers had their specialities and turned out articles in quantity.

I concentrated on the manufacture of 'gor blimey' caps and also rucksacks. My particular brand of cap, cut out of any suitably coloured blanket, having a peak stiffened with a piece of leather or other water-resisting stiffener and lined with a portion of coloured handkerchief and a soft-leather head-band, looked quite professional. My rucksacks were not always waterproof; they were made from dark-coloured or dyed, tough army material, with broad trouser braces adapted as straps, and the flaps and corners neatly edged with leather strips cut from boot tongues. They would pass in Germany as workmen's rucksacks.

Dyeing with 'ersatz' coffee or purple pencil lead became a fine art. The blue Royal Air Force uniform was readily adaptable and with skilful tailoring could become a passable civilian suit. Of course, real civilian clothing was what every officer ultimately aimed at possessing. This urgent desire accounts for the high premium set on the workmen's clothing which gave rise to the 'grand piano' incident.

A similar occasion arose once during one of the very rare visits of a German civilian dentist to supplement the work of our French army dentist. He was accompanied by two leech-like sentries, who kept so close to him that he hardly had room to wield his forceps.

The dentist's torture chamber was approached through a maze of small rooms and had two doors, one of which was supposed to be permanently locked but which we opened on our nefarious occasions with the aid of our universal keys. On the back of this door was a coat-hook, and on the hook our German dentist hung his Homburg hat and a fine fur-collared tweed overcoat.

This was indeed 'big game', and Dick Howe, with another British officer, 'Scorgie' Price, and a French officer named Jacques Prot were soon hot on the trail.

Dick arranged to pay an officer's dentist's bill. The dentist was paid in *Lagergeld* and Dick sought out an officer with a heavy bill – it came to a hundred marks. He collected the whole sum in one-mark notes. This would give him plenty of time. He arranged a signal with the other two. The operative word was 'Right'. When Dick said 'Right' loudly, Price was to open the locked door and remove the coat and hat.

Dick went to the dentist's room and insisted on interrupting the dentist's work to pay his brother-officer's bill. He drew him over to a table; the two sentries dutifully followed; and Dick started to count out laboriously his *Lagergeld*.

'*Eins, zwei, drei, . . .*' he started and carried on to *zehn*, at which point he looked up to see if he had the full attention of the dentist and his guards. 'Not quite', he thought, and he carried on painfully, '*elf, zwölf . . .*' By the time he reached *zwanzig* he had all their eyes riveted on the slowly rising pile of notes, so he said 'Right.' As he continued he sensed nothing had happened. At *dreizig* he repeated 'Right' a little louder. Again nothing happened. At *vierzig* he filled his lungs and shouted 'Right' again. Still nothing happened. Doggedly he continued, holding the attention of all three, as his reserves of *Lagergeld* dwindled. As *fünfzig, sechzig, siebzig* passed, his 'Rights' crescendoed, to the amusement of his three spectators. Nothing happened. An operatic bass would have been proud of Dick's final rendering at *achtzig, neunzig*, and *hundert*. The scheme had failed, and the only persons laughing were the Germans at Dick's, by this time, comic act.

The dentist, still guffawing, collected all the notes together and before Dick's crestfallen gaze started recounting them. As he reached *zehn* he shouted 'R-r-reight,' and Dick, to his own utter astonishment, felt rather than heard the door open behind them, and sensed an arm appearing around it. Before the dentist had reached *zwanzig* the door had closed again. Dick continued the pantomime and eventually, after assuring himself that the coat and hat had really disappeared, he retired from the scene with apologies – a shaken man.

The concealment of contraband material presented great difficulty, and many were the hours given up to devising ingenious ways of hiding our precious work. The common hiding-places and those at various times found out by the Germans were: behind false-backed cupboards and in trap-door hides, under floorboards, and sewn into mattresses and overcoat linings. Small items were often sealed in cigarette-tins, weighted and dropped into lavatory cisterns or concealed in stores of food. There were myriads of possibilities, and it is appropriate that the better ways remain undisclosed for the present. Men who may have nothing to think about for many a long, weary day in the years to come will rediscover them and sharpen their wits in the exercise.

* * *

To return to our twelve stalwarts perspiring with nervous anticipation, some even vomiting quietly in the seclusion of an *Abort*, waiting for the zero hour! At the appointed time, all was reported quiet on the other side of the wall. The hole was quickly broken out and the escapers started to squirm through in their correct order and at the appropriate intervals of time, while watchers at different vantage-points scanned the exits from the German quarters.

Soon reports began coming in: 'No exits'! and again 'No exits'! We persisted, however, for forty minutes by which time eight officers had passed through the hole. At this point I turned to the remaining four:

'I think it's too risky to continue without having a pause. What do you think?'

'It's suspicious that not one has poked his head out of the other end of the rabbit run yet!' said the next on the list to go.

'I don't think we can spoil anything by holding off and watching for results. If we go on pumping any more through as it is, they'll soon be bulging out of the *Kommandantur* windows.'

'Shall we stay on the field during half-time or go and have a drink?'

'Better stay here,' I advised. 'You may be wanted at a moment's notice, but have all your kit ready to hide too. Make a plan for a split-second hideaway in case the Jerries are on to the scheme and try to catch us in the rear.'

After fifteen minutes of inactivity the alarm was suddenly given. 'Jerries *en masse* entering courtyard, heading for our staircase!'

Well, that was the end of that! The Germans had laid a trap and we had walked into it, or eight of us had. The hole must have been marked during operations upon it, and a secret guard kept. As each of the eight escapers left the *Abort* and proceeded down a long corridor he was quietly shepherded into a room and put under guard!

Thus ended another depressing chapter for British morale in Colditz. The Germans had gained the upper hand and were playing with us. Our efforts were beginning to appear ridiculous.

II

Dutch Porcelain

BRITISH ESCAPING REPUTATION had reached rock bottom, and whatever conceit we had left was soon to receive a further blow, this time at the hands of the Dutch. From the beginning close relations were maintained with them, and, though at the start this did not involve revealing the full details of our respective plans, it soon developed into a very close co-operation, which was headed on the Dutch side by a Captain Van den Heuvel.

The Dutch were not very long at Colditz before Van den Heuvel warned me of an impending attempt. 'Vandy', as he was inevitably called, was a fairly tall, big-chested man with a round face, florid complexion, and an almost permanent broad grin. His mouth was large enough in repose, but when he smiled it was from ear to ear. He had hidden depths of pride and a terrific temper, revealed on very rare occasions. He spoke English well, but with a droll Dutch accent.

'How are you, Vandy?' I would ask him, to which his unvarying reply was: 'Rather vell, thank you,' with emphasis on the 'rather.'

'Patt,' he said to me one day, 've are about to trry our virst vlight vrom Golditz. I can only zay it is vrom the direczion ov the park and it vill take place on Zunday.'

Sunday passed calmly and in the evening I went to see Vandy.

'Well, Vandy, there's been no excitement. What have you got up your sleeve?' I asked.

'Aah! Patt,' he replied, with a mischievous twinkle in his eye, 'I haf two more op my sleeve vor next Zunday, two haf gone today!'

He was grinning as usual and was like a dog with two tails. His pleasure was infectious and I could not help laughing.

At the morning *Appell* on Monday, however, two Dutchmen were missing. Some time later (not the next Sunday, for technical reasons), two more disappeared.

The German were worried enough over the first two. They were 'hopping mad' when the number rose to four. When it had risen to six, they forgot even to hop. There was a series of searches of the camp premises, and the park was given a very careful scrutiny. I noticed the Jerries placed bars across the small wooden cover to a manhole in the football ground which had, in any case, one large nut and bolt securing it.

Eventually I managed to worm out of Vandy how he, a comparative newcomer to the camp, had managed with such ease to arrange the escape of his six Dutchmen from the fortress of Colditz.

His trick was so simple that it shook me to think that the rest of us – Poles, French, and British, numbering now some two hundred and fifty – could not have thought of it. The escape was indeed from the manhole in the football ground.

'All very well,' I said to Vandy. 'We've all looked at that manhole cover till we were blue in the face without arriving at a satisfactory scheme.'

'Ah!' he replied, 'Patt, vat is that game the Poles taught you? Gapin? Vell, I tought of Gapin and looked at the manhole cover vrom another angle!'

On the first two occasions in question, a few Dutchmen, led by a venerable-looking bearded one named Van Doorninck, had held Bible-reading meetings, curiously enough, around the manhole. Previously they had measured the size of the nut and bolt. During the Bible-reading, the bolt was undone with a pair of large home-made spanners filed out of iron bed-parts. The bolt had about a ¾-inch diameter thread. When the sentries' notice was attracted to a football game in progress, two Dutchmen disappeared into the manhole. Now this was the crux. Immediately after the reaction, and before the prisoners returned to the Castle, the football ground was carefully examined, invariably including the manhole, by two or three Jerries appointed for the purpose. They also let loose dogs to trace possible hideouts or graves among the trees.

'How,' I asked, 'did you conceal the opened manhole? That is what beats me.'

'Ve made another bolt; a fery special kind of bolt,' Vandy replied. 'It vas made of glass tubing with a vooden head, and painted just like the real vone.'

That in effect was the secret of this simple yet brilliantly conceived escape. The two escapers in the manhole had the real bolt with them. At nightfall they pushed up the lid, breaking the glass bolt. They cleaned away the bits as best they could before leaving, and replaced the original bolt exactly as it was before, applying mud and dirt to cover any marks left on the iron. Their exit thereafter, only impeded by a high wall and some barbed wire, presented no difficulty in the dark with the nearest guard over four hundred yards away. By this time the Germans had enforced no fewer than four roll-calls on the daily recreation parade: two in the park and two at the courtyard gate. How Vandy managed to cover these he kept a secret for a little while longer!

The first four who escaped were Captains A. L. C. Dufour and J. G. Imit (Royal Netherlands Indies Army) and Lieutenants E. H. Larive and F. Steinmetz (Royal Netherlands Navy), and the latter two reached Switzerland. The other two were caught on the frontier and eventually returned to Colditz. The third couple disappeared about a month after the others during a Polish-Dutch International Soccer match. They were Major C. Geibel and 2nd Lieutenant O. L. Drijbar, both of the Royal Netherlands Indies Army. They reached Switzerland safely.

The Germans still believed they could make Oflag IV C impregnable (from within), so that escapers, when recaught, were not sent elsewhere according to normal custom but invariably returned to Colditz. For this reason, it was always growing in population; a centre of gravity, towards which escapers moved from all over Germany, when not moving in the opposite direction under their own steam! It was likewise a fortress, which required an ever-increasing garrison. The Germans greatly outnumbered the prisoners. Admittedly our jailers were not class A1 soldiers. The swollen number of the garrison was probably a source of irritation to the German High Command, because they held a series of inspections at one period, including a visit by two German officers who had escaped from Allied hands. One was Hauptmann von Werra, the German airman who gave our

POW authorities much trouble and eventually escaped from Canada to the USA. The story has it that he jumped from a train near the St Lawrence River, stole a motor-boat in which he crossed and eventually reached the German Consulate in New York. He visited our camp during his leave to give the Commandant advice. Shortly afterwards he was reported to have been shot down and killed somewhere on the Russian front.

The return of escaped officers to their original camp provided certain advantages for the inmates, by which we were not slow to profit. It was inevitable, however, that, if the war lasted long enough, in the end the Germans would win the battle of Colditz and the camp would become practically unbreakable, but none of us thought that stage had arrived in the autumn of 1941. In fact, although every escape discovered meant that one more foxhole had been bunged up, the prisoners really never gave up trying until the Allied advance into Germany.

The *Prominente*, as they were called by the Germans, also drifted gradually towards Colditz. Winston Churchill's nephew, Giles Romilly, arrived. He was given the honour and the inconvenience of a small cell to himself, which had a sentry outside it all night. He was free to mix with the other prisoners during the day, but he had to suffer the annoyance of being called for by his guardian angel – a heavy-booted Hun – every night at 9 pm, and escorted to his bedroom and locked in!

Like everybody else, he wanted to escape, but it was naturally more difficult to arrange. I once succeeded in substituting him for one of several French orderlies who were off-loading coal from a lorry in the courtyard. The coal-dust was a helpful disguise – smeared over his face – but he did not pass the first gateway. It was obvious that he was either watched from within the camp by other than his ostensible jailers, or, which is equally likely in this case, a French orderly – perhaps the one substituted – reported to the Germans what was happening, to save his own skin. We never found out, but it was Hauptmann Priem himself who entered the courtyard when the lorry was ready to leave and calmly asked Romilly to step down from it. I think he was awarded only a week's solitary confinement and then returned to his normal routine.

It was also in the late summer of 1941, when I was doing one of my customary periods of solitary – three weeks in this case – that the cells became overcrowded and Flight-Lieutenant Norman Forbes joined me for a spell. The cells were tiny, about four yards by three yards. We were given a two-tier bed, however, which helped, but to compensate for this, our cell was built immediately over a semi-basement cellar in which the camp garbage-cans were housed.

Norman and I managed very well and did not get on each other's nerves. One day, shortly before his 'time' was finished, he remarked to me casually that he needed a hair-cut.

'Ah ha!' thought I, 'anything to relieve the monotony!'

'What a curious coincidence,' I said, 'that you should be doing "solitary" with an expert amateur barber. I learnt the art from my school barber, who said I had a natural talent for it.'

'Well, have a shot at mine, then,' was the reply.

Soon I was busy with a pair of nail-scissors and a comb, which I periodically banged together in a professional manner. I tried for a few minutes to cut his hair properly, then realized that a barber's skill is by no means easy to acquire. I carried on, extracting large chunks of hair here and there, until the back of his head looked more like a gaping skull than anything else. At the front of his head I cut a neat fringe. The rest of his head was a jumble. As the front was all that Norman could see in the tiny mirror we had, he was unaware of his predicament until a day or two later, when he rejoined the camp and became a standing joke for several days.

After Norman left, boredom settled on me once again. I was studying economics, but found it heavy reading when continued for weeks on end. One day I thought of my cornet. As a concession I had been allowed to take into 'solitary', along with books and other paraphernalia, my guitar and my brass cornet.

Norman had only just managed to withstand my guitar crooning, and categorically refused to let me practise my cornet. Now I was alone, I thought, and I could practise in peace. But so many objections were raised from nearby cells and also from the courtyard – which my cell faced – in the form of showers of pebbles, shouts, and insults, that I was driven to practising my cornet at the only time (apart from the dead of night) when nobody could stop me, which was during the half-hour of evening *Appell*.

This seemed to satisfy everybody; for the German officers and NCOs taking the parade could hardly hear themselves speak, and the numbers invariably tallied up wrong, necessitating several recounts. By the third evening the hilarity grew to such an extent that the parade almost became a shambles. Apparently many of the German troops thought the cornet practice funny too – which made it all the worse for the German officer-in-charge, who was beside himself. By the fourth day I was feeling so sorry for the Jerries having to put up with the ear-splitting noises which coincided with their commands, that I decided to show a gentlemanly spirit and refrain from practising that evening.

Evidently I was not the only one who had been reflecting, for when the evening *Appell* was assembled, and the German officer-in-charge entered the yard (Hauptmann Püpcke was his name), he made straight for my cell with two soldiers and swung open my door with violence.

'*Geben Sie mir sofort ihre Trompete*,' he shouted.

I was so taken aback by his abruptness after my good intentions and sympathy for the German position that I thought it was my turn to feel insulted.

'*Nein*,' I said. '*Ich will nicht; es ist meine Trompete, Sie haben kein Recht darauf*,' and with that I hid the cornet behind my back. He seized it and we began a violent tug-of-war. He ordered his two men to intervene, which they did by clubbing my wrists and arms with their rifle butts, and I gave up the unlucky instrument.

'You will have a court martial for this,' the officer screamed as he slammed the door behind him.

The court martial never came off, which was a pity, for it meant a journey, probably to Leipzig, and a chance of escape. Instead, I was awarded another month's 'solitary' which I began shortly afterwards in a different cell.

It was late September and the leaves were falling in the park, but all I could see from my tiny window by climbing on to my washstand was the wall of a section of our prison known as the theatre block. It was during one of my long periods of blank staring at this wall-face that a light suddenly dawned upon me. If I had not been an engineer, familiar with plans and elevations and in the habit of mentally reconstructing the skeletons of buildings, the idea would probably never have occurred to me. I suddenly realized that the wooden stage of the theatre was situated so that it protruded over a part of the Castle, sealed off from the prisoners, which led by a corridor to the top of the German guardhouse immediately outside our courtyard.

This discovery was a little goldmine. I tucked it away and resolved to explore further as soon as I was free.

12

The Riot Squad

As I have said, 'Never a dull moment' might well have been the motto on the armorial bearings of Oflag IV C. I had hardly finished ruminating on my discovery from the cell window when a fusillade of shots sounded from the direction of the park. I was tantalized to know what was happening. Soon the 'riot squad' dashed into the courtyard and headed for the British doorway. Any posse of Goons heading anywhere at the double in an excited manner with fixed bayonets was familiarly known as the 'riot squad'.

They did not leave for hours and there was an incredible amount of shouting and barracking, mostly in French. Eventually I heard the story from Harry Elliott, who passed in a note to me describing what had happened.

He was in the Dutch quarters when the shooting, and much shouting, began from the direction of the park. Everyone rushed to the windows to see what was happening, and they saw two Belgian prisoners (Lieutenant Marcel Leroy and Lieutenant Le Jeune) running up the steep hill towards the wall which surrounded the park. They had climbed the wire (or crawled under it) and were being fired at by the sentries. As the sentries stood in a circle, some of them on the uphill side of the park came close to being hit by the ones below them. The sentries surrounding the Castle walls joined in and a regular fusillade started. The shooting was, as usual, bad, and the Germans were rapidly losing their heads. It was a wonderful opportunity for the prisoners, who wasted no time in trying to distract the sentries by shouting all sorts of abuse at them. The Dutch, who were very correct on all occasions, did not join in with as much enthusiasm as the English. So Harry ran downstairs to the British quarters to assist in the fun from there. By the time he arrived, much of the shooting was directed against the windows of the Castle and bullets were thudding against it. The Belgians had reached the high wall, but found it impossible to climb at that point and eventually stood with their hands up, still being fired at by the Germans. Luckily they were not hit.*

Next, the sentries around the Castle walls came under fire from the sentries in the park, who began firing at the jeering mob at the Castle windows. The bullets were going over their heads, but must have seemed close and they were becoming jittery. The British found this the greatest fun, and continued laughing and teasing the sentries beneath them. Eventually Peter Storie Pugh (Lieutenant, Royal West Kents) produced a Union Jack which had been used in Christmas festivities long ago, and hung it out of the window. This produced an immediate response. The hoarse shouting of the Goons increased to a thunder and the shooting redoubled its intensity until the hills echoed. It was all directed at the Union Jack.

As the walls were of stone, from time to time bullets coming in at the window ricocheted round the room. The prisoners decided it was time to lie down. At this moment the riot squad, composed of the second in command (a major) and about a dozen Goons, with bayonets fixed, clattered into the courtyard. They dashed up the staircase, and burst into the British quarters, the major leading with his revolver in his hand, white to the lips and shaking all over. The riot squad were also terrified.

'Take that flag down,' said the major in German.

None of the prisoners moved – they were lying on the floor, chatting to each other – no one even looked up. There were a few loud remarks, such as—

'They seem pretty windy today,' and 'What the hell do they want?'

'The Herr Major says you are to take the flag down,' came from

* One Belgian, Captain Louis Remy, escaped successfully from the castle in April 1942 with Squadron Leader Paddon (British) and Lt. Just (Polish). The latter two were recaught. Remy reached Belgium, crossed France and Spain and swam to a British ship anchored off Algeciras. He was imprisoned for a month in England on arrival, being released only through the intervention of Paddon, who had again escaped – this time successfully – via Sweden! Remy joined the RAF, serving with Bomber Command (103 Squadron) until the end of the War.

the German interpreter as another round of shots thudded against the walls.

Not a move. The trembling major then went up to an Australian Squadron Leader named MacColm and, pointing a pistol at him, said:

'Take the flag down.'

'Why don't you take it down yourself?' replied MacColm.

The major continued to threaten until MacColm finally crawled over to the window and pulled the flag inside.

All the prisoners in the room were then made to go downstairs and parade in the courtyard. They were encircled by the Goons who kept their rifles in the rabbiting position. Heads started to pop out of windows and the Senior British Officer demanded to know what was happening to his boys. The Goons said, 'They fired first,' which caused great amusement.

The POWs waited patiently, making pointed remarks while nothing happened. The French, however, from their windows took up their favourite refrain:

'*Où sont les allemands?*'

'*Les allemands sont dans la merde,*' came the reply from about forty windows. And then the first chorus again:

'*Qu'on les y enforce,*' the reply to that being:

'*Jusqu' aux oreilles.*'

This always provoked the Germans, who understood what it meant, and after the litany had been chanted from the French and English quarters two or three times, the usual happened. The major started shouting at them; loud laughter from the prisoners and a few rude remarks in German; then the usual cry:

'Anyone looking out of the windows will be shot.'

The sentries were in a dilemma; they did not know whether to point their rifles at the British in the courtyard, or at the windows above. Eventually they all pointed at the windows and a few shots were fired. This was the signal for the British to sit down on the cobbles – a pack of cards was produced and four prisoners started playing bridge; the others chatted. When the Goons turned their attention away from the windows again and saw this they were 'hopping mad' and forced everybody to stand up once more at the point of the bayonet, but it was not long before small groups were again sprawling on the cobbles. The German major, having all this time received no orders from his higher command, departed. He was soon followed by the riot squad, who trailed despondently out of the gate, and the anticlimax was complete.

★ ★ ★

Beer had long since disappeared from the camp, and with the thought of a dreary winter ahead, a few of us put our heads together. With the help of Niki, who had already managed to procure some yeast from a German, we started a brewing society. Someone unearthed a curious medal struck to commemorate a brewing exhibition. I was elected Chief Brewer and dispensed the yeast, and wore the medal attached to the end of a large red ribbon. When asked by curious Goons what the medal represented, I proudly told them it was a war decoration for distinguished service in the boosting of morale.

Brewing soon became a popular pastime and, with a little instruction by the Chief Brewer and his stewards, was highly successful. Soon, at nearly every bedside could be seen large jars or bottles, filled with water and containing at the bottom a mash of sultanas, currants, or dried figs – produced from our Red Cross parcels – together with the magic thimbleful of yeast. Curiously enough, it was eventually found that the yeast was unnecessary, for there was enough natural yeast already on the skins of the fruit to start the fermentation process without assistance. The one difficulty was the provision of gentle heat, because fermentation requires a fairly consistent temperature of about 27 degrees Centigrade. This problem was overcome by the simple use of body heat, or 'hatching' as it was called. It was a normal sight to see rows of officers propped up in their beds for hours on end in the hatching position, with their jars and bottles nestling snugly under the blankets beside them. Fermentation was complete after a fortnight! Some of our amateur brewers were luckier than the ordinary run of broody officers in that their bunks were situated near an electric light. Large incubating boxes were manufactured out of cardboard and lined with German blanket. Jars were arranged in tiers in the boxes and the heat was turned on by placing the electric-light bulbs in the boxes attached to lengths of 'won' electric cable. A flourishing commerce in brewery shares arose and combines were started.

Soon we were having gay evening parties and started entertaining our fellow-prisoners of other nationalities.

One day our Brewing Association invited a 'brilliant lecturer' to expound the secrets of distillation! Human nature being what it was, we were soon distilling briskly. I tore down a long section of lead piping from one of our non-working lavatories and made a coil, which was sealed into a large German jam-tin about twenty inches high. This 'still' became the property of the Brewing and (now) Distilling Society. Almost every night distilling began after 'lights out', and continued into the early hours. We worked shifts and charged a small percentage (of the resultant liquor) for the distilling of officers' brews. I should explain that distillation is merely a method of concentrating any brew or wine. Brandy is distilled grape-wine. We named our liquor simply 'firewater', for that undoubtedly it was.

Over a period of time we used up nearly all the bed-boards in the British quarters as fuel for our witches' cauldron. Our rows of broody officers looked more odd than ever reposing on mattresses supported only by a minimum of bed-boards with pendulous bulges in between, the upper bunks in imminent danger of collapsing on the lower ones. In vain did the Germans make periodical surveys of the bed-boards, even to the extent of numbering them with chalk and indelible pencil. Alas! the numbers were consumed in the flames and did not survive the boards.

The distilling process was an eerie ceremony carried out in semi-darkness around the kitchen stove with the distillers listening over the cauldron for the telltale hiss of gentle distillation – their flickering giant-like shadows dancing on the walls – as the flames were carefully fed with fuel. Distilling required most concentrated attention because the work of a fortnight could be ruined in a minute if a brew, passing through the lead coils, became overheated and the alcohol boiled away. Distillation takes place between roughly 80 degrees and 90 degrees Centigrade.

Having no thermometers, we learned to judge the temperature by sound alone – hence our experts and our right to charge a premium for the process!

The liquor, as it appeared, drop by drop, from the bottom of the still, was pure white in colour. It was bottled and in a very short time the liquor became crystal clear, leaving a white sediment at the bottom. The clear liquid was run off and re-bottled. This was 'fire-water'. The white sediment was probably lead oxide – pure poison – but I was not able to check this, and nobody ever died to prove it.

With experience and Polish assistance we produced various flavoured varieties, which the Poles insisted on calling 'vodka'. We did not argue over the name, but I feel sure that our liquor would never have been a suitable accompaniment to caviar. It took the roof off one's mouth, anyway.

It was not long before the British had a good cellar and 'vintages' accumulating. Christmas 1941 looked rosily ahead of us.

13

A Staged Foursome

IMADE A RECONNAISSANCE of the stage in the theatre, which was on the third floor of the 'theatre block'. By removing some wooden steps leading up to the stage from one of the dressing-rooms, I was able to crawl underneath and examine that part of the floor over the sealed room leading to the German guardhouse. It was as I had hoped. There were no floorboards, only straw and rubble about four inches deep reposing on the lath-and-plaster ceiling of the room in question.

I next looked around for prospective candidates for the escape I was planning. I selected about half a dozen possibilities. To these I mentioned casually that I would get them out of Colditz if they, on the other hand, would produce first-class imitations of German officers' uniforms. It was a challenge and by no means an easy one.

We had made a start, however, on certain parts of German army accoutrements and this was reason for encouragement. What had been left over from the lead piping I removed to make the still had already been melted down and recast into perfect imitations of German uniform buttons and one or two of their insignia. The lead, unfortunately, did not go very far when melted down.

My offer was a test of ingenuity and enterprise, and it produced Lieutenant Airey Neave, R.A., an Etonian and a comparative newcomer to the Castle, and Hyde-Thompson of the 'recumbent palliasse' episode. They had teamed up and Airey promised to make the uniforms. He said he could not make them, however, without Dutch assistance, so eventually, with Van den Heuvel's agreement, two Dutch officers were selected to make the team up to four. The Dutch spoke German fluently, which was a great asset.

Neave and Scarlet O'Hara came to me in distress one day soon afterwards, while I was preparing our next evening's distilling operations. Airey said:

'We're running short of lead.'

Scarlet, who – it is scarcely necessary to mention – had gravitated to Colditz, was our foundry foreman. He added:

'The lead piping you gave me is finished. It didn't go very far. It's too darn thin – cheap German stuff – no weight in it.' He looked towards the still.

'What are you looking at?' I asked. 'I hope you're not hinting.'

'Wouldn't dream of it,' said Scarlet. 'I just don't know where I'm going to get any lead from. We've only got three lavatories working as it is. That's not many for forty officers. If I break one up, there will be a revolution.'

'H'm! This is serious.' I went into a huddle with Dick Howe, who was a keen distiller, and was at that moment repairing a water-leak at the bottom of our still.

'Dick, things look bad for the still. They've run out of lead. How much liquor have we? Would you say our cellar was reasonably stocked?'

'Our cellar is not at all well stocked,' Dick joined in, 'for the simple reason that it's a bottomless pit. But if there's a greater need, I don't see that we can avoid the issue. We'll probably be able to recuperate our loss in due course – from, say, a Dutch or a French lavatory.'

'Very good,' I said to Airey, 'your need is greater than ours. You'd better take the coil,' and then to Dick:

'It's probably just as well to lay up for the time being, as there's a search due one of these days and we've got some stock to carry on with. The still would cause a packet of trouble if found and it's useless trying to hide it.'

Dick stopped tinkering and the lead coil was handed over. It was melted down and poured into little white clay moulds which were prepared from beautifully carved patterns sculptured by a Dutchman. Replicas, conforming perfect as to colour (silver-grey) and size, were made of the various metal parts of German uniforms. Swastikas and German eagles, tunic buttons by the score and troops' belt-clasps with the 'Gott mit uns' monogram. The Brewing and Distilling

Society resumed the title of its earlier days and became 'The Brewing Society Only', a sad reminder of a glory that had passed.

The most important item of the German uniform was the long greatcoat of field-grey, and it was here that the Dutch came in; their greatcoats, with minor alterations, could pass in electric light as German greatcoats. The officers' service caps were cleverly manufactured by our specialists. Leather parts, such as belts and revolver holsters, were made from linoleum, and leggings from cardboard.

At a passing-out test we had to compliment Neave and the various Dutch and Britishers who had done the work. The uniforms would pass – though not in broad daylight at close range, yet under almost any other conditions.

In the meantime I had not been idle, having my share of the bargain to accomplish. From thin plywood I cut out an irregular oblong shape, large enough to fill a hole through which a man could pass. The edge was chamfered to assist in making a snug fit, and I gave one side a preliminary coat of white paint. To the reverse side I fixed a frame with swivelling wooden clamps, and I prepared wooden wedges. The result was christened 'Shovewood IV'!

I asked Hank Wardle to help me in the preparation of the escape. This tall, robust Canadian, with his imperturbable manner and laconic remarks, could be relied upon to do the right thing in an awkward moment. His brain was not slow, though his casual and somewhat lazy manner belied it.

Under the stage in the theatre we quietly sawed through the laths of the ceiling and then through the plaster. Small pieces of it fell to the floor with ominous crashes, but we were able to prevent most of it from capsizing. Then I had to descend with a sheet-rope to the room below, which was empty. The door connecting it to a corridor which passed over the main courtyard gate and thence to the attic of the guardroom was locked. I tested it with my 'universal key'. It opened easily, so I relocked and began work. I had prepared two collapsible stools which fitted one on top of the other. Standing on these, I could reach the ceiling. Hank held 'Shovewood IV' in position while I carved out the plaster of the ceiling to fit it. Eventually, when pressed home and wedged from above, it fitted well enough to give the impression of an irregular oblong crack in the real ceiling.

With a pencil I drew lines which looked like more cracks in various directions, to camouflage the shape of the oblong, and remove any impression that an observer might have of a concealed hole.

The colour of the ceiling was exasperatingly difficult to match and it took a long time to achieve a similarity of tint between it and 'Shovewood IV.' This latter work necessitated many visits, as each coat had to dry and then be examined in place.

Airey Neave was ready to go and was becoming impatient. 'Look here, Pat,' he protested, 'I've got pieces of German clothing and gear lying about all over our quarters. It's damn' tricky stuff to hide, and if the search comes I'm finished. When is your hole going to be ready?'

'Keep your hair on, Airey!' I retorted. 'You'll go in due course, but not before it's a finished job. Remember, I want others to use this exit too.'

'I wish you'd get a move on, all the same. The weather is fairly mild now, but remember, we've had snow already and we're going to have a lot more soon. I don't want to freeze to death on a German hillside.'

'Don't worry, Airey! I see your point of view,' I said sympathetically. 'I need two more days. You can reckon on leaving on Monday evening. The "take-off" will be immediately after evening *Appell*.'

Even when I finally launched Neave, I was not completely satisfied with my 'Shovewood'. It was so nearly perfect that I wanted to make it absolutely foolproof. Its position in the sealed-off room was unique, and I felt we could unleash officers at intervals 'until the cows came home'.

I made a reconnaissance along the German corridor and, unlocking a further door, found myself in the attic over the German guardhouse. Probably nobody had been near the attic since Niki climbed in through the skylight and left by the window at the end. The window had not been touched, but that route was no longer possible since a sentry had been positioned to cover the whole of that wall-face beneath the window. A staircase in the attic led down to the guards' quarters below. Layers of dust on everything, including the floor, were my greatest bugbear, and as I returned I had to waft dust painstakingly over fingerprints and footprints by waving a handkerchief carefully in the air over the marks.

The plan was simple enough. I would send the escapers out in two pairs on successive evenings immediately after a change of guard stationed at the front entrance to the guardhouse. Thus the new sentry would not know what German officers, if any, might have entered the guardhouse in the previous two hours. The two officers escaping would descend the guardhouse staircase and walk out through the hall. This was the most risky part of the attempt. The stairs and hall would be well lit, and a stray guardhouse Goon might wonder where two strange German officers had suddenly descended from. The moment of descent from the attic had therefore to be chosen when a period of comparative calm in guardhouse activity was anticipated. I insisted that the two officers, on reaching the guardhouse entrance, were to stop in full view of the sentry, put on their gloves and exchange casual remarks in well-prepared German, before marching boldly down the ramp to the first gateway. This 'act' was calculated to absorb any shock of surprise that the sentry might have if, for instance, two strange officers were to issue suddenly from the entrance and quickly march away.

The evening for the attempt arrived. After the last *Appell* all concerned with the escape disappeared into the theatre block instead of to our own quarters. Various senior officers and generals lived in the theatre block and movement in this direction did not arouse suspicion.

The two escapers, Airey Neave and Lieutenant Tony Luteyn (Royal Netherlands Indies Army), were wearing no fewer than three sets of apparel – apart from some delicate pieces of accoutrement, which were carried in a bag. Over everything, they wore British army greatcoats and trousers; underneath came their German uniforms and underneath again they carried their civilian attire.

Although we thought highly of the German uniforms, they were not good enough for a permanent disguise – the cardboard leggings, for instance, would not have looked very well after heavy rain! – and we decided they should be discarded and hidden in the woods outside the Castle.

Our stooges were posted and we climbed – the two escapers with some difficulty owing to their bulk – under the stage. I opened up 'Shovewood IV', and one after the other we dropped quietly into the room below. I led the way, opening the doors, along the corridor and into the German attic. British army attire had already been discarded. The German uniforms were brushed down and everything was checked. I said to Airey:

'It takes me eleven minutes to return, clean up and close "Shovewood". Don't move before eleven minutes are over.'

'Right!' replied Airey, 'but I'm not going to hang around long after that. I shall take the first opportunity of a quiet period on the staircase and landings underneath us.'

'Don't forget to take it easy at the guardhouse doorway,' I reminded him; 'remember, you own the place.'

'Good-bye and good luck!' I added, 'and don't come back here. Much as we like you, we don't want to see you again!'

We shook hands and I left them. I relocked doors, redusted traces, mounted the rope of sheets and, with Hank's assistance, wedged 'Shovewood IV' firmly in place. Before Hank and I had issued from under the stage, our watchers reported a perfect exit from the guard-house. The 'act' went off, the German sentry saluted smartly, and our two passed on. We did not expect much difficulty from the first gate. The guard on duty would see the officers coming and the gate itself was under a covered archway very dimly lit. After this, the two were to pass through the German courtyard under another archway, of which the gates at this hour were open. They would then reach the bridge over the moat, before having to pass the last sentry at the outermost gate. There was a possibility, however, of by-passing this last gate, which might require a password.

I knew of the existence of a small garden gate in the parapet at the beginning of the moat bridge. I had remarked on it on my first entry into the Castle just a year before. This gate gave on to a small path which led downwards into the moat. From what I knew of the geography of the camp, I always suspected this path might lead around to the roadway, down which we passed when going for exercise in the park. If our two officers could regain this roadway, they had merely to pass some occupied German barracks and proceed a hundred yards to a locked gate in the outer wall around the Castle grounds. This gate was not guarded as far as we knew, the area would be in pitch darkness, and the wall with its barbed wire could therefore be climbed.

Our first two disappeared towards the moat bridge, and we heard no more of them.

The next day we covered the two *Appells*. Van den Heuvel arranged this with perfect equanimity. It was another professional secret of his which he promised to reveal if I told him how I launched the escapers!

In the evening I repeated the performance of the night before and Hyde-Thompson and his Dutch colleague departed from the camp.

We could not conceal four absences, so that, at the next morning *Appell*, four officers were found missing. The Jerries became excited and everyone was promptly confined to barracks.

As the day wore on and the German searches proved fruitless, their impatience grew. So did that of the prisoners. Every German who entered the courtyard was barracked until, finally, the riot squad appeared.

With rifles pointed at the windows, orders were issued that nobody was to look out. Needless to say, this made matters worse. The French started shouting their usual colloquy, '*Où sont les allemands?*' and so on. The British began singing, '*Deutschland, Deutschland UNTER alles!*' – our revised version of the German National Anthem – to the accompaniment of musical instruments, imitating a German brass band. Mock heads began bobbing up and down at the windows and the inevitable shooting started, followed by the sounds of splintering glass.

From a protected vantage-point, I suddenly saw Van den Heuvel sally forth into the courtyard, having presumably opened the court-yard door with his own 'universal key'. His face was black with anger. He headed straight for the German officer in charge of oper-ations, and with indignation showing in his every movement, he told the Jerry in his own language what he thought of him and his race and their manner of treating defenceless prisoners. His anger was justified, for hardly had he finished speaking when the French announced in no uncertain terms from their windows that an offi-cer had been hit.

This calmed the Jerries at once. The German officer removed his riot squad and went to investigate. Lieutenant Maurice Fahy had received a ricochet bullet under one of his shoulder-blades. He was removed to hospital and peace settled on the camp once more. Fahy lost the use of one arm through this episode. In spite of this he was never repatriated to France because he was listed as '*Deutschfeindlich*', i.e. 'an enemy of Germany'. The personal particulars of every allied officer POW were annotated with either a little green or red flag. The latter meant '*Deutschfeindlich*'.

* * *

By the winter of 1941–42, when Neave's escape took place, the forging of escapers' credentials had improved considerably. A number of expert forgers were at work, with the result that every British officer was eventually equipped with a set of papers, as well as maps, a small amount of German money and a compass.

Identity papers were reproduced by various means. The imitation by hand of a typewritten document is very difficult. There were only two officers in Colditz capable of doing it, and they worked overtime. The German Gothic script, commonly used on identity cards, while appearing to be even more difficult is, in fact, easier to copy, and our staff employed on this form of printing was correspondingly larger. The day arrived when a Polish officer, Lieutenant Niedenthal (nicknamed 'Sheriff'), made a typewriter. This proved a great boon and speeded up the work of our printing department considerably. The typewriter was of the one-finger variety and its speed of reproduction could not be compared with any normal machine, but it had the great advantage of being dismountable into half a dozen innocent-looking pieces of wood which did not require to be concealed from the Germans. Only the letters attached to their delicate arms had to be hidden.

Each officer was responsible for the concealment of his own papers and aids; the idea being that, under such conditions, it was easier to make use of escape opportunities if they arose without warning. One or two such occasions did arise and were made good use of, thanks to this system. As for concealment of the contraband, many carried their papers about with them, relying on native wit to hide them in the event of a 'blitz' search by the Jerries.

Searches occurred from time to time at unpredictable intervals. Sometimes we had warning; at other times none.

On one of the latter occasions I was busily doing some work with a large hammer when the Goons entered our quarters.

I seized a towel lying on a nearby table and put the hammer in its folds. The method of search was systematic. All officers were herded into a room at one end of our quarters and locked in. The Germans then turned all the other rooms inside out. They tore up floorboards, knocked away chunks of plaster from the walls, jabbed the ceilings, examined electric lights and every piece of furniture, turned bedclothes and mattresses inside out, removed all the contents of every cupboard, turned over the cupboards, emptied the solid contents of all tins on the floor, poured our precious home-made brews down the sinks, broke up games, cut open pieces of soap, emptied water-closets, opened chimney flues, and spread the kitchen fire and any other stove ashes all over the floor.

Then, coming to the last room, each prisoner was stripped in turn, and even the seams of his clothing searched before he was released into the main section of the quarters, there to be faced with the indescribable chaos of the Germans' handiwork. The latter usually found some contraband, though rarely anything of major importance.

On this particular occasion when I had the hammer wrapped up in the towel, as soon as my turn came to be searched I put the towel casually on the table beside which the Jerry officer stood, and began stripping. When my clothing had been scrutinized, I dressed, picked up my 'loaded' towel and walked out of the room!

Then there was the time when the Gestapo decided to search the camp and show the German *Wehrmacht* how this should be conducted. They employed electric torches to search remote crevices and borrowed the keys of the camp to make the rounds. Before they had finished, both the keys and their torches had disappeared, and they left with their tails between their legs. The German garrison were as pleased as Punch. We returned the keys, after making suitable impressions, to their rightful guardians.

* * *

To return to the thread of my story. The four escapers were well equipped for their journey to the Swiss frontier towards which they headed. They travelled most of the way by train. Neave and Luteyn crossed the frontier safely. Neave was the first Britisher to make a home run from Colditz.*

Hyde-Thompson and his companion were caught by station controls at Ulm. They brought back the news that Neave and Luteyn had also been caught at the same station. There had been some RAF bombing, which was followed by heavy controls for the purpose of rounding up plane crews that had parachuted. Neave and Luteyn had, however, managed to escape again from the police-station during a moment's laxness on the part of their guards. By the time Hyde-Thompson reached Ulm, the Jerries were on their toes. Maybe they had received warning in any case, once he was suspected, he had no real hope of success.

Hyde-Thompson's bad luck taught us another lesson. We paid for our experience dearly! From now on, no more than two escapers at a time would travel the same route.

* Airey Neave has described his adventures in his book *They Have Their Exits* (Hodder & Stoughton). He was elected Conservative Member of Parliament for Abingdon in 1953.

14

The Informer

A S I HAVE mentioned, I was not completely satisfied with 'Shovewood IV.' When, after a week, the Germans had calmed down, Hank and I paid a surreptitious visit to the theatre and I applied a new coat of paint to the 'Shovewood', for I knew that when more officers escaped the German efforts to discover the exit would be redoubled.

When the paint was dry we paid another visit to check the colour, and during this visit I had a suspicion we had been followed – a vague impression and no more. I was more careful than ever about our movements and disappearance under the stage. It was curious, though, that the *fouine*, our German 'ferret,' paid a visit to the theatre and I even heard him speaking (presumably to a prisoner) close to the stage.

The next two officers were preparing for their exit, due for the following Sunday, when, on Saturday, we learnt that the Jerries had been under the stage and discovered my 'Shovewood'. This was more suspicious than ever, as no traces were left to indicate the position of the 'Shovewood', buried as it was under a four inch layer of dirt and rubble, which extended uniformly beneath the whole of the stage, an area of one hundred square yards.

My suspicions increased further when the German Regimental Sergeant-Major, Gephard, who on rare occasions became human, remarked in a conversation with Peter Allan:

'The camouflage was *prachtvoll*! I examined the ceiling myself, and would not have suspected a hole.'

'Well, how did you discover it then?' asked Peter.

'*Ach!* That cannot be revealed, but we would never have found it without help.'

'Whose help? A spy?'

'I cannot say,' replied Gephard with a meaning look, then, changing the subject:

'The photographer has been called to take photographs of the camouflage for the escape museum.'

'So you make records of our escapes?'

'*Jawohl!* We have a room kept as a museum. It is very interesting! After the war, perhaps you shall see it.'

The remark concerning 'help' was reported to the various senior officers and escape officers. It meant we had to act in future under the assumption that there was a 'stooge' or 'planted man' in the camp and, sure enough, it transpired that there was.

Gephard was a strange character. He gave the impression of being sour and ruthless with his harsh, deep voice and unsmiling face. But he was probably the most intelligent of the Jerries at Colditz. I am sure he was one of the first to realize who would win the war! Apart from this, under his gruffness, there was honesty, and it is possible he disliked the idea of sending blackmailed spies into a camp, enough to warrant his dropping hints about it.

The stooge was not unearthed for some time. There was no evidence from the theatre escape to commit anyone. However, certain Poles had been keeping their eye on one of their own officers over an extended period and had slowly accumulated evidence.

Not very long after the theatre escape, we heard a rumour that the Poles were about to hang one of their own officers. The same day a Pole was hurriedly removed from the camp.

What I gleaned from Niki and others – the Poles were reticent about the whole incident – was that they had held a court martial and found the man guilty of aiding the enemy, though under duress. The officer had been blackmailed by the Germans, having been tempted in a weak moment while he was ill in a hospital somewhere in Germany. He was allowed to return home and see his family, and thereafter was threatened with their disappearance if he did not act as an informer.

I would go so far as to say that the German army officers in the camp did not use him willingly. They were probably presented with an informer by the Gestapo and given orders to employ him. This would also account for Gephard's reaction in giving us the hint.

In any case, the upshot was that the Polish Senior Officer, rather than have a dead body on his hands, called on the German Commandant, told him the facts – which the Commandant did not deny – and gave the latter twenty-four hours to remove the man.

* * *

Towards the end of 1941 the Goons also tried to persuade the French and Belgian officer prisoners to 'collaborate' and work with them. Their efforts in Colditz had little success; only two or three Frenchmen disappeared. The Germans were keen to employ engineers and chemical experts. On a couple of days, a Goon officer addressed the French and Belgian officers at the midday *Appell* – by this time we were having three *Appells* daily – asking if there were any more volunteers for work, saying that officers should give in their names and state their professions in order to see if they could be fitted into the 'Economy of the Reich.' There was no response on the first day, except much laughter and derisive cheers. On the second day a French aspirant, Paul Durand, stepped smartly forward and said:

'I would like to work for the Germans.'

There was a gasp of surprise from the assembled parade and a beam from the Goon officer.

'You really want to work for the Reich?'

'Yes, I would prefer to work for twenty Germans than for one Frenchman.'

More gasps and looks of astonishment from the prisoners!

'All right! What is your name?'

'My name is Durand, and I wish to make it clearly understood that I would prefer to work for twenty Germans than for one Frenchman.'

'Good! What is your profession?'

'Undertaker!'

Jacques Prot, a *Sous-Lieutenant d'Artillerie*, was another Frenchman whose puckishness was irrepressible and whose quick-wittedness won him freedom and later glory. I have mentioned his name along with that of 'Scorgie' Price in connection with the requisitioning of the German dentist's hat and overcoat. Prot contrived to escape during a visit to the German dentist in the village of Colditz. The visit was an unheard-of relaxation, but he worked it. He set off under heavy guard with another Frenchman also suffering from some galloping disease of the teeth. 'Scorgie' Price's teeth did not warrant the visit and he was left behind. The other Frenchman was *Sous-Lieutenant d'Artillerie* Guy de Frondeville. They escaped from the guards when leaving the dentist's house, and that was that.

The two friends separated for safety at Leipzig. Prot, tall, dark, and well-built, aged about twenty-six, went through Cologne to Aix-la-Chapelle. As he neared the frontier he saw to his horror that his false papers were not at all like those in current use. The frontier station was heavily patrolled and guarded. He closely followed the crowd, mostly Belgian passengers, towards the barrier. He was at his wits' end. Then the light dawned! He grabbed a suitcase out of the hand of an astonished fellow-passenger and took to his heels, through the barrier and away. The psychology behind this move was inspired. For the passenger created a tremendous uproar, attracting everybody's attention for a few minutes – then, as soon as the Germans were fully aware of what had happened, they couldn't care less. An escaping French officer might have been something, but a thief running away with a Belgian's suitcase did not raise the slightest interest.

Nine days out from Colditz, Prot arrived in Paris, to the surprise and joy of his family, on Christmas Eve 1941.

He reached Tunis via the French Free Zone in 1942, and joined the 67th Artillery Regiment (Algerian). From Paris he returned the suitcase to the owner, whose address he found inside, and from Tunis he sent to the German dentist a large consignment of real coffee with apologies for the removal of his hat and coat. He fought through the Tunisian campaign to Cassino, where during the First Offensive (Mount Belvedere) on January 29th, 1944, he gave his life for France. May his honoured memory remain long with his countrymen as it is cherished by every Escaper of Colditz!

★ ★ ★

Christmas 1941 and New Year's Eve were gay affairs. There was deep snow everywhere and there was a spirit of hope, for the Germans were halted in Russia and having a bad time.

Our cellar of wines and firewater added to the fun! Teddy Barton produced another good variety show which played to overflowing houses for three nights. On New Year's Eve, towards midnight, the British started a 'snake chain'; men in single file each with an arm on the shoulder of the man in front. Laughing and singing, the snake passed through the various quarters of the Castle, growing in length all the time, until there must have been nearly two hundred officers of all nationalities on it. As midnight struck, the snake uncoiled itself into a great circle in the courtyard and struck up *Auld Lang Syne*. The whole camp joined in, as the courtyard refrain was taken up from the windows in the Castle. The snow was still falling. It had a peaceful and calming influence on everyone. If we prisoners could ever have felt happy and unrepressed, we were happy that evening.

15

Winter Medley

THERE WERE MANY heavy snowfalls during the winter of 1941–42. I used to pass hours in a sleepy trance looking out of my window, hypnotized by the slowly gyrating flakes. I think it was a Chinese philosopher who once said that everything in Nature can be turned to man's advantage, if only man can find the way! I pondered long over the possibilities of using snow in an escape. I thought of snowmen and then of snow tunnels, but the stuff melted so quickly. A short snow tunnel maybe – and as I stared out of my window, once more I saw an opportunity before my eyes.

There below, at the other end of the courtyard, was the canteen, and at a high level above the canteen were the dormer windows of that room into which only Niki had once been, over a year ago, and which was sealed off from the end room (the curved room) of our quarters. There was a small flat roof over the canteen doorway which abutted both a window of the curved room and also a vertical slate-covered gable of the sealed room. The window-sill was at the level of the roof. The snow on the flat roof was nearly three feet thick.

Here was an opportunity not to be missed. I had no idea where we could go from the sealed room, but Niki had reported a further door opening on to the German quarters.

'Scruffy' Orr Ewing and another British officer, Lieutenant Colin MacKenzie, M.C., Seaforth Highlanders, had always wanted to tackle this room, and as they were high on the escape roster I gave them the plan and offered to help. Our curved-room window was, as usual, barred, and the filing of bars would be visible to anyone in the courtyard under normal circumstances. Certainly any persons climbing out of the window would have been seen. Now the snow hid everything.

The bars were cut in no time and Scarlet O'Hara manufactured thin metal sleeves so that the cut bars could be replaced and the sleeves slid over the ends. The metal was worked to a superlative fit and when in place each broken bar could be shaken without its falling out. Quick-drying black paint completed the camouflage after every work-shift.

A short snow tunnel of four yards' length was burrowed. It was shaped like an arch, one foot nine inches high, resting on the flat roof. The snow roof caved in a little at one point but some cardboard helped to prop it. The tunnel did not melt with my body heat but, on the contrary, formed a compact, interior-ice-wall. On reaching the vertical gable I removed some slates and found only laths and plaster beyond. This presented no difficulty. After a day's work the hole was big enough and the three of us crawled through to inspect the sealed room – it was the middle of the afternoon. We were examining the door into the German quarters when we received an alarm signal. Hauptmann Priem and a couple of his stooges on one of their lightning 'catch you out' visits had entered the courtyard. He headed straight for the British door and immediately started a close scrutiny of the British quarters – starting, unfortunately, in the curved room. We were trapped and the bars which had been cut were not in place. It was also standard routine for the Jerries to tap all window bars. For one moment the officers in the room thought the Jerries might overlook our window as it opened into the courtyard and was not therefore as suspect as windows facing the outside of the Castle. But alas! They opened the window, saw the gaping hole in the bars, and then the fun began.

Priem sent an N.C.O. along the snow tunnel. We could see him coming. In a matter of seconds I gathered up the tools we had brought – a hammer, screwdriver, a small saw, a file and some keys, and forcing open one of the dormer windows I have already mentioned, I shouted to a couple of Britishers walking around the courtyard.

'Tools coming out; save them, for heaven's sake!'

Lockwood was one of the two Britishers; he immediately saw the position. The particular window I was at had never been opened since Colditz had become a prison! The tools descended and, before an astonished sentry's gaze, Kenneth collected them and headed for the Polish doorway. He had disappeared before the sentry, who was standing close to the canteen, had recovered from his surprise.

This was not the end; in another five seconds I followed, leaving the window just as the Jerry N.C.O. began waving his revolver, with his head and arm protruding through the hole in the gable. I was fed up with repeated 'solitary' confinements; this would mean another month and I was just not going to do it. Although the snow in the cobbled courtyard had been cleared, there was a thin film about half an inch thick on the ground. This might soften the drop, which was about twenty feet after a three-yard slide down to the gutter from the dormer window. I leaped out of the window, slithered, fell, and landed squarely, then doubled up forward, hitting my forehead hard on the ground. I wore a balaclava helmet with only eyes and nose showing, many layers of outer clothing, and thick leather gloves. To the sentry, just recovering from the rain of tools, the descending body must have looked like a man from Mars. As I picked myself up and ran for it, he stood transfixed and I was able to make a clean getaway. Orr Ewing and McKenzie did not follow. By that time the Jerry in the hole had advanced sufficiently to be able to make respectable use of his revolver.

After this setback we had another in which the Dutch came off badly. They lived on the floor just above us, and had discovered the existence of a hollow vertical shaft in the outer wall of the Castle. It was a medieval lavatory. The Castle had many curious buttresses and towers, and once before, during explorations, the Dutch had come across a secret staircase, bricked up in the thickness of one of the walls. Unfortunately, it led only to another floor-level and was of little use for escape purposes. It may have seen curious uses in bygone days!

The vertical shaft, on the contrary, held definite promise. Vandy constructed a superbly camouflaged entrance to it in the urinal wall of the Dutch lavatory. As the urinal was kept wholesome by applications of a creosote-and-tar mixture, Vandy had little difficulty in obtaining a supply of it from the Jerries, which served to hide the shaft entrance from even the most experienced snoop or 'ferret.' The entrance was about three feet from the ground and was closed with a thick concrete slab. Beyond the urinal was a small turret room. Through the outer wall of this turret, Vandy pierced a second hole which he camouflaged equally well by means of a door, made of the original stones of the wall cemented together. The door swung open on pivots and gave directly on to the vertical shaft, which was about one yard by four yards in size. The drop to the bottom was seventy feet. Vandy had a neat rope-ladder made for the descent.

At this stage he came to me with a proposal for a joint escape effort if I would provide him with some experienced tunnellers. This was not difficult. I proposed Jim Rogers, engineer of the long Laufen tunnel in which twelve hundred bedboards were used, and Rupert Barry, the best tunneller of our team, who had constructed the shorter Laufen woodshed tunnel. When Jim Rogers's huge bulk was not tunnelling, it was sitting on a stool playing the guitar. Jim took up the instrument on his arrival at Colditz, saying he would give his wife a surprise when he returned home after the war. He never mentioned it in his letters. By the time he left the prison camp years later, he was a highly proficient player. Without considering the diffi-cult classical music he played, it was sufficiently amazing to watch his massive fists manipulating the delicate strings. His index finger alone could easily 'stop' about three strings at once.

He and Rupert, with Dutch assistants, set to work at the bottom of the shaft, but the going was hard and rocky in parts. Tunnelling continued for a week and then the Jerries suddenly pounced. It was becoming painfully obvious by now that they had sound detectors around the Castle walls. Our tunnellers were experienced, knew exactly what they were up against and could be trusted not to do anything stupid. Yet again they were taken by surprise. This time Priem and his team of ferrets entered the Castle and made straight for the place where the shaft was located at ground-level. This implied that the Germans knew the invisible geography of the camp, presum-ably from plans of the Castle in their possession. Without a moment's hesitation, Priem set his men to attack a certain false wall with pick-axes, and in less than ten minutes they had pierced it and a man put his head and arm through and shone a torch up and down the shaft.

The two tunnellers on shift had succeeded in climbing the seventy feet, one at a time – for the rope-ladder was not reckoned strong enough to carry two – and Vandy was busy pulling up the ladder when the torch flashed around the shaft. A few seconds later and the ladder would have been out of sight. The Jerries would have had no clue as to the entrance and the betting was that they would not search for an underground tunnel entrance on the third floor of the Castle.

It was such a close shave that Vandy was not even sure they had seen the dangling ladder, but, unluckily for Vandy and his team, they had.

Nevertheless, the tunnellers had time to clear out and Vandy was able to complete the sealing of the two entrances, with the result that when the Jerries arrived in the upper stories they were at a complete loss. Eventually they pierced new openings on the same lines as the 'blitz' hole made down below. They first reached the small turret room, where, unluckily for all, they found important booty. Vandy had hidden much contraband in this room; no fewer than four complete German uniforms – our joint work – were found and also Vandy's secret *Appell* 'stooges.' After this debacle he told me the following story of his 'stooges.'

During one of the periodic visits of the Castle masons, doing repairs, he had managed to bribe one of them into giving him a large quantity of ceiling plaster. The Dutch amateur sculptor had carved a couple of life-size, officer-type busts which were cleverly painted (I saw one later) and as realistic as any of Madame Tussaud's waxworks. They were christened Max and Moritz by Vandy. Each bust had two iron hoops fixed underneath the pedestal, which was shaped to rest on a man's arm, either upright, or upside-down hanging from the hoops. A shirt collar and tie were fitted to the bust and, finally, a long Dutch overcoat was draped over the bust's shoulders.

When not in action the dummy hung suspended under the fore-arm of the bearer, concealed by the folds of the overcoat. In fact, to outward appearances the bearer was carrying an overcoat over his arm. When the *Appell* was called, officers would muster and fall into three lines. With a screen of two assistants and standing in the middle line of the three, the bearer unfurled the overcoat, an army cap was placed on the dummy's head by one assistant and a pair of top boots placed neatly under the coat in the position of 'attention' by the other assistant. The dummy was held shoulder high and the helpers formed up close to one another to camouflage the proximity of the 'carrier' office to his Siamese twin!

The ruse had worked perfectly for the *Appells* in connection with the Dutch park escape and the theatre escape. Although Max and Moritz were discovered by the Jerries in Vandy's hide, they were found as unclothed plaster busts and Vandy hoped that he might be able to play the trick again.

16

The Rhine Maiden

SINCE NIKI'S LAST escape attempt over the guardhouse roof, and two successive attempts from hospitals by a Lieutenant Joseph Just, which took him to the Swiss border but alas! not over it, the Poles seemed to retire from the escape front. Of course they were pestered for a long time by the 'informer', whom they must have suspected and who must have hampered their efforts greatly. They were also liable to be blackmailed for the slightest offence, as their families were at the mercy of the Germans. In January 1942, without any warning, they were told to pack. With many regrets we said good-bye, and as we shook hands we expressed the mutual wish:

'*Auf Wiedersehen – nach dem Krieg!*'

We saw very few of them again. They went to semi-underground fortress camps in the Posnan area. A very few managed to trek west-ward towards the end of the war. Niki died of tuberculosis.

For a long time the Polish rooms were vacant. Then, one spring morning, the 'ghetto' arrived. French Jewish officers sifted out from many camps were gathered together and sent to Colditz. Why were they being incarcerated here? The question made one reflect a little as to what was to be the ultimate fate of all the Colditz inmates. We were 'bad boys,' and a public danger and nuisance. I, personally, did not think that we had much hope of surviving the war. If the Allies won, which we considered almost a certainty, Hitler and his maniacs would see that all possible revenge was wreaked before they descended the abyss and their Fuhrer fulfilled the prophecy of his favourite opera, *Götterdämmerung*. The gathering of the French Jews was a bad omen. If the Germans won the war, they, at least, would not survive. Would we?

The French contingent had also been quiet for some time. They seemed to be resting on the laurels of Lebrun's escape for too long.

It was with pleasure therefore, although with considerable misgivings for its ultimate success, that I received the news of the commencement of a French tunnel. Its entrance was at the top of the clock-tower, a hundred feet from ground-level; that, at any rate, I thought, was a good beginning.

So many tunnels, and exits generally, begin at ground-level, that at Colditz, at least, it was almost a waste of time to start work in the conventional manner. If someone thought of a tunnel, we examined the attics; if someone thought of escaping by glider (do not laugh! for one was made in Colditz and is to this day, as far as I know, concealed there), we started, if possible, underground! The short Laufen tunnel and the Colditz canteen tunnel began at ground-level, although the entrances to both were under German lock and key. Clandestine entrances rose to the second-floor level in the theatre escape; hovered on the first floor with the snow tunnel; then rose to the third floor in the Dutch vertical-shaft tunnel, and now, the French capped all by starting their tunnel at the top of the clock-tower!

The most serious danger, of course, for all tunnel attempts nowadays in Colditz was that of sound detectors placed around the Castle. The lightning descents of Priem on our snow tunnel and on the Dutch tunnel were too speedy compared with what we could expect of normal Jerry vigilance. At the same time, as far as tunnel entrances were concerned, German scrutiny of floors and walls decreased in inverse ratio as one increased one's height from the ground!

The French tunnel was a gigantic undertaking. I shall leave it for the present at its entrance.

Further French originality displayed itself shortly after their tunnel had begun. One spring afternoon a mixed batch of French, Dutch and British were marching through the third gateway leading down to the exercise ground, or park as it was called. The majority had just 'wheeled right,' down the ramp roadway, when a gorgeous-looking German girl passed by. She haughtily disdained to look at the prisoners, and walked primly past, going up the ramp towards the German courtyard of the Castle. There were low whistles of admiration from the more bawdy-minded prisoners – for she was a veritable Rhine maiden with golden blonde hair. She wore a broad-brimmed hat, smart blouse and skirt, and high-heeled shoes – she was large as well as handsome – a fitting consort for a German Demi-God!

As she swept past us, her fashionable-looking wrist-watch fell from her arm at the feet of Squadron-Leader Paddon, who was marching in front of me. Paddon was familiarly known as 'Never-a-dull-moment' Paddon, because he was always getting into trouble! The Rhine maiden had not noticed her loss, but Paddon, being a gentleman, picked up the watch and shouted:

'Hey, Miss! You've dropped your watch.'

The Rhine maiden, like a barque under full sail, had already tacked to port, and was out of sight. Paddon thereupon made frantic signs to the nearest guard, explaining:

'Das Fräulein hat ihre Uhr verloren. Ja! – Uhr – verloren,' and he held up the dainty article.

'Ach so! Danke,' replied the guard, grasping what had happened. He seized the watch from Paddon's hand and shouted to a sentry in the courtyard to stop the girl.

The girl was, by now, primly stepping towards the other (main) gateway which led out of the camp. The sentry stopped her, and immediately became affable, looking, no doubt, deeply into her eyes from which, unfortunately, no tender light responded! 'Hm!' the sentry reflected, as she did not reply to his cajoling. 'She is dumb or very haughty or just plain rude.'

He looked at her again and noticed something – maybe the blonde hair had gone awry. The second scrutiny, at a yard's distance, was enough for him. By the time our guard arrived panting with the watch, the Rhine maiden stood divested of her *Tarnhelm*, a sorrowful sight, minus her wig and spring bonnet, revealing the head of Lieutenant Bouley (Chasseur Alpin), who unhappily did not speak or understand a word of German.

This escape had been the result of many months of patient effort and was prepared with the assistance of the officer's wife in France. The French were allowed to receive parcels direct from their next-of-kin, which made this possible. He had a complete lady's outfit including silk stockings. The golden hair was a triumph of the wigmaker's art, of real hair, collected, bleached, curled, and sewn together. The wig was put together in Colditz. The large straw bonnet was the product of French patterns and Colditz straw weaving.

The transformation had been practised for weeks and was a conjuring trick which, I regret, I never saw enacted. The 'conjurer' had three accomplices and the usual 'stooges' to distract momentarily the attention of the guards as he turned the corner out of the gateway leading to the park. At this point, the 'conjurer' could count on a few seconds of 'blind-spot', which might be drawn out to, say, ten or twelve seconds by a good 'stooge' attending to the guard immediately behind him. The guards were ranged along the ranks on both sides at intervals of ten yards.

Part of the transformation was done on the march, prior to arrival at the corner – for instance, strapping on the watch, pulling up the silk stockings, the rouging of lips and the powdering of the face. Once in the gateway, the high-heeled shoes were put on. The blouse and bosoms were in place, under a loose cloak around his shoulders. The skirt was tucked up around his waist. His accomplices held the wig, the hat, and the lady's bag.

There is a moral to this story which is worth recording. I had not been informed of the forthcoming attempt and certainly I sympathized with the French in their desire for complete surprise. It was much better, for instance, that the parade going to the park should be unconscious of what was taking place. The participants behaved naturally in consequence, whereas the least whispering or craning of necks or rising on tiptoe – any conscious movement – might have upset the effort. Yet the fact of having informed me would not have made much difference to all this. Neither would I have been able to warn all the British on the parade; it would have been dangerous. Nevertheless, the moral emerges: the fateful coincidence that I happened to be behind Paddon on the walk; that, if I had been warned, I might have nipped the watch incident in the bud, and the escape would probably have succeeded.

This escape, as usual, closed the park to the prisoners for a period. Hardly had walks recommenced, however, when Vandy announced another attempt to be made by his contingent. I asked from what direction, and he answered, 'Vrom the park, ov course!'

The 'privilege' of going to the park for a two-hour walk around a barbed-wire enclosure at the bottom of the valley was continually being withdrawn by the Goons, because of insubordination of the prisoners, in consequence of escapes or just to annoy us. During these periods in the late spring of 1942, when the privilege was not withheld, the Dutch used to sit together on the grass in the middle of the wire enclosure while one of them would read to the others. Personally, I did not go very often to the park – it used to depress me. The Goon sentries stood close up to the wire, so that when officers walked round the path of the perimeter, they came within a few yards of them. I am sure the Germans put English-speaking sentries on this job who listened to one's every word. They could not have been edified, because many prisoners made a point of saying exactly what they thought of the Goons, the German race, and the Third Reich in general, for their benefit.

On the day appointed by Vandy, I went there for a change, and noticed the Dutch in their usual group, with a huge, black-bearded man in his army cloak sitting in the centre, reading to them, I happened to notice also that he was fidgeting all the time, as if he had the itch. He held a book and continued reading for an hour and a half. The walk lasted officially two hours, but a quarter of an hour was allowed at the beginning and at the end to line us up and count the numbers present.

The whistle blew and the prisoners slowly collected near the gate where they lined up to be counted before marching back to the Castle. All went off as usual and we started to march back. It was the custom that, as soon as the prisoners left the park, the Goons unleased their dogs. Suddenly hoarse shouts were heard behind us. We were halted and again counted. This time the Goons found one prisoner missing.

What had happened was that the huge Dutchman with the black beard had been sitting on a small Dutchman who had been entirely hidden by his black cloak (an alternative to the Dutch colonial army overcoat) and who had dug a 'grave' for himself. The others had all helped to hide the earth and stones and cover the small Dutchman with grass. When the whistle blew they moved towards the gate, leaving the little man in his grave, ready to escape when the coast was clear. They managed to cover up the first count so that the Goons did not notice that a man was missing. By bad luck, one of the Alsatian police dogs took it into his head to chase another. The leading animal ran straight over the 'grave' and the other followed. When he reached the grave the second dog was attracted, possibly by the newly dug earth, and started digging; in a few seconds he unearthed the Dutchman.

Vandy had once more employed a dummy Dutchman – the third he had made. When the alarm was raised, however, he had not used it again. He knew the parade would be carefully scrutinized and he hoped to save the dummy. He was out of luck. The Germans searched all the officers carefully before they re-entered the Castle and the dummy was found in its full regalia.

It was always questionable whether a dog was much use immediately after a parade, unless he found himself almost on top of a body, because the ground must have reeked with the scent of many human beings who had just vacated the area. It cannot be denied, however, that in this case the dogs found the man; whether it was by coincidence or by astuteness, I do not know. The Germans were again having the better of the battle of Colditz. We would have to improve our technique . . . .

PART THREE
Escaper

17

The 1942 Feeling

IN APRIL 1942, I asked to be released from the post of escape officer. It was high time someone else took on the job. I had visions
of a month or two of rest, followed by an attempt in which I could
take part myself. As escape officer it had become morally impossible
for me to take part in any escape.

Colonel Stayner replaced Colonel German in the New Year as
Senior British Officer, after the latter's departure to another camp. I
think Colonel German was the only British officer who was removed
from Colditz, once having been incarcerated there. Needless to say
he returned about a year later on account of further 'offences' against
the German Reich.

I suggested Dick Howe as successor to the post of escape officer.
I deputized once again for him in July, while he did a month's 'solitary'. After that he carried on for a long time.

Throughout 1941 the British contingent had slowly risen from a
mere handful of seventeen officers to about forty-five. During 1942
the number rose further, until by the summer there were about sixty.
Late arrivals included Major Ronnie Littledale and Lieutenant
Michael Sinclair, both of Winchester and of the 60th Rifles, and ten
Naval officers and two Petty Officers from Marlag Nord. Group-
Captain Douglas Bader also arrived.

Ronnie Littledale and Michael Sinclair had escaped together from a
camp in the north of Poland and had travelled south. They were given
assistance by Poles and lived in a large town somewhere in Poland for a
while. When properly organized they headed for Switzerland, but were
trapped in Prague during a mass check-up of all its inhabitants on account
of the assassination of Heydrich. They were caught and put through the
mill, including torture, before they were despatched to Colditz.

Ronnie was a very rare specimen on this earth. There was not a flaw to be found in his character. Quiet and even shy in his ways yet firm in his opinions, he suffered 'the slings and arrows' of this world to strike harmlessly against him. He was very thin, too thin. He had 'been through it.' He looked a little older than his age, with hair thinning unmistakably in front. A sharp nose pointing towards a hatchet chin served to complete the impression of an ascetic, which, in fact, he was. He would never have admitted it, and, indeed, his human kindly side and his alert sense of humour belied his rigid self-discipline and dogged determination.

Fate was to draw us close together.

Before long Michael Sinclair, his colleague, had a court-martial charge read against him for an offence he had committed in his earlier camp. We waved him good-bye as he left for his trial under guard. He was completely equipped for a getaway with transformable clothing, chiefly of RAF origin. His court martial was at Leipzig, but he managed to elude his guards in a lavatory at a Leipzig barracks before it took place, and a few days later turned up in Cologne. There had been heavy Allied bombing and the colour of most of his clothing was unfortunate because a witch-hunt for RAF parachute survivors was in progress. He was caught in the meshes and duly returned to Colditz under a three-man guard.

Returning escapers were bad for morale. Each successful getaway was like a tonic for the rest of the prisoners even though it usually meant one less bolt-hole for those who remained. Michael Sinclair felt this very much, though he had no reason to. His record clearly showed that he was the type of man who would not miss a 'hundred to one against' chance of an escape.

It was, nevertheless, becoming obvious to everybody that, once out of the Castle, it was an escaper's duty to take very heavy risks rather than return to the fold within the oppressive walls of Colditz. It was in the summer of 1942 I resolved I would not come back if I ever escaped again, and I know it was the decision which many others made as the months of 1942 dragged on. We already had one temporarily insane officer on our hands (he recovered after the war). He remained with us for months before the Germans were convinced he was not shamming, and we had to maintain a permanent guard from among our own number to see that he did not attempt suicide. The guard, which was worked on a roster, soon had to do double duty to cope with a second officer who tried to slash his wrist with a razor, but, luckily, made a poor job of it and was discovered in a washroom before he had completed his work. This type of guard duty had a decidedly bad effect on the guards.

Then there was a third British officer who was not so mad as he looked. He confided to me one day, early in 1941, when he was perfectly normal:

'Pat, I think the only way I shall ever escape from Colditz is by going insane.'

'It's not a bad idea,' I replied, 'in so far as the Swiss have at last got things moving over the repatriation of wounded, sick, and insane POWs.'

'I know.'

'Do you realize what it means?' I said. 'Have you thought out all the ramifications?'

'Well, it'll be a long job, I know.'

'Much more than a long job! I read a book before the war called *The Road to En-Dor**. It is the best escape book I have ever read. In it a British officer feigned madness for months – and what he went through was nobody's business. He nearly hanged himself. Yet it was child's play compared with what you would have to do in this war by way of convincing experts.'

'I realize that,' said the officer, 'and I'm prepared for it. I'm ready to behave as insane before the whole camp and convince my friends also that I'm cuckoo.'

'More than that,' I said, 'you'll have to write insane letters to your people at home! Have you considered that?'

'No,' he admitted, 'it might be better not to write at all.'

'You're going to cause a lot of suffering, but if you're determined, go ahead. First, you'll have to have medical advice as to symptoms so that you can develop slowly and correctly. Your insanity will have to become your second nature. Do you realize there is a possibility of its becoming your real nature?'

---

* By E. H. Jones.

'I've heard it,' he agreed, 'but I'm prepared to risk it.'

'I shall have to obtain all the medical symptoms for you from the French camp doctor,' I continued. 'You must not approach him yourself because he is one of the first you will have to convince of your authenticity. The job will take six months at least before you get on to a repatriation train.'

'Good, I'm ready to start as soon as you've got all the dope.'

'All right,' I concluded. 'I'll let you know when I have it. I shall not tell anyone. If you mean to succeed, everyone around you must be convinced. It is the only way. If a rumour once starts that you're feigning, it will spread and eventually get to the Germans. Then you're finished for good.'

Two months after this conversation I handed over my job to Dick Howe and told him of the case of our pseudolunatic. Dick would not believe me at first. He thought that our pet lunatic (for he was of the harmless type) had pulled the wool over my eyes. It was a tribute to the officer's acting!

The arrival of the Navy in force gave rise to an incident which echoed through the halls of Colditz for many a day. The 'new boys' arrived one evening at about 9 p.m. Howard Gee, who had helped in the affair of the canteen tunnel, was a civilian. He had volunteered for the expedition to help the Finns against Russia, had been captured by the Germans in Norway, and inevitably gravitated to Colditz. He was a clever man, aged about thirty, dark and handsome; he loved adventure and sought it out; journalism was one of his hobbies and practical joking was another. He spoke German fluently – so, upon the arrival of the Navy, he dressed up as the German camp doctor in one of our German uniforms (between the Dutch and ourselves there were still several wardrobes available). Our 'medium-sized' RAF officer, as he called himself – he was 5 ft high – acted as his British medical orderly, wearing a white jacket and apron. Entering the room where the Navy had just bedded down and bellowing with rage, Gee ordered them all out of bed to parade in front of him in their pyjamas. He shouted for a *Dolmetscher* – that is, an interpreter – from among them. A fair-haired officer advanced and stood smartly at attention in front of him. In Colditz it was an unwritten law that nobody stood at attention before a German officer (except on *Appell*) unless ordered under threat to do so. The officer's action in this case, being unprecedented, inflamed our 'camp doctor' so much that he promptly ordered the *Dolmetscher* two months' *strenger Arrest*, otherwise 'solitary'. He then delivered a harangue, which the interpreter did his best to translate, saying the Navy were all lousy, that they should never have been allowed into the camp without first passing through the 'delouser' and consequently they would all be court-martialled. Then, with vociferous references to *les papillons d'amour* – he used the French term – he commanded his British orderly to produce the bucket of 'blue'. This is a strong, bright blue-coloured disinfectant which is applied to the body to kill lice, fleas, and so on. It is also a paint which takes weeks to remove. He made the parade strip naked and told the British orderly to apply a lavish coating of 'blue' to the bodies assembled. This done, he inspected the result, calling for more 'blue' where he thought it necessary, and then retired, still muttering threats and Prussian curses. The parade was left standing at attention, a row of bright blue nudists, while the laughter of the twenty or so 'old lags' who occupied the same room could be heard throughout the Castle.

The Navy saw the joke and Gee was known as the 'Herr Doktor' ever after.

Douglas Bader's arrival also heralded an increase in practical joking of the particular form which was known as 'Goon-baiting'. Bader, a character already famous for his exploits, was irrepressible, undaunted by catastrophe, a magnetic leader and a dangerous enemy. He had hardly been in Colditz a few weeks, when he – a man with no legs from the knees downwards – volunteered for partnership in an escape attempt over the roofs of the Castle!

Goon-baiting was a pastime indulged in when one had nothing better to do – a frequent occurrence in a POW camp. It varied from the most innocuous forms, such as dropping small pebbles from a hundred feet or so on the head of a sentry, through less innocent types as the release of propaganda written on lavatory paper and dropped out of windows when the wind was favourable, up to the more staged variety like the case of the 'corpse'.

A life-size 'lay figure' was made out of paliasses and straw by Peter Storie Pugh and clothed in a worn-out battle-dress. We were having frequent air-raid alarms by the summer of 1942, during which the normally floodlit Castle was blacked out. On one of these raids the 'lay figure' was eased through the bars of a window and left suspended with a long length of twine attached, some of which was held in reserve.

As soon as the floodlights went on again, the figure was jerked into movement and in less than no time the firing started.

After a good 'value for money' volley, the figure was allowed to drop to the ground. Goon sentries immediately rushed to recover the corpse, which thereupon came to life, and rose high into the air again. A Goon approached nearer and the lay figure was promptly dropped on his head!

It was difficult for the Jerries to find the culprits. It was even difficult for them to locate the window from which the figure had sallied, as thin twine was used. The result was the withdrawal of the 'park' privilege for the whole camp during a month.

At first sight it might appear to be unfair that other nationalities should suffer for our sins, but we were not the only sinners and we suffered reciprocally! It was the expression of our unity against the common enemy.

Harry Elliott also indulged in a cold war against the Goons, but of a type which they never actually discovered. In the intervals between escape attempts he was always inventing new ways of waging war inside the prison walls. Thus while languishing in 'solitary' after an 'attempt' from the air-raid shelter on the road to the park along with a Pole, Captain Janek Lados, in which he was caught by the German sleuthhounds, he conceived the 'Razor-blades in the Pig Swill' campaign. With the aid of volunteers and large numbers of broken razor-blades, the camp garbage was heavily and regularly impregnated. All razor-blade pieces were carefully inserted and hidden completely inside rotten potatoes and vegetable remains. The results of the campaign were never known except by inference. The Germans made it a court-martial offence, punishable by most severe sentences including the possibility of the death penalty, to endanger the lives of German animals by tampering with the camp swill. Incidentally, while Harry was hatching this scheme in one prison cell, Janek Lados succeeded in escaping from another – it was conveniently situated in the outer walls of the Castle. Janek cracked his shin-bone in the fall from the cell window. He reached the Swiss frontier, nevertheless, but was recaptured within sight of freedom.

Another campaign which Harry initiated was 'the Battle of the Dry Rot'. In conversation with a fellow-prisoner, Lieutenant Geoffrey Ransone, who was an architect by profession in peacetime, he learnt that dry rot could be propagated by making 'cultures' of it. He argued, quite logically, that whereas a RAF bomb could remove the roof of a building in a second or so, dry rot could do the same thing though in a somewhat longer space of time – say twenty years or so. The war, according to him, might easily last that long, so that in the end his work might equate to the work of a fair-sized bomb, and there was nothing that could please Harry more than the thought that he was dropping a bomb on Colditz – however long the time-fuse.

In less than no time rows of innocent-looking, almost empty jam-jars made their appearance in dark corners under the beds of Harry and his disciples. In each jar was a sliver of wood, but wedged to it somehow was 'the culture'. The jars had to be kept damp and in the dark. On their periodic searches the Jerries were always puzzled by these jars, but they looked so harmless that they never removed them, ignorant of the dangerous 'explosive' they contained. In due course, when ripe, the slivers of wood were distributed throughout the roof timbers of the camp, where no doubt they still repose.

Harry had another habit. At night, after 'Lights Out', he would often hold the stage as we all reclined on our beds in the darkness. A flow of funny stories would issue from the corner where he lay, and then he would start recounting some rather involved incident of his career – I think he did it on purpose. About halfway through it he would stop, and after a pause, during which heavy breathing would become audible, he would say:

'Don't you think so, Peter (or Dick, or Rupert)?'

A long pause was followed by:

'Hm! No answer. Time I turned in.'

And, to the sounds of grunts and rustling straw, Harry would turn in. The silence of 'a prisoner's vigil' would descent upon the rows of wooden bunks, faintly reflecting the glow of the searchlights outside.

18

Escape Strategy

MIKE SINCLAIR'S fear that he had closed another bunk-hole for his fellow-prisoners proved groundless. Soon after his attempt, Squadron-Leader 'Never-a-dull-moment' Paddon was called to face a court-martial charge at a former prison camp in the north-east of Germany. He was duly equipped for an escape and left for his destination under heavy guard. It was a long journey and he would be away several days. As the days turned into weeks, Colonel Stayner naturally became concerned, and demanded an explanation from the Camp Commandant. The latter replied with a resigned shrug of the shoulders:

'*Es war unmöglich, trotzdem is er geflohen*' – 'It was impossible, none the less he escaped!' Paddon eventually reached Sweden and then England safely. He was the second Englishman to do the home run from Colditz.

* * *

I was lying on my bunk one hot day in August 1942. 'Lulu' Lawton (Captain W. T. Lawton, Duke of Wellington's Regiment) was lying in another nearby. Lulu had one short break from Colditz and had been recaught after a few hours' journey outward bound. He was a Yorkshire-man and he naturally preferred the smell of the fresh air outside the precincts of the camp. He lay ruminating for a long time and then in a sad tone of voice, turning towards me, he said:

'As far as I can see, Pat, it's no good trying any more escapes from Colditz – the place is bunged up – a half-starved rat wouldn't find a hole big enough for him to squeeze through.' Then he added soulfully: 'I wouldn't mind havin' another go, all the same, if I could only think of a way.'

'You've got to consider the problem coldly,' I replied. 'The first principle for success in any battle is to attack the enemy in his weakest quarter, but what is always confused in the question of escape is our understanding concerning the enemy's weakest quarter. It isn't, for instance, the apparent weak point in the wire or the wall, for these are his rear-line defences. We have to go a long way before we reach them. It's his front-line defences that count, and they are inside the camp. Jerry's strongest weapon is his ability to nip escapes in the bud before they are ready. This he does right inside the camp and he succeeds ninety-eight per cent of the time. His weakest quarter inside the camp has therefore to be found; after that, the rest is a cakewalk.'

I added: 'For instance, if you were to ask me where the German weak spot in this camp is, I should say it's Gephard's own office. Nobody will ever look for an escape attempt being hatched in the German RSM's office.'

'That's all very well,' said Lulu, 'but Gephard's office has a cruciform lock and an ugly-looking padlock as well.'

'All the better,' I answered. 'You won't be disturbed then.'

'But how do I get in?'

'That's your problem,' I concluded.

I never dreamt he would take the matter seriously, but a Yorkshireman's thoroughness is not to be denied.

There was a Dutchman in the camp, the red-bearded Captain Van Doorninck. He used to repair watches in his spare time, and he even repaired them for the German personnel occasionally, in return for equipment with which to carry on his hobby. Thus, he possessed a repair outfit consisting of miniature tools and various oddments in the way of materials, which were rigorously denied to other prisoners. He never gave his parole as to the employment of the tools.

Van Doorninck was 'brainy'. He had a wide knowledge of higher mathematics, and at one period he gave me, along with one or two others, a university course in Geodesy – a subject. I had never thoroughly grasped as a student.

Besides tinkering with watches Van Doorninck was not averse to tinkering with locks, as Lulu Lawton found out, with the result that the former devised a method of lock-picking that any Raffles might have been proud of.

I have described the outward appearance of the cruciform lock before as resembling a four-armed Yale lock. Its essential internal elements consisted of between six and nine tiny pistons of not quite one-eighth of an inch diameter each. In order to open the lock these pistons had to be moved in their cylinders by the insertion of the key.

Each piston moved a different distance, the accuracy of which was gauged to a thousandth of an inch.

The principle involved was the same as that employed in the Yale lock. The keyhole, however, was like a cross, each limb being about one-sixteenth of an inch wide, whereas the Yale has a zigzag-shaped keyway. The latter keyway might have presented more difficulty to Van Doorninck, though I am sure he would have overcome it. However, he solved the cruciform problem by manufacturing a special micrometer gauge, which marked off the amount of movement that each piston required. He then made a key to conform, using his gauge to check the lifting faces of the key as he filed them. The key looked rather like a four-armed Yale key.

Van Doorninck succeeded brilliantly where I had failed miserably. I blushed with shame every time I recollected the tortures I had inflicted on so many wincing sufferers in the dentist's chair! The new key was a triumph. Moreover, Van Doorninck was in a position to 'break' all the cruciform locks, though each one was different. Thereafter, like ghosts we passed through doors which the Germans thought were sealed.

Returning to the door of Gephard's office: once the cruciform lock was 'broken' the other lock, the padlock, presented no difficulty.

The plan evolved. Lulu Lawton had teamed up with Flight-Lieutenant. 'Bill' Fowler, RAF, and then made a foursome with Van Doorninck and another Dutchman. Dick Howe, as escape officer, was in charge of operations. He came to me one day.

'Pat, I've got a job for you,' he said. 'Lulu and three others want to break out of Gephard's office window. Will you have a look at it? I'd also like you to do the job for them.'

'Thanks for the compliment,' I replied. 'When do we start?'

'Any time you like.'

'I'm not so sure of the window idea, Dick,' I said, 'but I'll check up carefully. It's pretty close to a sentry and it may even be in his line of sight.'

'Kenneth Lockwood will go sick whenever you're ready,' Dick continued, 'and he'll live in the sick-ward opposite Gephard's office and manipulate all the necessary keys.'

'Good! There's no German medical orderly at night, so I can hide under Kenneth's bed after the evening *Appell* until lights out. Then I can start work. I'll take someone with me.'

'Yes, do,' said Dick, 'but don't take Hank this time. He's an old hand. We've got to train more men in our escape technique. Choose someone else.'

I had a look at the office. It was small and oblong in shape, with a barred window in an alcove at the far end from the door. Gephard's desk and chair were in the alcove. The remainder of the office was lined with shelves on which reposed an assortment of articles. Many of them, such as hurricane lamps, electric torches, dry batteries, and nails and screws, would have been useful to us, but we touched nothing. The window exit was thoroughly dangerous. I saw by careful inspection and a few measurements that with only a little more patience we could rip up Gephard's floor, pierce a wall eighteen inches thick, and have entry into a storeroom outside and below us. From there, by simply unlocking a door, the escapers would walk out on to the sentry path surrounding the Castle. There was one snag. Did the storeroom have a cruciform or an ordinary lever lock?

This was checked by keeping a watch from a window for many days upon the area of the storeroom. The storeroom door was not visible, but a Jerry approaching it would be visible and, in due course, a Jerry was seen going to the door holding in his hand an ordinary lever key! Van Doorninck would take a selection of keys and there should be no difficulty. The alternative, which would have taken much longer, would have been for me to construct a camouflage wall and examine the storeroom at leisure. This escape was to be a blitz job. The hole would be ready in a matter of three days. Experience was proving that long-term jobs involved much risk due to the time element alone. I often mused on the chances of the French tunnel which was advancing slowly day by day . . .

The work would have to be done at night; Gephard's office was in use all day. The office was situated near the end of a ground-floor corridor, on the opposite side of which was the camp sick-ward. This ward was across the courtyard from our quarters, so that the undertaking involved entering the sick-quarters before the main doors were locked up for the night and hiding there, under the beds, until all was quiet – there was a sentry in the courtyard all day and night nowadays. The hospital beds were not high off the ground and were rather crammed together, giving ample concealment for super-ficial purposes.

I chose Lieutenant Derek Gill (Royal Norfolks) to come along and help me; he was the right type – imperturbable. We started operations as soon as Kenneth was snugly ensconced in his sick-bed, with serious stomach trouble. When the doors were locked and the patrols departed Kenneth manipulated the keys, opened the sick-ward door and then Gephard's door, locked us in for the night and returned to bed.

I removed the necessary floorboards underneath the window and also, incidentally, under the desk at which Gephard sat every day! I started work on the wall. The joints between the stones were old, as I suspected, and by the morning the two of us had reached the far side. I noticed there was plaster on the other side. This was what I expected; it was the wall-face of the storeroom. That was enough for the first night. Most of the large stones were removed in a sack, and in the under-floor rubble a passage was cleared at a forty-five-degree angle so that a person could ease himself down into the hole. Blankets were laid down so as to deaden the hollow sound, and the floor under Gephard's desk was then very carefully replaced. Nails were reinserted and covered with our patent dust-paste. All cracks were refilled with dirt. In the early hours, Kenneth, by arrangement, let us out and locked up. We retired to the sick-ward, the door of which also had to be locked, and rested comfortably until the German medical orderly arrived on his morning rounds, when we retired under the beds.

The next night Derek and I went to work again. This time the job was more difficult; the hole in the wall had to be enlarged enough to allow a large-sized man's body (Van Doorninck) to pass through. At the same time, the plaster on the further face was to be left intact. I knew the hole was high up in the storeroom wall, probably eight to ten feet from the floor-level. We finished the task successfully and in the morning retired as before.

The escape exit was now ready. Dick, Lulu, Bill, and myself worked out the plan together. It was based on the fact that German NCOs occasionally came to the storeroom with Polish POWs who were working in the town of Colditz. They brought and removed stores, baskets of old uniforms, underclothing in large wooden boxes, wooden clogs and a miscellaneous assortment of harmless soldier's equipment, as far as we could see. They came at irregular hours, mostly in the mornings, sometimes as early as 7 am and seldom more often than twice a week. These habits had been observed and noted over a period of a month. It was agreed that the escape party should be increased to a total of six. Two more officers were therefore selected. They were 'Stooge' Wardle, our submarine type, and Lieutenant Donkers, a Dutchman. It was arranged that Lulu should travel with the second Dutchman, and Bill Fowler with Van Doorninck.

Sentries were changed at 7 am, so the plan was made accordingly. Van Doorninck, who spoke German fluently, would become a senior German NCO and Donkers would be a German private. The other four would be Polish orderlies. They would issue from the storeroom shortly after 7 am. Van Doorninck would lock up after him. The four orderlies would carry two large wooden boxes between them, the German private would take up the rear. They would walk along the sentry path past two sentries, to a gate in the barbed wire, where Van Doorninck would order a third sentry to unlock and let them pass. The sentries – with luck – would assume that the 'fatigue' party had gone to the storeroom shortly before 7 am. Once through the barbed wire the party would proceed downhill along the roadway which went towards the park. They would, however, turn off after fifty yards and continue past a German barracks, and farther on they would reach the large gate in the wall surrounding the Castle grounds; the same over which Neave and Thompson had climbed in their escape. At this gate, Van Doorninck would have to use more keys. If he could not make them work, he had to use his wits. Indeed, if he managed to lead his company that far, he could probably ring up the Commandant and ask him to come and open the gate!

The plan necessitated the making of two large boxes in sections so that they would be passed through the hole into the storeroom, and yet of such construction that they could be very quickly assembled.

The day for the escape was fixed shortly after a normal visit to the storeroom, in order to lessen the chances of clashing with a real 'fatigue' party. We prayed that a clash might not occur, but the visits were not accurately predictable and we had to take this chance.

The evening before the 'off', after the last *Appell*, nine officers ambled at irregular intervals into the sick-ward corridor. There was other traffic also, and no suspicion was aroused. The sections of the wooden boxes had been transferred to the sick-ward at intervals during the day under coats. Eight officers hid under the beds, while Kenneth retired to his official one and saw to it that the hospital inmates remained quiet and behaved themselves. They were mostly French and were rather excited at the curious visitation. Kenneth had a way of his own of dealing with his brother officers of whatever nationality. He stood on his bed and addressed the whole sick-ward:

'I'll knock the block off any man here who makes a nuisance of himself or tries to create trouble. *Comprenez? Je casse la tête à n'importe qui fait du bruit ou qui commence à faire des bêtises.*'

Of course, Kenneth knew everybody there intimately and could take liberties with their susceptibilities. He continued:

'What is going on here is none of your business, so I don't want to see any curiosity; poking of heads under beds for instance; no whispering. When the patrol comes round everybody is to behave quite normally. I'll be sitting up looking around. If I see the slightest unnecessary movement, I'll report the matter to General Le Bleu as attempted sabotage.'

Kenneth's mock seriousness had an edge to it. Among those in the sick-ward were a few more or less permanent in habitants – the neurotic ones. They were capable of almost any absurdity and a firm line was the only one to take in their case.

The sick-ward was duly locked and night descended upon the Castle. Quietly the nine arose, and as Kenneth unlocked one door after another with ease, we 'ghosted' through. Eight of us squeezed into the small office and Kenneth departed as he had come.

'Derek,' I whispered, 'we've got a long time in front of us before we start work. There's no point in beginning too early in case of misfires and alarms.'

'How long do you think it will take to break out the hole?' " he questioned.

'About an hour, I should say, but we'll allow double that amount.'

'That means,' said Derek, 'we can start at, say, four am.'

'Better make it three am. We must allow much longer than we anticipate for pushing this crowd through, along with all the junk. There's also the hole to be made good. Have you brought the water and the plaster?'

'Yes. I've got six pint bottles and enough plaster to do a square yard.'

'Good. What time do you make it now?'

'Nine-forty-five,' Derek replied. We sat around on the floor to pass the vigil.

At midnight there was an alarm. We heard Germans unlocking doors and the voice of Priem in the corridor. He went into the sickward for five minutes, then came out and approached Gephard's office door. We heard every word he said as he talked with the night-duty NCO. The latter asked:

'Shall I open this door, Herr Hauptmann?'

'Yes, indeed, I wish to control all,' answered Priem.

'It is the office of *Oberstabsfeldwebel* Gephard, Herr Hauptmann.'

'Never mind. Open!' came the reply.

There was a loud noise of keys and then Priem's voice:

'Ah! of course Herr Gephard has many locks on his door. I had forgotten. Do not open, it is safe.'

The steps retreated and then died away as the outer door was relocked. We took several minutes to recover from this intrusion. Eventually Lulu Lawton, who was beside me, whispered into my ear, 'My God! You were right, and how!'

It was uncanny the way Priem scented us out and nearly caught us in spite of all our precautions.

In the dog-watch, I started work quietly by making a small hole through the plaster and then cutting and pulling inwards towards myself. Minute pieces fell outside and made noises which sounded like thunder to me, but which were not, in reality, loud. In due course the hole was enlarged for a hand to pass through, then the rest was removed with ease. I had a sheet with me to help the escapers down into the storeroom beyond. Van Doorninck went first. He landed on some shelves and, using them as a ladder, descended safely to the floor. A few minutes later he reported that the outside door of the storeroom had a simple lock and that he had tried it successfully. This was good news. The other five officers followed: then the sections of the two boxes; the various bundles of escape clothing; the Polish troops' uniforms; the German soldiers' uniforms, and lastly, the plaster and the water. We could have made good use of a conveyer belt!

Derek and I wished them all good luck and, wasting no time, we started to refill the hole in the wall as neatly as possible, while Van Doorninck on the other side applied a good thick coat of plaster. The wooden boxes would come in very handy for carrying away the empty water-bottles and surplus plaster as well as all the civilian outfits! Finally, as the last stone was ready to go into place, Van Doorninck and I checked watches and I whispered Goodbye and 'Good luck' and sealed the hole.

Derek and I then replaced blankets and floorboards carefully. By 6 am the operation was finished, just as we heard Kenneth whispering through the door: 'Is all well, are you ready?'

'Yes, open up.'

Kenneth manipulated the locks and we retired to the sick-ward.

From there we would not see the rest of the act. The escapers would leave at 7.10 am, while the sick-ward would not open up until 7.30 am. Morning *Appell* was at 8.30. This was where the fun would start!

At about 7.30 am we sallied forth unobtrusively. Dick was waiting for us and reported a perfect take-off!

Van Doorninck's uniform was that of a sergeant. The sentries had each in turn saluted smartly as the sergeant's 'fatigue' party wended its way along the path towards the barbed-wire gate. Arrived here, the sentry in charge quickly unlocked it, and the party passed through and was soon out of sight of our hidden watchers in the upper stories of the Castle.

As minutes passed and there were no alarms, we began to breathe more freely. By 8 am we could almost safely assume they were away.

The *Appell* was going to cause trouble. We had for the time being exhausted all our tricks for the covering of absentees from *Appell*. We had tried blank files, with our medium-sized R.A.F. officer running along, bent double, between the ranks and appearing in another place to be counted twice. We had tried having a whole row of officers counted twice by appropriate distraction of the NCOs checking off the numbers. We had tried bamboozling the Germans by increasing the returns of officers sick. The Dutch dummies were no more.

If the escape had been in the park, we had a greater variety of methods from which to choose. Park parades, in the first place, did not cover the whole prisoner contingent. We could add bodies to begin with; as we had done, for instance, by suspending our medium-sized officer, on occasion, around the waist of a burly Dutch officer, whose enormous cloak covered them both with ease! On another attempt, we had staged a fake escape to cover the real one, by having two officers cut the park wire and run for it – without a hope of escape, of course. The deception, in this case, was that the two officers acted as if a third was ahead of them among the trees. They shouted encouragement and warning to this imaginary one, whom the Jerries chased round in circles for the remainder of the day!

By now we had temporarily run out of inspiration. We might manage to conceal one absence, but six was an impossibility. So we did the obvious thing. We decided to lay in a reserve of spare officers for future escapes. We concealed four officers in various parts of the Castle. There would be ten missing from the *Appell*! With luck the four hidden in the Castle would become 'ghosts.' They would appear no more at *Appells* and would fill in blanks on future escapes. The idea was, by now, not unknown to the Germans, but we would try it.

The morning *Appell* mustered and, in due course, ten bodies were reported missing. There were hurried consultations, and messengers ran to and fro between the *Kommandantur*. We were counted again and again. The Germans thought we were playing a joke on them. Guardhouse reports showed there had been a quiet night, after Priem's visit, with no alarms.

The Germans kept us on parade, and sent a search-party through all the quarters. After an hour, they discovered two of our ghosts.

This convinced them we were joking. They became threatening, and finally held an identification parade while the Castle search-party continued its work. Eventually the latter found two more ghosts. By 11 am, not having found any further bodies, they concluded that perhaps six had escaped after all. The identification parade continued, until they had established which officers were missing, in the midst of tremendous excitement as posses of Goons were despatched in all directions around the countryside.

We were satisfied at having increased the start of our six escapers by a further three hours. Later in the day we heard that the Jerries, after questioning all sentries, had suspected our fatigue party, and working backwards to the store room, had discovered my hole. There was much laughter, even among the Jerries, at the expense of Gephard, under whose desk the escape had been made! I leave it to the reader to imagine the disappointment and fury of Priem at our having eluded his grasp so narrowly during the night!

Before the evening was over, we had our disappointment too; Lulu Lawton and his companion were recaught. I was sorry for Lulu. He had put so much effort into the escape. It was largely his own idea and he had displayed cleverness and great pertinacity. These qualities, I thought, deserved better recognition than a month of 'solitary' in the cells.

Lulu told us how Van Doorninck led the fatigue party past the German barracks and onwards to the last gateway. As he approached it, a Goon from the barracks ran after the party and asked Van Doorninck if he wanted the gate opened. 'Naturally,' replied the latter!

The Goon hurried off and returned shortly with the key. He opened the gate and locked it again after them!

A day later, Stooge Wardle and Donkers were recaptured.

Bill Fowler and Van Doorninck carried on happily. They slipped through the net and reached Switzerland safely in six days. That was in September 1942. Two more over the border! We had no reason to be ashamed of our efforts!

19

Forlorn Hope

It was high time Bruce, our medium-sized officer, was given a chance of escape. He had done such good work unobtrusively! The opportunity arrived when the Germans decided we had too much personal property in our rooms. It was September, and they issued orders that all private kit not immediately required, as, for instance, summer clothing, was to be packed. The Jerries provided large boxes for the purpose. We were informed on the word of honour of the Camp Commandant that the cases would be stored in the German *Kommandantur* (the outer part of the Castle) and would be made available again in the spring.

The cases were duly packed, closed, and removed on a lorry. Several of them were Tate and Lyle sugar-boxes, about three feet square by three feet high, which had contained bulk consignments of Red Cross food, and in one of these travelled our medium-sized officer!

He had his civilian clothes and escape equipment with him, as well as a knife to cut the cords holding down the lid of his case, and about a forty-foot length of rope in the form of sheets. We knew the cases were to be stored in an attic at the top of a building which we could see from our windows.

Bruce reached Danzig, bicycling much of the way. Unfortunately, he was recaught on the docks, trying to stow away on a neutral ship, and returned in due course to Colditz where he was placed in solitary confinement.

I would like to have heard the full story but I never saw him again. I was doing two successive bouts of 'solitary' in the 'cooler' when he returned, and I did not even meet him during the daily exercise hour.

My 'solitary' was due to two abortive escape attempts. The first was a short tunnel, mostly vertical, built to connect up with the drains in the courtyard, which I have mentioned before. Rupert Barry and Colin McKenzie were my confederates. I had long noticed, on a photograph of the prisoners' courtyard taken before the war, a manhole cover near the entrance gateway. This manhole cover no longer existed and I was sure it had been covered over for a good reason. We were trying to find out why, by means of the tunnel, when the unannounced arrival of a batch of Russian prisoners proved our undoing. Our vertical shaft began in what was known as the 'delousing shed', a temporary structure in the courtyard built to house the portable ovens, which looked like boilers and into which clothing was put and baked in order to kill lice and other pests.

The sudden arrival of the Russians necessitated the use of these portable ovens, and Rupert and I were caught red-handed. McKenzie was lucky. He was doing earth-disposal duty and was not in the shed! The boilers were hardly used once in six months, and it was unfortunate the Russians arrived just during our working hours!

The incident, however, enabled us to meet the Russian soldiers, who were to be housed in the town where normally we should never see them. They were a sight of which the Germans might well have been ashamed. Living skeletons, they dragged their fleshless feet along the ground in a decrepit slouch. These scarecrows were the survivors of a batch ten times their number which had started from the front. They were treated like animals, given no food and put out into the fields to find fodder amidst the grass and roots. Their trek into Germany took weeks.

'Luckily,' said one of them, 'it was summer-time. In the winter,' he added, 'nobody bothered even to move us to the hinterland from the front. We died where we were captured.'

How many times, in my life as a prisoner, did I murmur a prayer of thanksgiving for that blessed document, 'the Geneva Convention', and for its authors! But for its humane principles, I saw myself standing in the place of these wretched creatures. Needless to say, as between Germany and Russia, there were no recognized principles for the treatment of prisoners-of-war. Neither of them had signed the Convention.

My second bout of 'solitary' was due to the fact that I tried to escape from my prison cell. It happened to be in the town jail because, as usual, all the camp cells were full, and the overflow nowadays went to the jail.

By placing my cell table on the bed, I could reach the ceiling of the cell. I had a small saw, which was normally hidden in my guitar. Breaking through the plaster one evening, I started work on the wood. I had to work noiselessly, for the guards lived next door. In spite of every effort, I was not finished by morning and, of course, the jailer saw my handiwork when he came with my bread and ersatz coffee.

I was evidently doomed to spend another winter in Colditz.

★   ★   ★

September was nearly over. Dick Howe came up to me one day.

'I have another job for you, Pat,' he said. 'Ronnie Littledale and Billie Stephens have teamed up and are clamouring to leave. Their idea isn't in the least original, but that doesn't stop their clamouring,' he added.

He then described to me roughly what they intended to do.

'That old chestnut,' I commented, 'has grown a long beard by now. It has about as much chance of success as the famous camel that tried to go through the eye of a needle! What's the idea, Dick?' I asked. 'I thought we were going to keep that type of lunacy till the very end, and that we wouldn't even consider it until every hole in the camp was completely bunged and we were desperate?'

'We're not desperate, Pat. I hope we never shall be. Still, I don't mind letting them have a shot. I want you to go with them,' he added as an aside, 'just to see they don't get into any trouble!'

'Well! I seem to be doomed. I'll do it for the fun of the thing, but it's a mad idea and it will mean another month in the "cooler" for me without a shadow of a doubt,' I concluded.

I knew the scheme well. A child could have thought of it. It involved making a sortie from one of the windows of the kitchen over the low roofs of various store buildings in the adjoining German *Kommandantur* courtyard. Then, descending to the ground, one had to cross over the path of a sentry's beat, when his back was turned, and then crawl across the dimly lit area in front of the *Kommandantur* to a small open pit, in the far corner of the courtyard, which was visible from our windows. That was as far as the plan went! We were still in the midst of the enemy and how we were supposed to extricate ourselves was a mystery to me.

Dick, Ronnie, Billie Stephens, and myself discussed the plan.

I suggested an adition to the team:

'We may as well be hung for a sheep as a lamb, so why not add a fourth to our group of three! Then, when we get out, *if* we get out, we can travel in independent groups of two each.'

'All right,' said Dick, 'who do you suggest?'

'Well, if Ronnie and Billie are going to travel together, it's rather up to me, I suppose, to choose someone. I think Hank Wardle is the man. It's time he had a turn.'

'Good. I don't think there will be any objections, but I'll just confirm this,' rejoined Dick. 'He's the right man as far as I'm concerned. He has all the qualifications; he's high on the roster and has helped other escapes; and he's RAF.'

Ronnie put in: 'This attempt will be an "All Services" venture then, Billie being a naval type. A good idea, I think!'

'You'll have to travel by different routes, of course,' said Dick. 'What do you suggest?'

'Well, if it's all the same to Ronnie and Billie,' I answered, 'I've studied the route from Penig via Zwickau to Plauen, Regensburg and Munich, and thence to Ulm and Tuttlingen. I'd like to stick to it. How about it, Ronnie? You could go from Leisnig to Dobeln, then via Chemnitz to Nürnberg and Stuttgart.'

'That suits us,' said Ronnie. 'We prefer Leisnig, as it's only a few kilometres away and we reckon to catch a train before the morning *Appell*.'

'All right,' said Dick, 'you're agreed then. We'll go into questions of detail, dress, food, and so on, nearer to the date for the "off". Let me know if you are stuck for anything.'

Lieutenant-Commander William Stephens, RNVR (Billie), had been captured during the St Nazaire raid, when the dock gates were blown up in an effort to imprison a large number of German U-boats. He had tried to escape twice, and was a new arrival at Colditz. In fact, when he arrived he was promptly put into 'solitary' for several weeks to complete his sentences before he was let loose into the camp. His school was Shrewsbury and he came from Northern Ireland. He was handsome, fair-haired, with piercing blue eyes and Nelsonian nose. He walked as if he was permanently on the deck of a ship. He was a daredevil, and his main idea appeared to be to force his way into the German area of the camp and then hack his way out with a metaphorical cutlass.

The one hope I could see was of forcing an entry into the tall block of buildings, at the top of which our medium-sized officer had been deposited in his Tate and Lyle sugar-box. As he had been able to make an exit from there, maybe we could also. It was important to have Bruce's comments, and I managed to pass a message to him in some food and, eventually, had an answer. Once inside his building, it was possible to descend from unbarred windows on the far side into the moat of the Castle. The top floors were unoccupied, but care was necessary to avoid noise as Germans occupied floors below. There was a large heavy door into the building which was visible from our quarters and which gave on to an unused staircase leading to the top.

There were two principal snags: the door mentioned above was visible from almost everywhere and in full view of the sentry in the German courtyard; secondly, the door was locked. We could assume the lock was not cruciform in type, but beyond this we knew nothing. At night, when the floodlights were blazing, this door was in shadow. I might be able to work at the lock, but the risk was tremendous because the door was beside the main path, leading from the outer Castle gateway to the entrance of the *Kommandantur* – all pedestrians passed within a yard of it. Besides, would the shadow be sufficient to hide a man from the eyes of the sentry? Lastly, the door was twenty yards from the pit of which I have spoken – and the nearest place of concealment – so that a person going to and from the door had to flit twenty yards each way in a penumbra where movement would be visible.

When Hank's nomination had been agreed, I broached the subject to him:

'Ronnie and Billie want you and me to join them on about the most absurd escape attempt I know,' I opened by way of invitation.

'One thing seems to be as good or as bad as another in this camp nowadays,' was Hank's reply.

'That means you're not fussy, I take it?'

Hank's answer was a typical shrug of the shoulders and 'I couldn't care less, I've got nothing to do till the end of the war, so it's all the same to me!'

I described the plan to him in fair detail, and when I had finished he said:

'I'll try it with you. I agree there's no hope of success, but we've got to carry on trying just the same.'

The whole scheme assumed that we could reach the pit safely and hide inside it. For all we knew it might have been deep. Our hope that it was shallow was based on the fact that the pit was not balustraded and a man might easily have fallen into it. To reach the pit would be a prolonged nightmare.

The camp kitchen was in use all day. Towards evening it was locked up. It was in full view of the sentry in the prisoners' courtyard. A pane of glass in one of the metal-framed windows was half-broken. I had preparatory work to do in the kitchen and this window was my only means of entry. I employed a stooge to help me. After the evening *Appell* on the first day of operations, he sat on a doorstep near the kitchen, watching the sentry, while I remained out of sight behind the protruding wall of the delousing shed, about five yards from the window. The sentry's beat varied between eight and twelve seconds. I had to be inside before he turned round.

My stooge gave me the OK signal. I ran and hopped on to the sill. Reaching through the broken pane of glass on tiptoe, I could just grasp the lever which opened the window. I pulled it upwards gently, withdrew my arm carefully so as not to break what was left of the glass pane, opened the window and crept through. If the sentry stopped short or turned in the middle of his beat, I was caught. I jumped down on to the kitchen floor and silently closed the window. I was safely inside, with a second to spare.

Leaving the kitchen was a little easier, as one faced the sentry and could see him through cracks in the white paint of the lower glass panes of the window.

I repeated this performance five evenings running along with one assistant. We usually entered after the evening *Appell*, at about 6 pm, and returned again before locking-up time, at 9 pm.

During these periods of three hours, we worked hard. The windows on the opposite side of the kitchen opened on to the flat roofs of a jumble of outhouses in the German courtyard: all the roofs were about twelve feet above the ground. The kitchen windows on this side, as well as the whole wall of the building, were in bright floodlight from dusk onwards.

I opened one of the windows by removing a number of wire clips which were supposed to seal it, and examined the bars beyond. I saw that, by removing one rivet, I could bend a bar inwards, providing enough room for a body to pass. The hole through the bars opened on to the flat roof.

The rivet was the next problem. I could saw off the head, but it was old and rusty and would obviously require great force to withdraw it. Yet the method would involve much less sawing. 'Silence was golden'. A sentry plied his beat just beyond the outbuildings, about fifteen yards away. Luckily the window was not in his line of vision, unless he extended his beat to nearly double its normal length. This he did from time to time. Of course, the window and the flat roof were in full view of all the windows of the *Kommandantur* above the ground floor!

The less sawing I did, the better. Sawing the head off the rivet was the solution, if only I could withdraw it afterwards.

My assistant was ERA 'Wally' Hammond, RN. He was one of the naval types who had been painted blue! He and his friend ERA 'Tubby' Lister arrived by mistake at Colditz, this being an officers' camp, while they were Chief Petty Officers. They made good use of their sojourn.

Soon afterwards, when they were removed to their rightful prison, they escaped, and with the advantage of their Colditz 'education' behind them, they reached Switzerland with comparative ease!

These two submarine men deserve to be placed on pedestals in a conspicuous place somewhere in England. They were the quintessence of everything for which our island stands. If a hundred Englishmen of every rank and county were put together in a pot and boiled down, the remaining crust would be Wally Hammond and Tubby Lister. Their sense of humour was unbeatable. It rose to meet dangers, knocking them on the head with a facetiousness capable of dispersing the most formidable army of adversities.

During their escape, for instance, for lack of a better language they spoke pidgin-English with the Germans throughout, posing as Flemish collaborators. They stayed at middle-class German hotels, and before leaving in the mornings, usually filled any army top-boots which happened to be outside the doors of neighbouring rooms with water, as a mark of their respect for the *Oberkommando der Wehrmacht* – the German High Command! . . . . Their full story belongs to another book*; their journey through Germany was a pantomime.

★　★　★

To return to the story of the rivet which required attention; the head was sawn through during the fourth evening shift. Next, we needed a high-powered silent-working punch which would force the rivet out of its socket.

Wally Hammond made one in the space of a few hours out of a bar used for closing the grate door of a German heating stove. The bar was about a foot long. At each end he made clamps which could be fixed to the iron bar outside the kitchen window. In the centre there was, already, a half-inch-diameter screw. The end of this was filed to fit the quarter-inch-diameter rivet-hole. The head of the screw was a knurled wheel of two inches diameter. To the latter, Hammond arranged to clamp a lever one foot long.

On the fifth evening of work I applied Hammond's punch, turned the lever, and the rivet, which had been corroded in its position for probably twenty years, slid smoothly and silently out of its hole and the job was done!

I camouflaged the joint with a clay rivet, sealed the window as usual, and, redusting everything carefully, we left the kitchen as we had come.

The escape was on and we wasted no time. Our two groups would travel by different routes to the frontier crossing-point on the Swiss border – a Colditz secret! Although I had never been there, I knew the area in my mind's eye like the back of my hand. Every Colditz

---

* *The Latter Days at Colditz*, by P. R. Reid (see also page 211).

escaper's first and last duty was to learn this crossing by heart; for I had forbidden frontier-crossing maps to be carried many months ago. We had the master map in the camp and it was studied by all.

We each had our identity papers, our general maps, money, and compass. We kept them usually in small tubes. I had once received a present from friends in England which actually arrived – two boxes of twenty-five Upmann Havana cigars. The cigars were in light metal containers about five inches long. These cases were much in demand. All the above documents, money, and a compass fitted into the metal tube, which was easily carried and could be easily concealed, even by sleight of hand if necessary.

I had printed my own identity papers. German Gothic script is not easy to copy, but it was possible with practice. We had a primitive, yet highly successful, system of duplicating, and reproduced typewritten orders and letters as desired. A multitude of lino-cut stamps provided all the officialdom necessary, and photographs were managed in various ways. The brown-coloured *Ausweis* was of thick white paper dyed the correct tint with a patent mixture of our own manufacture.

Our clothes had long since been prepared. I would wear one of my mass-production cloth caps, converted RAF trousers, a fawn-coloured windjacket I had concealed for a year, and finally an overcoat (necessary at this time of year, early October) which I succeeded in buying from a French officer who had obtained it from a French orderly who, in turn, had access to the village.

It was a dark-blue civilian overcoat with black velvet lapels and it buttoned, double-breasted, high up on the chest! I imagine it was a German fashion of about 1912. I wore black shoes.

It was essential to remove every single trace of the origin of anything we wore or carried, such as lettering inside shoes, name tags and 'Made in England' marks. We were to live our false identities, and were prepared to challenge the Germans to prove the contrary, if we were held for questioning. Thus Hank and I became Flemish workmen collaborating with the Germans. As *flamands* we could pass off our bad German and our bad French – a useful nationality! Not being a common one, the Germans would take a long time to find someone who spoke Flemish and could prove we were not *flamands*.

We were concrete or engineering contractors' workmen. My

German wallet contained my whole story. I was permitted to travel to Rottweil (some thirty miles from the Swiss border), in reply to newspaper advertisements – I had the cuttings – requiring contractors' men for construction work. I also had a special and very necessary permit to travel close to the frontier. Part of my story was that my fianceé worked at Besançon as a telephone operator for the Germans. She was a Walloon – or French-speaking Belgian girl. I kept a fictitious letter from her (prepared for me by a Frenchman) in my wallet asking me to spend my few days' leave with her in Besançon before going to work in Rottweil. By a curious coincidence the railway line going to Besançon from my direction passed within fifteen miles of the Swiss frontier!

My trump card was a real photo, which I had, of a girl I met in France. One day, while looking through a German weekly newspaper, I had come across a German propaganda photograph showing German and foreign girls working together for the Germans in a post office and telephone exchange. One of the girls in the picture was the double of the girl whose photo I carried. I immediately cut out the press photo and kept it as a treasured possession. It would prove to any German where my imaginary fianceé's loyalties lay. My private snapshot was conclusive evidence and I was prepared to battle with any German who dared to doubt my identity.

The other three of our team had different case-histories, more or less as conclusive as mine.

Towards the end of our final preparations I held a last consultation and, among many items, we discussed food.

'You all realize that we can't take anything with us by way of food except normal German rations,' I pointed out.

'Yes, I agree,' said Billie, 'But all the same I'm taking enough corned beef and tinned cheese to make sure of one good meal before we board the train.'

'Our sugar is all right too,' added Ronnie. 'We can carry that with us indefinitely. It looks the same as the German and would pass.'

'Now I've got a sticky proposition to make,' I began, changing the subject. 'There are a few of those small ersatz leather suitcases lying about – you know, the ones that came with the last batch of parcels. They had army clothing in them. I propose we each carry one.'

'H'm! That's a tall order!' retorted Billie. 'It's going to be hard enough to get out of the camp, climbing over roofs and walls and down ropes, without being pestered with suitcases into the bargain.'

'I agree, but remember, Billie, when we *do* get out of the camp we are a long way from Switzerland and freedom,' I argued; 'it's no use planning only for the beginning and leaving the rest to look after itself. The rest in this case is just as important, and a little extra risk to begin with – in conditions over which we have some control – may be amply repaid later on, in circumstances over which we have no control at all.'

'What does all that imply?' queried Billie.

'It means,' I said, 'that I don't think it's such a tall order. Once outside the camp, a suitcase becomes the hall-mark of respectability and honesty. How many people travel long journeys on main-line expresses in wartime with nothing at all in their hands? Only fugitives and railway officials. And the Germans know this well. They know that to look out for an escaped prisoner means to look out for a man travelling light, with no luggage – without a suitcase.'

'I see your point, Pat,' agreed Billie.

'At railway-station controls or in a round-up, a suitcase will be invaluable,' I continued. 'You can wave it about and make it prominent and the betting is it'll help a lot. Moreover, it will be useful for carrying articles of respectability: pyjamas – without tags and hallmarks – razors, bootbrushes, and German boot polish, German soap, and, of course, your German food. Otherwise your pockets are going to be bulgy, untidy, and suspicious-looking. I know it's going to be hell lugging them with us out of the camp, but I think it will be worth the effort in the end.'

They all agreed and so it was fixed. We procured four of the small fibreboard suitcases and packed away our escape-travelling kit.

I could hardly believe we were going to do the whole four-hundred-mile journey by train. I thought of our naïve escape from Laufen and realized how much experience counted in escaping.

20

The Walls are Breached

I<small>T WAS OCTOBER</small> 14th, 1942. As evening approached, the four of us made final preparations. I said 'Au revoir till tomorrow' to Van den Heuvel, and to Rupert, Harry, Peter Allan, and Kenneth and Dick. Rupert was to be our kitchen-window stooge. We donned our civilian clothing, and covered this with army trousers and greatcoats. Civilian overcoats were made into neat bundles.

In parenthesis, I should explain why we had to wear the military clothes over everything. At any time a wandering Goon might appear as we waited our moment to enter the kitchen, and there might even be delays. Further, we had to think of 'informers' – among the foreign orderlies, for example, who were always wandering about. If orderlies saw one of us leap through the kitchen window, it was just too bad – we might be after food – but it would be far worse if they saw a number of civilian-clothed officers in a staircase lobby – the orderlies' staircase as it happened – waiting, apparently, for their taxi to arrive!

Our suitcases were surrounded with blankets to muffle sound, and we carried enough sheets and blankets to make a fifty-foot descent, if necessary. Later we would wear balaclava helmets and gloves; no white skin was to be visible. Darkness and the shadows were to be our friends, we could not afford to offend them. Only our eyes and noses would be exposed. All light-coloured garments were excluded. We carried thick socks to put over our shoes. This is the most silent method of movement I know, barring removal of one's shoes – which we were to do for the crossing of the sentry's path.

Squadron-Leader MacColm was to accompany us into the kitchen in order to bend the window bar back into place and seal up the window after we had gone. He would have to conceal the military clothing we left behind in the kitchen and make his exit the next morning after the kitchen was unlocked. He could hide in one of the enormous cauldrons so long as he did not oversleep and have himself served up with the soup next day.

Immediately after the evening *Appell* we were ready and started on the first leg of our long journey. It was 6.30 pm.

I was used to the drill of the entry window by now. At the nodded signal from Rupert, I acted automatically; a run, a leap to the sill, one arm through the cracked pane of glass, up with the window lever, withdraw arm carefully, open window – without noise – jump through, and close again softly. I was through. Only two had done it before at any one session. The question was, would five succeed? One after another they came. At least, they had not the window-lever latch to bother about.

The sentry was behaving himself. At regular intervals, as he turned his back, the signal was given. I could not see Rupert – but he was timing perfectly. I could see the sentry from behind the window throughout his beat.

Each time, as the sentry turned away, I heard a gentle scurry. I automatically opened the window, in jumped a body, and I closed the window again, breathing a heavy sigh. The drill was becoming automatic. It was taking as little as five seconds. Then, suddenly, just as the last of the five was due, I sensed – I do not know how – an uncertainty, a hesitation in the manner of the sentry as he turned away. I knew that he would behave oddly during this beat. My heart was in my mouth, for I expected to hear the scurry and anticipated a clash. But there was no scurry, and in the next instant the sentry stopped dead and turned around! It was nothing less than intuition on Rupert's part that saved us.

On the next turn of the sentry's beat, I heard the scurry, opened and closed again. At last all five of us were safe.

We removed our military clothing and handed it to MacColm.

I set about the window overlooking the German courtyard, and as darkness fell and the floodlights went on, I heaved on the bar until it was bent horizontal, and immediately attached to the unbent portion a long strip of black-painted cardboard resembling the bar. This hung downwards in the correct position and camou-flaged the opening.

'All set!' I whispered to the others. 'I'm going out now. Hank! Wait until I'm hidden by the shadows of the large ventilator out there. Then join me as quickly as you can. Billie and Ronnie, remember not to follow until we have crossed the sentry's path safely.'

I squirmed through the hole in the bars on to the flat roof beyond. The roof joined the kitchen wall just below our window-sill. I crept quietly forward in a blaze of light. The eyes of a hundred windows glared down upon me.

The impression was appalling. 'Does nobody ever look out of a window at night?' I kept asking myself.

Happily there was shelter from the glare about halfway across the roof. The high square ventilator provided a deep shadow behind which I crawled. Hank soon followed. The sentry plied his beat not fifteen yards away.

For several days we had arranged music practices in the evenings in the senior officers' quarters (the theatre block). The music was to be used for signalling, and we had to accustom the sentry in front of us to a certain amount of noise. While Major Anderson (Andy) played the oboe, Colonel George Young played the concertina, and Douglas Bader, keeping watch from a window, acted as conductor. Their room was on the third floor, overlooking the German court-yard. Bader could see our sentry for the whole length of his beat. He was to start the practice at 7.30 pm, when the traffic in the courtyard had died down. From 8 pm onwards he was to keep rigid control on the players so that they only stopped their music when the sentry was in a suitable position for us to cross his path. It was not imperative that they stopped playing every time the sentry turned his back, but when they stopped playing that meant we could move. We arranged this signalling system because, once on the ground, we would have little concealment, and what little there was, provided by an angle in the wall of the outbuildings, prevented us from seeing the sentry.

At 8 pm Hank and I crawled once more into the lime-light and over the remainder of the roof, dropping to the ground over a loose, noisy gutter which gave me the jitters. In the dark angle of the wall, with our shoes around our necks and our suitcases under our arms, we waited for the music to stop. The players had been playing light jaunty airs – and then ran the gauntlet of our popular-song books. At

8 pm they changed to classical music; it gave them more excuse for stopping. Bader had seen us drop from the roof and would see us cross the sentry's path. The players were in the middle of Haydn's oboe concerto when they stopped.

'I shall make this a trial run,' I thought.

I advanced quickly five yards to the end of the wall concealing us, and regarded the sentry. He was fidgety and looked up at Bader's window twice during the five seconds' view I had of his back. Before me was the roadway, a cobbled surface seven yards wide. Beyond was the end of a shed and some friendly concealing shrubbery. As the sentry turned, the music started again. Our players had chosen a piece the Germans love. I only hoped the sentry would not be exasperated by their repeated interruptions. The next time they stopped we would go.

The music ceased abruptly and I ran – but it started again just as I reached the corner. I stopped dead and retired hurriedly. This happened twice. Then I heard German voices through the music. It was the duty officer on his rounds. He was questioning the sentry. He was suspicious. I heard gruff orders given.

Five minutes later I was caught napping – the music stopped while I was ruminating on the cause of the duty officer's interrogation and I was not on my toes. A late dash was worse than none. I stood still and waited. I waited a long time and the music did not begin again. A quarter of an hour passed and there was still no music. Obviously something had gone wrong upstairs. I decided therefore to wait an hour in order to let suspicions die down. We had the whole night before us, and I was not going to spoil the ship for a ha'p'orth o' tar.

All this time Hank was beside me – not a word passed his lips – not a murmur or comment to distract us from the job on hand.

In the angle of the wall where we hid, there was a door. We tried the handle and found it was open, so we entered in pitch-darkness and, passing through a second door, we took temporary refuge in a room which had a small window and contained, as far as we could see, only rubbish – wastepaper, empty bottles, and empty food-tins. Outside, in the angle of the wall, any Goon with extra-sharp eyesight, passing along the roadway, would spot us. The sentry himself was also liable to extend his beat without warning and take a look around the corner of the wall where we had been hiding. In the rubbish room we were much safer.

We had been in there five minutes when, suddenly, there was a rustling of paper, a crash of falling tins, and a jangling of overturned bottles – a noise fit to waken the dead. We froze with horror. A cat leaped out from among the refuse and tore out of the room as if the devil was after it.

'That's finished everything,' I exclaimed. 'The Jerries will be here in a moment to investigate.'

'The darn thing was after a mouse, I think,' said Hank. 'Let's make the best of things, anyway. They may only flash a torch round casually and we may get away with it if we try to look like a couple of sacks in the corner.'

'Quick, then,' I rejoined. 'Grab those piles of newspapers and let's spread them out a little over our heads. It's our only hope.'

We did so and waited, with our hearts thumping. Five minutes passed, and then ten, and still nobody came. We began to breathe again.

Soon our hour's vigil was over. It was 9.45 pm and I resolved to carry on. All was silent in the courtyard. I could now hear the sentry's footsteps clearly – approaching – and then receding. Choosing our moment, we advanced to the end of the wall as he turned on his beat. I peeped around the corner. He was ten yards off and marching away from us. The courtyard was empty. I tiptoed quickly across the roadway with Hank at my heels. Reaching the wall of the shed on the other side, we had just time to crouch behind the shrubbery before he turned. He had heard nothing. On his next receding beat we crept behind the shed, and hid in a small shrubbery, which bordered the main steps and veranda in front of the entrance to the *Kommandantur*.

The first leg of our escape was behind us. I dropped my suitcase and reconnoitred the next stage of our journey, which was to the 'pit'. Watching the sentry, I crept quickly along the narrow grass verge at the edge of the path leading away from the main steps. On one side was the path and on the other side was a long flower-bed; beyond that the balustrade of the *Kommandantur* veranda. I was in light shadow and had to crouch as I moved. Reaching the pit, about twenty-five yards away, before the sentry turned, I looked over the edge. There was a wooden trestle with steps. The pit was not deep. I dropped into it. A brick tunnel from the pit ran underneath the veranda and gave perfect concealment. That was enough. As I emerged again, I distinctly heard noises from the direction of the roofs over which we had climbed. Ronnie and Billie, who had witnessed our crossing of the roadway, were following. The sentry apparently heard nothing.

I began to creep back to the shrubbery where Hank was waiting. I was nearly halfway when, without warning, heavy footsteps sounded; a Goon was approaching quickly from the direction of the main Castle gateway and around the corner of the Castle building into sight. In a flash I was flat on my face on the grass verge, and lay rigid, just as he turned the corner and headed up the path straight towards me. He could not fail to see me. I waited for the end. He approached nearer and nearer with noisy footsteps crunching on the gravel. He was level with me. It was all over. I waited for his ejaculation at my discovery – for his warning shout to the sentry – for the familiar '*Hände hoch!*' – and the feel of his pistol in my back between the shoulder-blades.

The crunching footsteps continued past me and retreated. He mounted the steps and entered the *Kommandantur*.

After a moment's pause to recover, I crept the remainder of the distance to the shrubbery and, as I did so, Ronnie and Billie appeared from the other direction.

Before long we were all safe in the pit without further alarms, the second lap completed! We had time to relax for a moment.

I asked Billie: 'How did you get on crossing the sentry's beat?'

'We saw you two cross over and it looked as easy as pie. That gave us confidence. We made one trial, and then crossed the second time. Something went wrong with the music, didn't it?'

'Yes, that's why we held up proceedings so long,' I answered. 'We had a lucky break when they stopped for the last time. I thought it was the signal to move, but I was too late off the mark, thank God! I'd probably have run into the sentry's arms!'

'What do you think happened?' asked Ronnie.

'I heard the duty officer asking questions,' I explained. 'I think they suspected the music practice was phoney. They probably went upstairs and stopped it.'

Changing the subject, I said: 'I heard you coming over the roof. I was sure the sentry could have heard.'

'We made a noise at one point, I remember,' said Ronnie, 'but it wasn't anything to speak of. It's amazing what you can hear if your ears are expecting certain sounds. The sentry was probably thinking of his girl friend at that moment.'

'If it wasn't for girl friends,' I chimed in, 'we probably wouldn't be on this mad jaunt anyway, so it cuts both ways,' and I nudged Hank.

'It's time I got to work,' I added grimly.

My next job was to try to open the door of the building which I have described as the one from which our medium-sized officer escaped. The door was fifteen yards away; it was in deep shadow, though the area between the door and the pit was only in semi-darkness. Again watching the sentry, I crept carefully to the door, and then started work with a set of *passe-partout* keys I had brought with me. I had one unnerving interruption, when I heard Priem's voice in the distance returning from the town. I had just sufficient time to creep back to the pit and hide, before he came around the corner.

We laughed inwardly as he passed by us along the path talking loudly to another officer. I could not help thinking of the occasion when he stood outside Gephard's office and did not have the door unlocked!

Poor old Priem! He was not a bad type on the whole. He had a sense of humour which made him almost human.

It was 11 pm when Priem passed by. I worked for an hour on the door without success and finally gave up. We were checked, and would have to find another exit.

We felt our way along the tunnel leading from the pit under the veranda, and after eight yards came to a large cellar with a low arched ceiling supported on pillars. It had something to do with sewage, for Hank, at one point, stepped off solid ground and nearly fell into what might have been deep water! He must have disturbed a scum on top of the liquid because a dreadful stench arose. When I was well away from the entrance, I struck a match. There was a solitary wheel-barrow for furniture, and at the far end of the cavern-like cellar, a chimney flue. I had previously noticed a faint glimmer of light from this direction. Examining the flue, I found it was an air-vent which led vertically upwards from the ceiling of the cavern for about four feet, and then curved outwards towards the fresh air. Hank pushed me up the flue. In plan it was about nine inches by three feet. I managed to wriggle myself high enough to see around the curve. The flue ended at the vertical face of a wall two feet away from me as a barred opening shaped like a letter-box slot. The opening was at the level of the ground outside, and was situated on the far side of the building – the moat side for which we were heading, but it was a practical impossibility to negotiate this flue. There were bars, and in any case only a pigmy could have wriggled round the curve.

We held a conference.

'We seem to have struck a dead end,' I started; 'this place is a cul-de-sac and I can't manage the door either. I'm terribly sorry, but there we are!'

'Can anyone think of another way out?' asked Ronnie.

'The main gateway, I think, is out of the question,' I went on. 'Since Neave's escape nearly a year ago, they lock the inner gate this side of the bridge over the moat. That means we can't reach the side gate leading down into the moat.'

'Our only hope is through the *Kommandantur*,' suggested Billie. 'We can try it either now, and hope to get through unseen – or else try it early in the morning when there's a little traffic about and some doors may be unlocked.'

'Do you really think we'll ever pass scrutiny at that hour?' questioned Ronnie. 'If we must take that route, I think it's better to try it at about 3 am when the whole camp is dead asleep.'

I was thinking how impossibly foolhardy was the idea of going through the *Kommandantur*. I remembered that other attempt – years ago now it seemed – when we had pumped men through the hole in the lavatory into the *Kommandantur*. I had considered then that the idea was mad. I thought aloud:

'There are only three known entrances to the *Kommandantur*: the main front door, the French windows behind, which open on to the grass patch right in front of a sentry, and the little door under the archway leading to the park. The archway gate is locked and the door is the wrong side of it.'

In desperation, I said: 'I'm going to have another look at the flue.'

This time I removed some of my clothing and found I could slide more easily up the shaft. I examined the bars closely and found one was loose in its mortar socket. As I did so, I heard footsteps outside the opening and a Goon patrol approached. The Goon had an Alsatian with him. A heavy pair of boots trampled past me. I could have touched them with my hand. The dog pattered behind and did not see me. I imagine the smell issuing from the flue obliterated my scent.

I succeeded in loosening one end of the bar and bent it nearly double. Slipping down into the cellar again, I whispered to the others: 'There's a vague chance we may be able to squeeze through the flue. Anyway, it's worth trying. We shall have to strip completely naked.'

'Hank and Billie will never make it,' said Ronnie. 'It's impossible; they're too big. You and I might manage it with help at both ends – with someone pushing below and someone else pulling from above.'

'I think I can make it,' I rejoined, 'if someone stands on the wheelbarrow and helps to push me through. Once I'm out, I can do the pulling. Hank had better come next. If he can make it, we all can.'

Hank was over six feet tall and Billie nearly six feet. Ronnie and I were smaller, and Ronnie was very thin.

'Neither Hank nor I,' intervened Billie, 'will ever squeeze around the curve on our tummies. Our knees are not double-jointed and our legs will stick. We'll have to come out on our backs.'

'Agreed,' I said. 'Then I go first, Hank next, then Billie and Ronnie last. Ronnie, you'll have no one to push you, but if two of us grab your arms and pull, we should manage it. Be careful undressing. Don't leave anything behind – we want to leave no traces. Hand your clothes to me in neat bundles, and your suitcases. I'll dispose of them temporarily outside.'

After a tremendous struggle, I succeeded in squeezing through the chimney and sallied forth naked on to the path outside. Bending down into the flue again, I could just reach Hank's hand as he passed me up my clothes and my suitcase, and then his own. I hid the kit in some bushes near the path and put on enough dark clothing to make me inconspicuous. Hank was stripped and struggling in the hole with his back towards me. I managed to grab one arm and heaved, while he was pushed from below. Inch by inch he advanced and at the end of twenty minutes, with a last wrench, I pulled him clear. He was bruised all over and streaming with perspiration. During all that time we were at the mercy of any passer-by. What a spectacle it must have been – a naked man being squeezed through a hole in the wall like toothpaste out of a tube! To the imaginative-minded in the eerie darkness, it must have looked as if the massive walls of the Castle were slowly descending upon the man's body while his comrade was engaged in a desperate tug-of-war to save his life!

Hank retired to the bushes to recover and dress himself.

Next came Billie's clothes and suitcase, and then Billie himself. I extracted him in about fifteen minutes. Then Ronnie's kit arrived. I gave him a sheet on which to pull in order to begin his climb. After that, two of us set about him, and he was out in about ten minutes. We all collapsed in the bushes for a breather. It was about 3.30 am and we had completed the third leg of our marathon.

'What do you think of our chances now?' I asked Billie.

'I'm beyond thinking of chances,' was the reply, 'but I know I shall never forget this night as long as I live.'

'I hope you've got all your kit,' I said, smiling at him in the darkness. 'I should hate to have to push you back down the shaft to fetch it!'

'I'd give anything for a smoke,' sighed Billie.

'I see no reason why you shouldn't smoke as we walk past the barracks if you feel like it. What cigarettes have you got?'

'Gold Flake, I think.'

'Exactly! You'd better start chain-smoking, because you'll have to throw the rest away before you reach Leisnig. Had you thought of that?'

'But I've got fifty!'

'Too bad,' I replied. 'With luck you've got about three hours; that's seventeen cigarettes an hour. Can you do it?'

'I'll try,' said Billie ruefully.

A German was snoring loudly in a room with the window open, a few yards away. The flue through which we had just climbed gave on to a narrow path running along the top of the moat immediately under the main Castle walls. The bushes we hid in were on the very edge of the moat. The moat wall was luckily stepped into three successive descents. The drops were about eighteen feet and the steps were about two yards wide, with odd shrubs and grass growing on them. A couple of sheets were made ready. After half an hour's rest, and fully clothed once more, we dropped down one by one. I went last and fell into the arms of those below me.

On the way down, Billie suddenly developed a tickle in his throat and started a cough which disturbed the dogs. They began barking in their kennels, which we saw for the first time, uncomfortably near the route we were to take. Billie in desperation ate a quantity of grass and earth, which seemed to stop the irritation in his throat. By the time we reached the bottom of the moat it was 4.30 am. The fourth leg was completed.

We tidied our clothes and adjusted the socks over our shoes. In a few moments we would have to pass underneath a lamp at the corner of the road leading to the German barracks. This was the road leading to the double gates in the outer wall around the Castle grounds. It was the road taken by Neave and by Van Doorninck.

The lamp was situated in full view of a sentry — luckily, some forty-five yards away — who would be able to contemplate our back silhouettes as we turned the corner and faded into the darkness beyond.

The dogs had ceased barking. Hank and I moved off first — over a small railing, on to a path, past the kennels, down some steps, round the corner under the light, and away into the darkness. We walked leisurely, side by side, as if we were inmates of the barracks returning after a night's carousal in the town.

Before passing the barracks I had one last duty to perform — to give those in the camp an idea as to what we had done, to indicate whether other escapers would be able to follow our route or not. I had half a dozen pieces of white cardboard cut into various shapes – a square, an oblong, a triangle, a circle, and so on. Dick Howe and I had arranged a code whereby each shape gave him some information. I threw certain of the cards down on to a small grass patch below the road, past which our exercise parade marched on their way to the park. With luck, if the parade was not cancelled for a week, Dick would see the cards. My message ran:

'Exit from pit. Moat easy; no traces left.'

Although I had pulled the bar of the flue exit back into place, we had, in truth, probably left minor traces. But as the alternative message was: 'Exit obvious to Goons' – which would have been the case, for instance, if we left fifty feet of sheet-rope dangling from a window – I preferred to encourage other escapers to have a shot at following us.

We continued another hundred yards past the barracks, where the garrison was peacefully sleeping, and arrived at our last obstacle – the outer wall. It was only ten feet high here, with coils of barbed wire stretched along the top. I was on the wall heaving Hank up, when, with a sudden pounding of my heart, I noticed the glow of a cigarette in the distance. It was approaching. Then I realized it was Billie. They had caught us up. We had arranged a discreet gap between us so that we did not look like a regiment passing under the corner lamp.

The barbed wire did not present a serious obstacle when tackled without hurry and with minute care. We were all eventually over the wall, but none too soon, because we had a long way to go in order to be safe before dawn. It was 5.15 in the morning, and the fifth leg of the marathon was over. The sixth and last stage – the long journey to Switzerland – lay ahead of us!

We shook hands all round and with '*Au revoir* – see you in Switzerland in a few days,' Hank and I set off along the road. Two hundred yards behind us, the other two followed. Soon they branched off on their route and we took to the fields.

As we trudged along, Hank fumbled for a long time in his pockets, and then uttered practically the first words he had spoken during the whole night. He said:

'I reckon, Pat, I must have left my pipe at the top of the moat.'

21
Liberty Express

Hank and I walked fast. We intended to lie up for a day. Therefore, in order to be at all safe we had to put the longest distance possible between ourselves and the camp. We judged the German search would be concentrated in the direction of a village about five miles away, for which Ronnie and Billie headed and in which there was a railway station. The first train was shortly before morning *Appell*. Provided there was no alarm in the camp before then, and if the two of them could reach the station in time for the train (which now seemed probable), they would be in Leipzig before the real search started. This was the course Lulu Lawton had taken, but he had missed the train and had to hide up in a closely hunted area.

Hank and I chose a difficult route, calculated to put the hunters off the scent. We headed first south and then westwards in a big sweep in the direction of the River Mulde which ran due north-wards towards the Elbe. In order to reach a railway station we had to trek about twenty miles and cross the river into the bargain. It was not a 'cushy' escape-route and we relied on the Germans thinking likewise.

We walked for about an hour and a half, and when it was almost daylight entered a wood and hid up in a thicket for the day. We must have been five miles away from the camp. Although we tried to sleep, our nerves were as taut as piano wires. I was on the alert the whole day.

'A wild animal must have magnificent nerves,' I said to Hank at one point.

'Wild animals have nerves just like you and I. That's why they are not captured easily,' was his comment.

Hank was not going to be easy to catch. His fiancée had been waiting for him since the night when he took off in his bomber in April 1940. It would plainly require more than a few tough Germans to recapture him. It gave me confidence to know he was beside me.

I mused for a long time over the queer twists that Fate gives to our lives. I had always assumed that Rupert and I would escape finally together. Yet it happened to be Hank's turn, and here we were. I had left old and tried friends behind me. Two years of constant companionship had cemented some of us together very closely. 'Rupert, Harry, Dick, Kenneth and Peter. Would I ever see them again?' Inside the camp the probability of early failure in the escape was so great that we brushed aside all serious thought of a long parting.

Here in the woods it was different. If I did my job properly from now on, it was probable that I would never see them again. We were not going back to Colditz; Hank was sure of that too. I was rather shaken by the thought, realizing fully for the first time what these men meant to me. We had been through much together. I prayed that we might all survive the war and meet again.

As dusk fell we set off across the fields. Sometimes when roads led in our direction we used them, but we had to be very careful. On one occasion we only just left the road in time as we saw a light ahead (unusual in the blackout) and heard voices. A car approaching was stopped. As we by-passed the light by way of the fields, we saw an army motor-cyclist talking to a sentry. It was a control and they were after us. We passed within fifty yards of them!

It seemed a long way to the river. As the night wore on, I could hardly keep my eyes open. I stumbled and dozed as I walked, and finally gave up.

'Hank, I'll have to lie down for an hour and sleep. I've been sleep-walking as it is. I don't know where we're going.'

'OK. I'll stay on guard while you pass out on that bank over there under the tree,' said Hank, indicating a mound of grass looming ahead of us.

He woke me in an hour and we continued, eventually reaching the river. It was in a deep cutting, down which we climbed, and there was a road which ran along its bank. Towards our left, crossing the river and the cutting, was a high-level railway bridge. I decided to cross it. We had to reclimb the cutting. Sleep was overcoming me once more. The climb was steep and over huge rocks cut into steps like those of the pyramids. It was a nightmare climb in the pitch-darkness, as I repeatedly stumbled, fell down, and slept where I lay. Hank would tug at me, pull me over the next huge stone and set me on my feet without a word, only to have to repeat the performance again in a few moments. Halfway up the embankment we stopped to rest. I slept, but Hank was on the qui vive and, peering through the darkness, noticed a movement on the railway bridge. It needed a cat's eye to notice anything at all. He shook me and said:

'Pat, we're not going over that bridge; it's guarded.'

'How the hell do you know for certain?' I asked, 'and how are we going to cross the river, then?'

'I don't mind if we have to swim it, but I'm not crossing that bridge.'

I gave way, though it meant making a big half-circle, crossing the railway line and descending to the river again somewhere near a road bridge which we knew existed farther upstream.

Reaching the top of the railway-bridge embankment we crossed the lines, and as we did so we saw in the distance from the direction of the bridge the flash of a lighted match.

'Did you see that?' I whispered.

'Yes.'

'There's a sentry on the bridge, sure enough. You were right, Hank. Thank God you insisted.'

Gradually we edged down the hill again where the river cutting was less steep, and found that our bearings had not been too bad; for we saw the road bridge in the foreground. We inspected it carefully before crossing, listening for a long time for any sound of movement. It was unguarded. We crossed rapidly and took to the bushes on the far side, not a moment too soon; a motor-cycle came roaring round a bend, its headlights blazing, and crossed the bridge in the direction from which we had come.

We tramped wearily across country on a compass bearing until dawn. Near the village of Penig, where our railway station was situated, we spruced ourselves up, attempted a shave and polished our shoes. We entered the village – it was almost a small industrial town

– and wended our way in the direction of the station. I was loth to ask our way at this time of the morning when few people were about. Instead, we wandered onwards past some coalyards where a tram-line started. The tracks ran alongside a large factory and then switched over to the other side of the road, passing under trees and beside a small river. We followed the lines, which eventually crossed a bridge and entered the town proper. I was sure the tram-lines would lead us to the station. The town was dingy, not at all like Colditz, which was of pleasing appearance. Upkeep had evidently gone to the dogs. Broken window-panes were filled with newspaper, ironwork was rusty, and the front doors of the houses, which opened directly on the street, badly needed a coat of paint.

We arrived at the railway station. It was on the far edge of the town and looked older and out of keeping with the buildings around it. It had a staid respectable atmosphere and belonged to a period before industry had come to Penig. We entered and looked up the trains. Our route was Munich via Zwickau. I saw we had a three-hour wait and then another long wait at Zwickau before the night express for Munich. Leaving the station, we walked out into the country again and settled down for a meal and a rest behind a barn near the road. It is dangerous to wait in railway stations or public parks and advisable to keep moving under any circumstances when in a town.

We returned to the station towards midday. I bought two third-class tickets to Munich and we caught the train comfortably. Our suitcases were a definite asset. My German accent was anything but perfect, but the brandishing of my suitcase on all occasions to emphasize whatever I happened to be saying worked like a soporific on the Germans.

In Zwickau, having another long wait, we boarded a tram. I tripped on the mounting-step and nearly knocked the conductress over. I apologized loudly.

'*Entschuldigen Sie mich! Bitte, entschuldigen, entschuldilgen! Ich bib ein Ausländer.*'

We sat down, and when the conductress came round I beamed at her and asked in broken German:

'*Gnädige Fräulein!* If you please, where is the nearest cinema? We have a long time to wait for our train and would like to see a film and the news pictures. We are foreigners and do not know this town.'

'The best cinema in Zwickau is five minutes from here. I shall tell you where to alight.'

'How much is the fare, please, *Fräulein?*'

'Twenty pfennigs each, if you please.'

'*Danke schön,*' I said, proffering the money.

After five minutes the tram stopped at a main thoroughfare junction and the conductress beckoned to us. As we alighted, one of the passengers pointed out to us with a voluble and, to me, incoherent stream of German exactly where the cinema was. I could gather that he was proud to meet foreigners who were working for the victory of 'Unser Reich'! He took off his moth-eaten hat as we parted and waved a courteous farewell.

Zwickau was just a greatly enlarged Penig as far as I could see. Dilapidation was visible everywhere. The inhabitants gave me an impression of impoverishment, and only the uniforms of officials, including the tram conductress, and those of the armed forces bore a semblance of smartness.

Hank and I spent a comfortable two hours in the cinema, which was no different from any other I have seen. German officers and troops were dotted about in seats all around us and made up ninety per cent of the audience. I dozed for a long time and I noticed Hank's head drooping too. After two hours I whispered to him:

'It's time to go. What did you think of the film?'

'What I saw of it was a washout,' Hank replied. 'I must have slept though, because I missed parts of it. It was incoherent.'

'This cinema seems to be nothing more than impromptu sleeping-quarters. Look around you,' and I nudged Hank. The German Army and Air Force were dozing in all sorts of postures around us!

'Let's go,' I said, and, yawning repeatedly, we rose and left the auditorium.

Returning to the station in good time, we boarded the express to Munich. It was crowded out, for which I was glad, and Hank and I spent the whole night standing in the corridor. Nobody paid any attention to us. We might as well have been in an express bound from London to the North. The lighting, however, was so bad that few passengers attempted to read. It was intensely stuffy owing to the over-crowding, the cold outside, and the blackout curtains on all windows. The hypnotic drumming and the swaying of the train pervaded all.

Our fellow-travellers were a mixed bag; a few army and air force other ranks, some workmen, and a majority of down-at-heel-looking business men or Government officials. There was not a personality among them; all were sheep ready to be slaughtered at the altar of Hitler. There was a police control in the early hours. I produced my much-soiled German leather wallet, which exposed my identity card or *Ausweis* behind a grimy scratched piece of celluloid. The police officer was curt:

'*Sie sind Auslander?*'

'*Jawohl.*'

'*Wo fahren Sie hin?*'

'*Nach München und Rottweil.*'

'*Warum?*'

'*Betonarbeit*' (that is, concrete work).

Hank was slow in producing his papers. I said:

'*Wir sind zusammen. Er ist mein Kamerad.*'

Hank proffered his papers as I added, taking the officer into my confidence:

'*Er ist etwas dumm, aber ein guter Kerl.*'

The control passed on and we relaxed into a fitful doze as we roared through the night towards Munich – and Switzerland.

We arrived in Munich in the cold grey of the morning – several hours late. There had been bombing and train diversions.

I queued up at the booking-office, telling Hank to stand by. When my turn came I asked for, '*Zweimal dritte Klasse, nach Rottweil.*' The woman behind the grill said:

'*Fünfundsechzig Mark, bitte.*'

I produced fifty-six marks, which almost drained me right out. The woman repeated:

'*Fünfundsechzig Mark, bitte – noch neun Mark.*'

I was confusing the German for fifty-six with sixty-five.

'*Karl,*' I shouted in Hank's direction, '*geben Sie mir noch zehn Mark.*'

Hank took the cue, and produced a ten-mark note which I handed to the woman.

'*Ausweis, bitte,*' she said.

I produced it.

'*Gut,*' and she handed my wallet back to me.

I was so relieved that as I left the queue, forgetting my part completely, I said in a loud voice:

'All right, Hank, I've got the tickets!'

I nearly froze in my tracks. As we hurried away I felt the baleful glare of a hundred eyes burning through my back. We were soon lost in the crowd, and what a crowd! Everybody seemed to be travelling. The station appeared to be untouched by bombing and traffic was obviously running at high pressure. We had another long wait for the train which would take us to Rottweil via Ulm and Tuttlingen. I noted with relief that the wait in Ulm was only ten minutes. Hyde-Thompson and his Dutch colleague, the second two officers of my theatre escape, had been trapped in Ulm station. The name carried foreboding and I prayed we would negotiate this junction safely. I also noticed with appreciation that there was a substantial wait at Tuttlingen for the train to Rottweil. It would give us an excuse for leaving the station.

In Munich I felt safe. The waiting-rooms were full to overflowing and along with other passengers we were even shepherded by station police to an underground bomb-proof waiting-room – signposted for the use of all persons having longer than half an hour to wait for a train.

Before descending to this waiting-room, however, I asked for the *Bahnhofswirtschaft* and roving along the counter I saw a notice '*Markenfreies Essen*', which meant 'coupon-free meals'! I promptly asked for two and also *Zwei Liter Pilsner*. They were duly served and Hank and I sat down at a table by ourselves to the best meal provided us by the Germans in two and a half years. The *Markenfreies Essen* consisted of a very generous helping of thick stew – mostly vegetable and potatoes, but some good-tasting sausage-meat was floating around as well. The beer seemed excellent to our parched gullets. We had not drunk anything since our repast on the outskirts of Penig when we had finished the water we carried with us.

We went to the underground waiting-room. We were controlled once in a cursory manner. I was blasé by now and smiled benignly at the burly representative of the *Sicherheitspolizei* – security police – as he passed by, hardly glancing at the wallets we pushed under his nose.

In good time we boarded the train for Ulm. Arriving there at midday, we changed platforms without incident and quickly boarded our next train. This did not go direct to Rottweil, but necessitated changing at Tuttlingen. Rottweil was thirty miles, but Tuttlingen only fifteen miles from the frontier! My intention was to walk out of the station at Tuttlingen with the excuse of waiting for the Rottweil train and never return.

This Hank and I duly did. As I walked off the station platform at Tuttlingen, through the barrier, we handed in our tickets. We had walked ten yards when I heard shouts behind us:

'Kommen Sie her! Hier, kommen Sie zurück!'

I turned round, fearing the worst, and saw the ticket-collector waving at us.

I returned to him and he said:

'Sie haben Ihre Fahrkarten abgegeben, aber Sie fahren nach Rottweil. Die müssen Sie noch behalten.'

With almost visible relief I accepted the tickets once more. In my anxiety I had forgotten that we were ostensibly due to return to catch the Rottweil train and, of course, still needed our tickets.

From the station we promptly took the wrong road; there were no signposts. It was late afternoon and a Saturday (October 17th). The weather was fine. We walked for a long time along a road which refused to turn in the direction in which we thought it ought to turn! It was maddening. We passed a superbly camouflaged factory and sidings. There must have been an area of ten acres completely covered with a false flat roof of what appeared to be rush matting. Even at the low elevation at which we found ourselves looking down upon it, the whole site looked like farmland. If the camouflage was actually rush matting, I do not know how they provided against fire risks.

We were gradually being driven into a valley heading due south, whereas we wished to travel westwards. Leaving the road as soon as possible without creating suspicion, we tried to make a short-cut across country to another highway which we knew headed west. As a short-cut it misfired, taking us over hilly country which prolonged our journey considerably. Evening was drawing in by the time we reached the correct road. We walked along this for several miles, and when it was dark, took to the woods to lie up for the night.

We passed a freezing, uncomfortable night on beds of leaves in the forest and were glad to warm ourselves with a sharp walk early the next morning, which was Sunday. I was thankful it was a Sunday because it gave us a good excuse to be out walking in the country.

We now headed along roads leading south-west, until at 8 am we retired again to the friendly shelter of the woods to eat our breakfast, consuming most of what was left of our German bread, sugar, and margarine.

We had almost finished our repast when we were disturbed by a farmer who approached and eyed us curiously for a long time. He wore close-fitting breeches and gaiters like a typical English game-keeper. I did not like his attitude at all. He came close to us and demanded what we were doing. I said:

'*Wir essen. Können Sie das nicht sehen?*'

'*Warum sind Sie hier?*' he asked, to which I answered:

'*Wir gehen spazieren; es ist Sonntag, nicht wahr?*'

At this he retired. I watched him carefully. As soon as he was out of the wood and about fifty yards away, I saw him turn along a hedge and change his gait into a trot.

This was enough for me. In less than a minute we were packed and trotting fast in the opposite direction, which happened to be southward! We did not touch the road again for some time, but kept to the woods and lanes. Gradually, however, the countryside became open and cultivated and we were forced once more to the road. We passed a German soldier, who was smartly turned out in his Sunday best, with a friendly '*Heil Hitler!*' Church bells were ringing out from steeples whch rose head and shoulders above the roofs of several villages dotted here and there in the rolling country around us.

We walked through one of the villages as the people were coming out of church. I was terrified of the children, who ran out of the church shouting and laughing. They gambolled around us and eyed us curiously, although their elders took no notice of us at all. I was relieved, none the less, when we left the village behind us. Soon afterwards, the country again became wooded and hilly, and we disappeared amongst the trees, heading now due south.

As the afternoon wore on I picked up our bearings more accurately, and we aimed at the exact location of the frontier crossing. A little too soon – I thought – we reached the frontier road, running east and west. I could not be sure, so we continued eastwards along it to where it entered some woods. We passed a fork where a forest track, which I recognized, joined it. I knew then that we were indeed on the frontier road and that we had gone too far eastwards. At that moment there were people following us, and we could not break off into the woods without looking suspicious. We walked onward casually and at the end of the wooded portion of the road we heard suddenly:

'*Halt! Wer da!*' and then, more deliberately, '*Wo gehen Sie hin?*'

A sentry-box stood back from the road in a clump of trees and from it stepped forth a frontier guard.

'*Wir gehen nach Singen,*' I said. '*Wir sind Ausländer.*'

'*Ihren Ausweis, bitte.*'

We produced our papers, including the special permit allowing us to travel near the frontier. We were close to him. His rifle was slung over his shoulder. The people who had been following us had turned down a lane towards a cottage. We were alone with the sentry.

I chatted on, gesticulating with my suitcase brazenly conspicuous.

'We are Flemish workmen. This evening we take the train to Rottweil, where there is much construction work. We must be there in the morning. Today we can rest and we like your woods and countryside.'

He eyed us for a moment; handed us back our papers and let us go. As we walked on I dreaded to hear another 'Halt!' I imagined that if the sentry were not satisfied with us he would, for his own safety, move us off a few yards so that he could unsling his rifle. But no command was given and we continued our 'Sunday afternoon stroll'. As we moved out of earshot Hank said to me:

'If he'd reached for his gun when he was close to us just then, I would have knocked him to Kingdom come.'

I would not have relished being knocked to Kingdom come by Hank and I often wonder if the sentry did not notice a look in Hank's eye and think that discretion was perhaps the better part of valour! A lonely sentry is not all-powerful against two enemies, even with his gun levelled. Our story may have had a vague ring of truth, but none the less, we were foreigners within half a mile of the Swiss frontier!

Soon we were able to leave the road and we started to double back across country to our frontier crossing-point. Just as we came to a railway line and climbed a small embankment, we nearly jumped out of our skins with fright as a figure darted from a bush in front of us and ran for his life into a thicket and disappeared. I could have assured him, if only he had stopped, that he gave us just as big a fright as we gave him!

By dusk we had found our exact location and waited in deep pine woods for darkness to descend. The frontier was scarcely a mile away. We ate a last meal nervously and without appetite. Our suitcases would not be required any more, so they were buried. When it was pitch-dark, we pulled on socks over our shoes, and set off. We had to negotiate the frontier-crossing in inky blackness, entirely from memory of the maps studied in Colditz. We crossed over more railway lines and then continued, skirting the edge of a wood. We encountered a minor road, which foxed me for a while because it should not have been there according to my memory, but we carried on. Hearing a motor-cycle pass along a road in front of us, a road running close to and parallel with the frontier, warned us of the proximity of our 'take-off' point. We entered the woods to our left and proceeded parallel with the road eastwards for about a hundred yards and then approached it cautiously. Almost as we stumbled into it, I suddenly recognized the outline of a sentry-box hidden among the trees straight in front of us!

We were within five yards of it when I recognized its angular roof. My hair stood on end. It was impossible to move without breaking twigs under our feet. They made noises like pistol shots and we could be heard easily. We retreated with as much care as we could, but even the crackle of a dried leaf caused me to perspire freely.

To compensate for this unnerving encounter, however, I now knew exactly where we were, for the sentry-box was marked on our Colditz map and provided me with a check bearing. We moved off seventy yards and approached the road again. Peering across it, we could discern fields and low hedges. In the distance was our goal: a wooded hill looming blacker than the darkness around it, with the woods ending abruptly halfway down its eastern slopes, towards our left. This end of the woods was our 'pointer.' There was no 'blackout' in Switzerland, and beyond the hill was the faintest haze of light, indicating the existence of a Swiss village.

At 7.30 pm we moved off. Crouching low, and at the double, we crossed the road and headed for our 'pointer'. Without stopping for breath we ran – through hedges – across ditches – wading through mud – and then on again. Dreading barbed wire which we could never have seen, we ran, panting with excitement as much as with breathlessness, across fields newly ploughed, meadows and marsh-land, till at last we rounded the corner of the woods. Here, for a moment, we halted for breath.

I felt that if I could not have a drink of water soon I would die. My throat was parched and swollen and my tongue was choking me. My heart was pounding like a sledge-hammer. I was gasping for breath. I had lived for two and a half years, both awake and in sleep, with the vision of this race before me and every nerve in my body was taut to breaking-pitch.

We were not yet 'home'. We had done about half a mile and could see the lights of the Swiss village ahead. Great care was now necessary, for we could easily recross the frontier into Germany with-out knowing it, and stumble on a guard-post. From the corner of the wood we had to continue in a sweeping curve, first towards our right, and then left again towards the village. Where we stood we were actually in Switzerland, but in a direct line between us and the Swiss village lay Germany.

Why had we run instead of creeping forward warily? The answer is that instinct dictated it and, I think in this case, instinct was right. Escapers' experience has borne out that the psychological reaction of a fleeing man to a shouted command, such as 'Halt', varies. If a man is walking or creeping the reaction is to stop. If he is running the reaction is to run faster. It is in the split seconds of such instinctive decisions that success or failure may be determined.

We continued on our way at a rapid walk, over grass and boggy land, crouching low at every sound. It was important to avoid even Swiss frontier-posts. We had heard curious rumours of escapers being returned to the Germans by unfriendly Swiss guards. However untrue, we were taking no risks.

We saw occasional shadowy forms and circled widely around them and at last, at 8.30 pm, approached the village along a sandy path.

We were about a thousand yards inside the Swiss frontier. We had completed the four-hundred-mile journey from Colditz in less than four days.

Under the first lamp-post of the village street, Hank and I shook hands in silence . . .

* * *

We beat Ronnie and Billie by twenty-six hours. At 10.30 pm the following evening they crossed the frontier safely!

Epilogue

A MONTH AFTER I reached Switzerland, the invasion of North Africa occurred and the Germans took over the south of France. Switzerland became a neutral island in a belligerent's home waters. The British Legation in Berne had only the Swiss Postal wireless telegraphic facilities of communication with London.

I had made a short report on Escape from Colditz in general, which never reached home. In that report, I made a statement which I would like to repeat here. It was:

Although in one case or another the name of practically every officer could be included in a list of those who worked for the common good at the expense of their own, I mention especially the following – not in order of priority:

Lieutenant-Colonel Guy German, Leicester Regiment; Lieutenant-Colonel G. Young, RE; Major W. F. Anderson, RE; Squadron-Leader H. M. MacColm, RAF; Captain R. Barry, 52nd Light Infantry; Captain R. Howe, RTR; Captain K. Lockwood, QRR; Flight Lieutenant N. Forbes, RAF; Flight Lieutenant H. Wardle, RAF; Lieutenant W. L. B. O'Hara, RTR; Lieutenant D. Gill, Royal Norfolks; Lieutenant 'Rex' Harrison, Green Howards; Lieutenant J. K. V. Lee, RCS; E.R.A. W. Hammond, RN.

In general these officers all placed at the disposal of the camp some flair or technical qualification without regard to personal consequences.

This story brings the war history of Colditz up to November 1942. The camp was relieved by the Americans on April 15th, 1945. The prisoners had therefore nearly another two and a half years in front of them when I left. I pay tribute to their endurance, for I could not picture myself lasting that length of time at Colditz without becoming a neurasthenic.

Two other British officers made successful escapes from the camp: Harry Elliott and 'Skipper' Barnet (Lieutenant R. Barnet, RN). Elliott foxed German Medical Boards for years on end, suffering from terrible stomach ulcers produced on substitute X-ray plates. He lost weight regularly and to an astonishing degree by having himself weighed, to begin with, loaded with bags of sand concealed under his pyjamas. Thereafter, weight-losing was a simple procedure, and like an observation balloon he jettisoned ballast at will. Skipper Barnet practised 'Yoga' for a long time until, by muscular control, he could raise his blood pressure to incredible heights. The Germans finally repatriated him, convinced he would never survive the excitement of a homecoming. Skipper, incidentally, was the boxer at Laufen who nearly knocked Harry Elliott out with a stout door between them.

One or two French officers, also removed to hospital at death's door, managed to rise from their beds and escape successfully to France.

A time came when it was no longer worth while trying to escape. This period probably started around 'D' Day, June 1944. Then it became a question of waiting patiently for the sound of the guns and the arrival of the Allies at the gates of the Castle.

Many events of interest took place, however, before that time. There were several brilliant, though unsuccessful, escape attempts, made under the guidance of Dick Howe. Rupert Barry made another game bid for freedom but was recaught while innocently trundling a wheelbarrow out of the last gateway of Colditz. Michael Sinclair, whose name is rapidly becoming legendary among escape fans, made three more attempts. On the first occasion he did not go far; he was shot through the chest at the Castle gateway. He recovered. On his next attempt he reached Rheine, twenty-five miles from the Dutch frontier, along with his companion Flight Lieutenant J. W. Best, RAF, before recapture. On his third attempt he was shot dead some yards from the wire of the Colditz park recreation ground. His memory is especially honoured by every man who knew him.

Best was chiefly known for his 'mole' escape from an Air Force camp (Sagan, I think), which brought him to Colditz. In this attempt he and another officer, Bill Goldfinch, made a sufficiently long tunnel to house themselves with some space to spare for what is known as 'bulking'. They laid in a stock of provisions and had an air-tube. They then carried on digging at their leisure, and eventually surfaced at a reasonable distance from the camp and walked off!

The French tunnel was still under construction when I left. It is worth a chapter to itself. The Dutch departed from Colditz and, unhitching their railway coach in motion on the way to their next camp, the whole contingent escaped in various directions when it came to a standstill! The escape of ERAs Hammond and Lister, which I have mentioned in this book, is among the cream of escape stories. Dick Howe, from somewhere high up in the Castle eventually made contact with the concealed manhole (which I had tried to reach from the delousing shed) in the prison courtyard. From there he carried on through a maze of drains until he reached the main Castle outfall sewer. The Germans, unfortunately, discovered this attempt before it reached fruition. Dick also took over magnificently concealed wireless sets left by the French and gave the prisoners daily News Bulletins. More *Prominente* arrived of various nationalities – General Bor Komorowsky, Captain the Earl of Hopetoun, Lieutenant Alexander, Lieutenant Lascelles, First Lieutenant John Winant (USAF), and others. American POWs joined the serried ranks of the hardbitten Colditz convicts! Finally the 'Relief of Colditz' was dramatically exciting, and carried with it a touch of pathos which it would be difficult to describe. All this and much more has been incorporated in my book *The Latter Days at Colditz*, which concludes the Saga of the Fortress Prison.

The thrilling sequel to THE COLDITZ STORY

THE LATTER DAYS AT COLDITZ

In THE COLDITZ STORY, Pat Reid told the story of the escape academy that sprang up inside the most impregnable German POW camp of the Second World War, ending appropriately with his own incredible escape from Colditz.

But Reid's own break-out was by no means the last. In this enthralling sequel, he follows the fortunes of the escape academy right up until the arrival of the allied forces in April 1945. These tales of fantastic bravery and stunning ingenuity are every bit as mesmerising as the original.

HODDER &
STOUGHTON

www.hodder.co.uk

HISTORY LIVES

at Hodder

From Anya Seton and Mary Stewart to Thomas Keneally and Robyn Young, Hodder & Stoughton has an illustrious tradition of publishing bestselling and prize-winning authors whose novels span the centuries, from ancient Rome to the Tudor Court, revolutionary Paris to the Second World War.

———

Want to learn how an author researches battle scenes?

Discover history from a female perspective?

Find out what it's like to walk Hadrian's Wall in full Roman dress?

Visit us today at **HISTORY LIVES** for exclusive author features, first chapter previews, book trailers, author videos, event listings and competitions.